Pages à photocopier

14-15
19-20
211-222

Getting Canada Online

Getting Canada Online

Understanding the Information Highway

DAVID JOHNSTON
DEBORAH JOHNSTON
SUNNY HANDA

Stoddart

Published in 1995 by
Stoddart Publishing Co. Limited
34 Lesmill Road
Toronto, Canada
M3B 2T6
Tel. (416) 445-3333
Fax (416) 445-5967

Stoddart Books are available for bulk purchase for sales promotions,
premiums, fundraising, and seminars. For details, contact the
Special Sales Department at the above address.

Electronic Addresses
http://www.zoo.net/I_way/
The authors can be contacted at:
I_way@zoo.net

Canadian Cataloguing in Publication Data

Johnston, David L.
Getting Canada online: understanding the information highway

Includes index.
ISBN 0-7737-5778-3

1. Information superhighway – Canada.   I. Johnston,
Deborah.   II. Handa, Sunny.   III. Title.

HE7572.C3J6 1995   384.3'3   C95-932588-3

The authors would like to thank the
Information Highway Advisory Council
for permission to use its glossary of terms.

Cover Design: the boy 100 and Tannice Goddard
Text Design: Tannice Goddard

Printed and bound in Canada

*Stoddart Publishing gratefully acknowledges the support of the
Canada Council, Ontario Ministry of Citizenship, Culture and Recreation,
Ontario Arts Council, and Ontario Publishing Centre in
the development of writing and publishing in Canada.*

CONTENTS

PREFACE

As Adam and Eve left the Garden of Eden, one said to the other, "We are in a period of profound change." So are we today; and so have been many periods of history in between. Today's information revolution will be as deep and momentous as any other scientific movement in history. But, with one striking difference. Rather than evolving over years, decades and even centuries as did the agricultural and industrial revolutions, this change is unfolding before us in weeks and months. In one generation — ours — it will change dramatically how we work, live and play.

Such change at such a dazzling pace presents formidable challenges. We must first try to understand the change. What drives it? What are its consequences? Second, we must steer it in directions that foster the highest and broadest good. We must foster a collective desire to use our individual skills and knowledge to find our way onto the information highway, to begin to drive in a fashion appropriate to each of us.

The setting of this book is the society we know best: Canada. With all its imperfections, it is a remarkably civic society — one which has learned to live with difference and make it an invigorating strength. These differences include language, ethnic makeup, change of seasons, vastly varying regional societies spread across the largest governed land mass in the world bordering on three oceans, with two principal legal systems, and a pioneering tradition. From this have come tolerance, a capacity to collaborate, a carefully calibrated balance between individual and collective rights and responsibilities, and finally, adaptability, the quality that will be most needed to deal with change.

This all seems positive. Responding to change has been, throughout Canadian history, invigorating and filled with the promise of a new and better life. But this change has a dark side. There are destructive repercussions and losers — societies and individuals. The sheer magnitude and the pace of change evoke misgivings. Can we adapt and, if so, how?

We have written this book in the belief that our society will respond positively, relying on its tradition of embracing change and moving forward. We hope this book will help. It aims to leave the reader with a deeper understanding of the information highway in its Canadian context and to sketch its scientific, legal, socio-economic and cultural implications. We are surrounded by the buzz of the information highway. We understand that it is transforming and will continue to transform our lives. Yet, many do not know how this change will occur. Will we be better off? One of our purposes in writing this nontechnical text is to provide all Canadians with an opportunity to understand and use this vast communications infrastructure known as the information highway.

The book is divided into four. First, we introduce the reader to the information highway, paying special attention to the Internet. Second, we explore the scientific foundations. How exactly does information travel on the highway? How does a computer function? Third, we discuss the "players" — the content suppliers, content carriers and rules on the highway. How do we address privacy, security, censorship and intellectual property rights? How effective are our current laws in the information age? What changes are necessary? Finally, the book reviews some of the information highway's socio-economic implications. How will it affect the Canadian economy, employment, education and health care?

Our message is simple. We live in a period of dramatic change. It will propel us down the information highway. We, as individuals and as a nation, have a choice: to understand and use the change to our advantage, or to be overwhelmed by it and be casualties in its wake.

We each brought very different backgrounds to this project. David completed a fifteen-year term as Principal of McGill University in 1994 and returned to his position as Professor of Law at McGill. He teaches in the areas of science, information technology and securities regulation. David just completed a year as Chair of the Information Highway Advisory Council for the government of Canada, struck in April 1994. David's work with the Council served as the immediate stimulus for the book. It released its final report in September 1995. Its compelling message was the importance of understanding and adapting. The Council's broad objectives were job creation through innovation and investment, reinforcing Canadian sovereignty and cultural identity, and ensuring universal access at reasonable cost. Its objectives, principles and issues are instructive in identifying the public policy challenges in Canada.

While this book may be regarded as complementing that report, it was not written as a supplement. It stands on its own as an independent work. It represents the three authors' journey in understanding and adapting. The Council's report and its recommendations will appear frequently as it represents a first comprehensive Canadian attempt to come to grips with the information highway.

Sunny is a lawyer and is currently a doctoral candidate in McGill's Law Faculty. He also teaches courses in copyright and information technology, shared with David, and computers and the law. Sunny's background is in computer technology. Sunny is the civil libertarian in the group; preserving the individual's freedom of expression and limiting government involvement in new technologies is a high priority. So too is the advancement of knowledge and progress.

Deborah has just completed two law degrees at McGill, is in the process of qualifying for the Quebec Bar and coordinates the legal and research methods course in McGill's Law Faculty. Her interests lie in criminal and information law, aboriginal justice and, more specifically, law reform.

It quickly became clear during the writing of this text that in analysing the information highway we examine fundamental values and beliefs. As lawyers recommending how the information highway should be built, we have had to work hard to comprehend the law as it is, and even harder, the law as it ought to be and how and why we get it there. The chapters, as written, reflect compromises reached — a truly Canadian trait. Each of us holds different views on many I-way issues such as privacy, control of content and economic regulation. Early drafts of the manuscripts reflected these differences. We have attempted, through subsequent revisions, to sublimate our own political views (though these cannot be totally suppressed). Where possible, we present several sides to important social issues, leaving their resolution to the reader.

We hope our efforts to understand and adapt as set out in these pages will be helpful to Canadians and all citizens of the global village. We dedicate this book to family, students and colleagues. For David, this dedication begins with his co-authors Sunny and his daughter, Deborah. The dedication embraces so many others who are part of our journey in lifelong learning, particularly the journey towards understanding the information highway. We should mention here especially students at McGill, who have taught us much. Warm thanks to our editor, Don Bastian, and to Mark Potter and other Advisory Council colleagues who have read and improved particular chapters. A special tribute goes to Ann Brodie, who manages our office in the Law Faculty like a magician. Ann lives the "iron fist in velvet glove" maxim so adroitly that she can reduce dictator and diplomat alike to envy.

I

THE HIGHWAY

1

WHAT IS THE INFORMATION HIGHWAY?

"A world community can exist only with world communication,
which means something more than extensive shortwave facilities scattered
about the globe. It means common understanding, a common tradition,
common ideas, and common ideals."
— Robert M. Hutchins

What is the information highway?
The term "information highway" (or "I-way" or "electronic superhighway") is a household phrase. Its high level of public awareness in
Canada is steadily increasing. In a May 1995 Andersen Consulting survey, 70 percent of Canadians claimed familiarity. One year earlier, the
figure was 54.4 percent. By comparison, public awareness of important
issues ranges from one-third to under one-half.[1] However, despite the
widespread public *awareness*, few people actually *understand* what this
sweeping concept means. In the same Andersen survey, almost 60 percent
of Canadians did not know who was responsible for the information
highway. If we are to fully develop and exploit the I-way, we must
bridge this gap between public awareness and public understanding.

The I-way is defined in many ways. The April 1994 mandate for
the government of Canada's Information Highway Advisory Council
(IHAC) states:

The terms *information highway* or *electronic highway* denote the advanced information and communications infrastructure that is essential for Canada's emerging information economy. Building on existing and planned communications networks, this infra-structure will become a "network of networks," linking Canadian homes, businesses, governments and institutions to a wide range of interactive services from entertainment, education, cultural products and social services to data banks, computers, electronic commerce, banking and business services.[2]

The concept embraces existing and future public and private networks. They include cable and satellite television, digital and traditional airwave radio, broadband, narrowband and wireless (e.g., cellular) telephone, plus local area (LANs) and wide area (WANs) computer networks, and databases.[3] The idiom "network of networks" refers to the joining, or "convergence," of these systems to create a seamless communications infrastructure. It includes both the *means* of conveyance — the carriers — and the *content* placed on the carriageway.

Why is there such confusion about the I-way metaphor?

Partly because the information highway is transforming so rapidly. Partly because the metaphor identifies different aspects of the current electronic revolution for different audiences. It is a chameleon. The metaphor symbolizes both physical and abstract elements. Moreover, it is too limiting.

How?

Some use the term "information highway" as a catch-all to describe the technological revolution, the transformative process that is sweeping most of the globe. For others, the words "information highway" identify the individual technological innovations that affect our every-day life: most prominently, the Internet, interactive television and electronic banking. Yet others view it as a massive infrastructure, constituting a "seamless and transparent network of networks" capable of transmitting a full range of interactive, audio, video and data services.

Where did the I-way metaphor come from?

U.S. Vice-President Al Gore popularized it in the 1992 presidential campaign. It is instructive that the term gained prominence as a political vision. The parentage is natural. Vice-President Gore's father, Senator Albert Gore of Tennessee, founded the U.S. interstate highway system through legislative initiatives over thirty years ago. But Vice-President Gore and President Clinton have taken it further. As they prepare for the 1996 presidential campaign, they speak of the Global Information Infrastructure (GII) and a predominant U.S. role for both carriage and content.

There are both similarities and distinctions between traditional transportation systems and the I-way, the contemporary metaphorical equivalent.[4] Both require substantial capital investment. Both provide a basic infrastructure for modern society. But the term "I-way," drawn from the more understandable transportation highway, is imprecise in several respects. First, I-way ownership will be less public, more private and more varied. Second, its creation will engage a substantial number of technological systems. Third, it will be interactive, with intelligence and flexibility.

The I-way metaphor is the leading wave of the current information revolution. The two words "information highway" represent its principal functions. The first describes the content. The second describes the carriageway. However, it masks the scope and depth of changes in society. It may submerge the aspirations and concerns of individual Canadians.[5] It evokes the image of a massive physical structure. It ignores the essential element of people and communities maintaining contact with one another. Consequently, a more embracing metaphor envisages a global village square uniting people for the purposes of commerce, leisure, learning and worship, rather than a highway on which people operate as self-contained units. It is not simply a source of information; it is a means of communication. The IHAC captured this in its November 1994 Progress Report:

> The Information Highway, in our view, is not so much about information as it is about communication in both its narrowest and broadest senses. It is not a cold and barren highway with exits and entrances that carry traffic, but a series of culturally rich and dynamic intersecting communities, large and small, north and south, east and west, populated by creative thinking people who reach out and enrich one another. Rather than a highway, it is a personalized village square where people eliminate the barriers of time and distance, and interact in a kaleidoscope of different ways. It really is the next step en route to the global village that Marshall McLuhan described so forcefully and eloquently.[6]

Why distinguish between carriage and content?

Traditionally, government regulators have distinguished between carriers of information, e.g., telephone, cable and satellite companies, and suppliers of content, e.g., radio and television broadcasters, database services and publishers. Content simply refers to the information transmitted over a communications system. Carriage is the mode of transmission. Additionally, some communications enterprises, such as cable companies, serve hybrid functions, providing both content and conveyance. The Canadian regulatory body the Canadian Radio-television and Telecommunications Commission (CRTC) governs carriers and content suppliers. The Telecommunications Act[7] regulates carrier companies. The Broadcasting Act[8] governs content providers.

In May 1995, the CRTC concluded seven months of hearings on the "convergence" of the traditionally distinct domains of cable and telephone carriers.[9] The resulting decision opened the door to direct competition between cablecos and telcos in their respective markets.

Convergence of telecommunications and computer technologies, bolstered by the CRTC Convergence Report, has eroded these traditional distinctions and raised numerous regulatory issues. It is now difficult to say where carriage ends and content begins.

What has disturbed these tranquil two solitudes?

The computer. We speak of three different communications systems carrying three different types of content or information: telephone for voice communication; cable, airwaves and satellite for television and radio; computer networks for data. What synthesizes or amalgamates the three is the computer and digitization, the ability to store bits of information as 1s and 0s, pluses or minuses, in an electronic circuit. What propels computer usage is speed, capacity and flexibility in manipulation of data. Through innovation, the computer has become central to all three modes of communication. The result? Convergence of these technologies and increased capabilities and sophistication of each.

What does convergence mean?

It means many things. In its simplest form, convergence means the joining or interconnection of formerly distinct entities. For information technology, this entails the merger of communications and computer technology based on a common digital language. Radio and television transmissions, traditionally in analog form, will be increasingly digitized. This will result in higher quality, speed and capacity. Similarly, computer technology will spawn increasing audio and video capacities, resembling radio and television.

Apart from technological convergence, we have business convergence. This describes the increasing consolidation of the telecommunications and broadcasting industries with the incorporation of computer technology and now embraces information and entertainment creators and providers. In the past, Canadian law has prohibited a single enterprise from delivering information, entertainment and communications

7

together. Separate telecommunications, cable and over-the-air broadcasting industries functioned as independent regulated monopolies. Telephone companies provided voice, fax and modem connections. Cable and (more recently) satellite companies delivered video. Broadcasters supplied over-the-air programming. Traditional justification for these monopolies was twofold: they ensured (1) universal access on carriageways and (2) Canadian cultural sovereignty in programming. Today, the computer, consumer electronics, entertainment and publishing, and (telecommunications and cable) distribution industries are thrust together by the changing face of the technology that each traditionally has exploited. Because of these forces, some of the world's largest companies are forming new cross-industry allegiances to seek competitive advantage. For example, companies such as Apple Computer Inc., American Telephone and Telegraph (AT&T) and Time Warner Inc. have recently approached one another to combine their technologies for the impending multimedia explosion. Similar alliances are formed irrespective of company size or market share. Convergence is at the core of the information revolution. The term is used to describe a variety of different changes.

Where does the information highway run?

Everywhere. It pervades every aspect of our lives. Consider these examples. ATM banking and direct-payment systems in stores have transformed our cash economy into a credit economy. Direct satellite broadcasts of the O. J. Simpson trial continent-wide dramatized the American justice system in homes across North America. Through worldwide instantaneous communications technology, a newspaper can list the world's weather with temperatures and climatic conditions drawn from over fifty cities around the world, reinforcing our mutual dependence in the global village. New digital cameras holding fifty pictures per disk are rendering photographic film obsolete. Once the pictures are downloaded to a video recorder or computer, the disk can be reloaded into the camera and reused.

When was the information highway built?

Suggestions that the I-way is a new structure or yet to be built are misleading.[10] Despite the recent coinage of the phrase, the I-way is not new. While it is continually under construction to reflect changing technologies and needs, it builds upon existing and planned structures. Two Canadian railways provide useful analogies. Building the Canadian Pacific Railway was a condition of Confederation in 1867, the promise to link Canada coast to coast. That transportation corridor established an East-West trade and communication axis that countered natural North-South forces then (and still) pervading. The East-West premise and promise of communication continues to guide Canadian policy.

Today, many features already exist for new telecommunications, broadcasting and information technology. The next stage is to link and standardize these technologies.[11] The construction of the Canadian National Railway provides an apposite analogy on how standardization or interconnectivity and interoperability will occur.[12] In its early days, different sections of the railway had different rail widths. As a result, railway traffic could not travel from one rail system to another. The development of a common gauge (the distance between widths of rails) resolved the problem by standardizing the rail system. Similarly, standardizing current telecommunications technologies will enable the exchange of electronic traffic between different technologies.[13] Mindful of Pierre Berton's book *The Last Spike*,[14] which describes the role of the Canadian Pacific Railway in nation building, one student of Canadian history labelled Canada's information highway "The Next Spike."

Are there Canadian I-way builders?

Indeed. Alexander Graham Bell invented the telephone near Brantford, Ontario, in 1876. An Italian inventor, Marchese Guglielmo Marconi, sent the first transatlantic wireless radio communication from St. John's, Newfoundland, to England in 1901. In 1969, the Canadian government and private industry joined forces through TELESAT to launch the first domestic geostationary satellite communications network dedicated to peaceful functions. Its celestial presence conquered geographical barriers with a "footprint" that gave telecommunications and broadcasting services to the entire country. Canada is the world leader in digital switching of telephone communications. Virtually all businesses and 99 percent of Canadian homes have telephones. As well, 98 percent of our country's households have televisions, 75 percent have cable television and 40 percent have computers.[15] These are world-leading figures.

Why has Canada been a leader in telecommunications?

Two reasons, which both reflect national objectives. Geography first. Because our land is so vast and sparsely populated, we have required enhanced communications networks. Accordingly, "national purpose" has demanded basic communications services not only for urban areas but also for rural and isolated regions. Second, political philosophy. There is a desire to provide equality of opportunity, to create sustainable communities and to connect these communities coast to coast to coast and build a nation linked across its regions.

Who builds the information highway and who owns it?

This question goes to the core of information-highway policy. Yet, at present, it is beset with uncertainty. The corporate sector, government, and individual users are the three principal architects, builders and financers. The more pointed issue, however, is the allotment of responsibility amongst the three. How extensive a role, if any, should government play in building the I-way? Should the role be supervisory, regulatory and/or financial? What is industry's role? What slices of the information-highway pie should be held by the telephone, cable, wireless, satellite and computer industries? Should slices be won or allotted? Because the I-way is evolving at a dazzling pace, because the attention it attracts is relatively recent, decisive answers are elusive. Moreover, because the I-way is multifaceted, the questions are complex. Finally, because the information highway is continually under construction, the answers will continually change.

The I-way can be a lucrative creation. Yet, building Canada's information highway and ensuring accessibility to Canadians will be expensive. Consequently, the question of who pays for this massive initiative is germane to any discussion of its present and future development. The federal government's IHAC strongly endorsed private-sector construction.[16] The Council emphasized government's role in policy and rule making, as "referee" in defining the environment within which the highway will be built and operated.[17]

How does this information revolution fit into a historical context?

Three epic economic and social changes have profoundly shaped our Western civilization: the agricultural (technological phase), industrial and information revolutions. The first two, distorting the term "revolution," evolved in progressive stages over decades and centuries. The last, symbolized by the I-way, originated within the past two decades. It accelerates in intervals measured in months and years. Each revolution has had enormous economic and societal impact. At each stage, society has exploited an innovative tool or tools to replace human labour and, increasingly, to complement the human mind. The metal plow spearheaded agricultural change. James Watt's steam engine drove the Industrial Revolution. The computer gave birth to the information society. And as we envision the future, we picture chips replacing neurons.

The Industrial Revolution began in Great Britain in the 1760s. It spread throughout the Western world and beyond to become the defining characteristic of the so-called developed world. Much like the current "digitization" of society, industrialization profoundly transformed economies, employment opportunities, the workplace, the family structure and population distribution. A striking difference, however, is the speed with which the information revolution transforms society. The pace of this transformation produces and demands rapid adaptation. It also provokes fear and uncertainty. Although each revolution has occurred with increasing speed, the current need to adapt profoundly, in one generation, is almost unique in history. It is dazzling in defining opportunity, disturbing in dislocation. Some observers summarize this transformation by another metaphor — the wave. The race will go to those who make or ride the wave. Others it will engulf or swamp.

As a result of the Industrial Revolution, Great Britain emerged in the nineteenth century as the world's economic, political and technological leader. It created unprecedented wealth based on ideas and innovation and intellectual property. It harnessed brainpower, to use a mixed metaphor appropriate for the time. Why was Britain the cradle of the Industrial Revolution? The reasons include the comparative absence of war and its island status, emerging political pluralism and evolving democratic institutions, efficient administration with fair laws and taxes, increasingly progressive legislation, an open society spearheaded by the cities, and flexibility in business organization. These were conditions which encouraged adaptability to technological change. The United States became a global superpower in the twentieth century as a result of industrialization and, in particular, electrification, led by Thomas Edison. Today, Japan has emerged as one of the world's most powerful nations due to its role as a technological pioneer, innovator and manufacturer. There is a clear correlation between technological innovation, adaptability and global strength. The challenge for Canada is to become an international information technology leader.

One discerning analysis of the foundation of the information era suggests that the tools for an information society have existed for some time.[18] They include the calculator, the typewriter, the filing cabinet, the television and the telephone. The calculator helps us work with numbers, the typewriter with characters. The filing cabinet stores information to be retrieved. The television portrays our ideas. The telephone permits voice communications. The key element in the evolution from an industrial to an information society, however, is the computer. The computer performs all of these tasks, merging and enhancing these individual technologies.

What is so unique about the computer?

Several qualities. First, its ability to concentrate or compress data allows the storage and transmission of much greater amounts of information. Second, its speed. Third, the computer's ability to perform tasks mimicking certain lower-level aspects of human intelligence. It manipulates data. To a certain extent, the computer can replicate some aspects of human thought. It is no accident that the term "artificial intelligence" is used to describe these conquests.

What about the human factor?

Intelligent and sensible human intervention is essential to the I-way's success. The human element will determine whether this technology works for or against us, whether we ride the technological wave or are engulfed by it. The Newfoundland poet E. J. Pratt captured its significance in his epic poem *The Titanic*. It described an earlier human triumph over nature. He dramatized the ancient Greek concept of hubris — people believing that they had advanced technology sufficiently that nature and fate no longer held sway. The "unsinkable" *Titanic* set forth on its maiden voyage in 1912 from England to America. It struck icebergs off the coast of Newfoundland and sank quickly, losing most of its passengers. For the whole of the day before the sinking, the *Titanic*'s telegraph operator rejected iceberg warnings from other ships in the area. Its telegraph and limited airwaves were preoccupied transmitting passengers' maiden voyage messages of greeting to shore. At nightfall, the captain of the *California*, the ship closest to the *Titanic*, gave strict instructions that he not be disturbed before morning. When the *Titanic* was struck and began to sink, it sent telegraphic SOS messages, one of the first occasions on which they were used. The *California* received them. However, its radio operator did not awaken the captain, who alone could order a change of direction. Had it steamed directly to the scene, it would have saved many of the passengers.

The tragedy of the *Titanic* teaches that technology is only as reliable as the people who use it. At this stage, computers cannot think or reason. They merely execute instructions from the human user. Consequently, we must not be deceived by our own hubris to believe that, if sufficiently advanced, technology can entirely replace human beings. Ultimately, it is vulnerable to nature and to human intervention. Moreover, the value of technology stems from its human element: it is ours to use, abuse or ignore.

It is people who use technology and it must be geared to the human user's needs and aspirations. There is a convergence between humanity and technology as well as between technologies.[19]

What does the information highway mean for Canada?

It depends on how we use it. This infrastructure represents the foundation for Canada's economic prosperity and for social and cultural growth in a knowledge-based global society. It provides new dimensions for learning, creativity and entrepreneurship.[20] Most experts in the technological and telecommunications industries agree that Canadians need an interactive, high-speed network. This will open the gates to a wide variety of services and encourage a broad base of users.[21] But deciding how to do it is much more difficult than declaring what is to be done.

The information highway will unquestionably change how we function as a society. It can enrich the lives of all Canadians. It can strengthen the entire Canadian economy. Domestically, it can improve the efficiency and service delivery of businesses and organizations. Externally, it can boost Canadian businesses to expand their markets and increase their competitiveness nationally and globally. The use of communal databases can enhance the information flow in various businesses, professions, learning communities and individual lives. It can also change the nature of consumerism, drastically increasing new forms of shopping and furthering our credit economy.

However, like the Roman god Janus who looked in both directions, there is a second face to this technological wave. Job dislocation, acute for those without skills or without the learning base to adapt, creates widespread anxiety. The accumulation of personal data, the capacity to manipulate it and disseminate it in unimagined ways and to ubiquitous destinations, creates understandable fear for one's privacy and dignity. The demanding and discriminating nature of these new tools and their lack of "user-friendliness" threatens a society of "haves and have-nots" within the nation and between nations around the world.

As the information revolution is in its infancy, we cannot yet accurately and comprehensively describe its full impact on the lives of Canadians. But, we must not embrace this transformation blindly. Technology is changing so rapidly that there is virtually no time to assess its impact thoughtfully and comprehensively. We must address the very real and substantial security and regulatory concerns. We must gauge the social impact of the information highway. How will the I-way modify human interaction? To what extent will computer interaction replace human interaction? In the 1950s, television drastically transformed society. Similarly, information technology will fundamentally alter the way we communicate, learn, work and play. The choice is ours.

This is our challenge. To embrace this change. To use it wisely to our advantage. To recognize its more sinister potential. And, like the ancient Greeks, to understand that pride in human intelligence is powerfully creative. But hubris is powerfully destructive.

2

THE INTERNET

"What I have perceived in this Global Village created by
instantaneous information is a threat to human identity
and the erasure of our way of life."
— Marshall McLuhan

The Internet is a microcosm of the information highway. While the
two are not wholly synonymous, the legal, economic and social issues
posed by the Internet mirror those of the I-way. Because of its prominence and its extraordinary growth and potential, we explore the
Internet separately.

What is the Internet?

It is a network of interconnected computer networks. It links educational and research institutions, homes, military, business and other
organizations worldwide. It is often referred to as the world's largest
computer network. One writer zestfully described it as "a global
network of chatty computers crammed with a galaxy of information."[1]
Like the concept "information highway," however, the Internet is
more than a physical infrastructure. It is a burgeoning collectivity of
people exchanging ideas and information globally.

The Internet is a dramatic example of the power and convergence of database, telecommunication, and digital technologies. In contrast to a centralized database stored in one computer, the Internet operates as a "distributed database." Data are distributed among computers across the globe. These computer sites are linked via telephone lines, dedicated telecommunication lines, microwave towers and satellites. At present, one central database cannot store all of the information accessible on the Internet. This is one advantage of a "distributed" storage method. Much greater amounts of information may be accumulated and accessed. It also opens more doors to international dialogue on a vast spectrum of issues.

Understandably, in an increasingly knowledge-based society, the Internet is an invaluable tool. Canadians grasp this. A May 1995 Andersen Consulting survey found that over half of Canadians were familiar with the Internet.[2] An overwhelming 12 percent of Canadians (approximately 3.5 million people) have used the Internet. International awareness and use of the Internet grows in leaps and bounds. Current plans are underway for the Internet 1996 World Exposition in Montreal. This year-long fair will take place across the globe online and offline, largely through virtual (e.g., home pages) and "real world" (e.g., museums) pavilions. Core servers in major Internet access points such as San Francisco, Amsterdam and Tokyo will be linked via an "Internet Railroad." The exposition will provide information on government, technology, culture and education.[3] Since the nineteenth century, world expositions have often promoted and explained innovations such as electric light, television, the telephone and railroads and signified their profound implication for us all.

Where did the Internet originate?

It was a creature of the United States Defense Department, a classic example of swords into ploughshares. During the 1960s, the Cold War between the United States and the Soviet Union intensified, due principally to three events: the 1962 Cuban Missile Crisis, which brought the two countries to the brink of nuclear war; the nuclear arms build-up; and, finally, the escalation of the Vietnam War. The Americans feared a Soviet nuclear strike. The U.S. Defense Department designed the Advanced Research Projects Agency network (ARPAnet), the Internet's precursor, for military research. It was built in the 1970s as a "fail-safe" communications network capable of surviving a nuclear attack. If a nuclear bomb struck one or several parts of the United States, alternate communications networks through undamaged areas would carry commands from government to defence establishments. The idea was to distribute information over many different locations and establish alternate access routes. Thus, if any single communications link was destroyed, information could travel via another path. Shortly thereafter, the defence establishment employed the same communications methods to link with university researchers doing contract research.

Contemporaneously, the British and French governments developed a new inter-computer communications technique immune to nuclear attack.[4] Called "packet switching," it transferred data between two points without a direct fixed connection such as a direct phone line. The information broken into addressable "packets" or "posted letters" was routed through a succession of interconnected computers until it reached its final destination where the data would be reassembled. It functioned much like our postal system, in which individual letters pass through different collection, sorting and distribution stations. Letters can take various routes to their final destination. The U.S. government adopted the packet-switching technology to establish a national attack-proof computer network.

Analogy

The ARPAnet was a success. Researchers began to use it to communicate with one another. Not surprisingly, universities around the world employed it to communicate among themselves. It became a favoured medium for universities implementing LANs in the early 1980s. Consequently, newer network facilities adopted the ARPAnet standards in their design. Eventually, a sufficiently large number of individual computing facilities had implemented the ARPAnet model to create a relatively uniform standard. ARPAnet became the *de facto* international standard for local computer networking.

In the late 1980s, the American National Science Foundation (NSF) set up supercomputer facilities at five American universities. Their mandate was to promote academic research. This initiative thereby extended the scope of the network beyond military and limited academic research. In view of the geographical spread of academic centres across the United States, it was extremely costly to supply each academic facility with individual connections to the NSF. Consequently, the NSF developed a system linking academic centres within individual geographical regions. Each regional network then was connected to the NSF. Each academic centre acted as a node which relayed the communications traffic towards its ultimate destination.

How do the early days compare with today's Internet?

There has been phenomenal change. Over the past twenty years, the network's equipment and users have evolved remarkably. Equipment upgrades have vastly enhanced capacity and speed with higher bandwidth transmission lines to handle the increased network traffic. Software programs controlling the traffic have significantly improved. Internet users have increased and diversified dramatically, aided by increasingly user-friendly software navigation tools.

Who uses the Internet?

It is difficult to quantify the number of computers on the Internet because of the proliferation of personal computers and LANs. However, a conservative estimate in May 1995 suggests over 30 million computer users with Internet links. The number more than doubles each year.[5] In terms of individual users, this communication medium now vastly exceeds the exclusive domain of the academic researcher and the military. There is a gender gap in Internet use. More men than women use the Internet. According to a Matrix

Information & Directory Services (MIDS) study, the figure at the end of 1994 was slightly below a 2:1 male-female ratio. Moreover, although it originated as a noncommercial network, today, just over 50 percent of subscribers to the worldwide Internet are commercial bodies. Many companies realize that direct contact with other computer users anywhere in the world boosts their research and development and more broadly their advertising and sales. The Internet is used widely in educational institutions because, in many countries, there is no direct cost to the student.

Who pays for the Internet?

There is no ubiquitous "Revenue Internet" or "Internet Inc." collecting subscriber fees from its networks and users.[6] Rather, the costs are distributed among individual network users, such as universities, and commercial online services. They pay for their portion of the network by charging user fees to their subscribers. CA*net, the Canadian heart of the Internet, pays to lease lines interconnecting regional networks and linking them to international sites. A university, e.g., pays for its connection to a regional network (usually at subsidized rates). It may or may not charge its students through direct fees, computer facility charges or tuition charges or its professors through research grant computer charges or departmental telecommunications levies.

Numerous individual Internet users, particularly within educational institutions, have access to the net "free of charge." This has bred a widespread belief that the Internet is costless. One should bear in mind the timeless phrase: "There is no free lunch." Internet costs include local phone hookups, long-distance inter-computer telecommunications charges and computer-server charges. When a user has "free" access to the Internet, someone subsidizes that connection, generally those with the deeper pockets. While certain categories of individuals do not pay for Internet access, subscriber services and institutions usually pay a connection fee. The Internet is like the telephone: its increase in value for any one person depends on the total number of users. Hence, one rationale for cost redistribution is that it is worthwhile subsidizing users initially to develop a "critical mass."[7] The dramatic point of the Internet, however, is its relative cheapness, even when summing all the special subsidies built into its financing.

*What is the CANARIE/CA*net network?*

The federal government's industry ministry created the Canadian Network for the Advancement of Research, Industry and Education (CANARIE) to stimulate the development of high-bandwidth applications and to link Canadian educational and research institutions via a high-speed network.[8] CA*net was established in 1989 to interconnect provincial networks. CA*net is the Canadian core of the Internet.

CA*net leases carrier lines to link ten regional computer networks to a nationwide research and development and educational network.[9] Each of these regional networks operates as a subsidiary of CA*net. In Quebec, for example, Réseau interordinateurs scientifique Québécois (RISQ) charges preferential rates to educational institutions to hook onto the national network. It is subsidized by revenue from lines leased to the public at much higher rates. CA*net also links Canada to the worldwide Internet. Additionally, CA*net administers the "ca" domain, i.e., the Canadian portion of the Internet.

CANARIE Inc. was federally incorporated in March 1993 as a nonprofit organization. It is governed by a board of directors. It is supported by members who pay fees on a sliding scale. They include representatives from the telecommunications and computer industries, educational and nonprofit institutions, and nonvoting associate members. CANARIE serves three principal functions: (1) as an operative network with CA*net, (2) as a high-speed experimental network, and (3) as a funding source for high-speed R&D communication projects.[10]

What is the difference between a LAN and a WAN?

A local area network (LAN) is a telecommunications network of two or more computers joined together in a geographic area of less than sixteen kilometres.[11] Most universities and large companies have LANs. They interconnect individual computers within the organization. LANs contrast with wide area networks (WANs), groups of computers linked via dedicated lines or via satellite in a geographic area exceeding sixteen kilometres.[12]

LANs have superseded the older mini- and mainframe computer-centred architecture. In so doing, they have threatened temporarily the existence of traditional mainframe suppliers like IBM who were slow to adjust to this change. In the age of "distributed computing," data is no longer stored in one enormous mainframe computer. Rather, it is dispersed among a series of small computers linked through a network. In a LAN, each computer has the ability to perform processing functions, and frequently provides local storage capabilities. Often, LANs have one or more servers which make files available on the network. When a non-server computer, or node, requests the use of an application, the server "serves" the application through the network to the node. LANs enable network users to share system resources to communicate with one another.

How is the Internet used?

A computer user — whether it be an individual, a business or government — equipped with a modem and an Internet account, can use the Internet for a multitude of activities. The user can access foreign sites, browse, and download and upload lists of information, applications and computer files from these sites. Presently, the most popular Internet service is the World Wide Web. It provides multimedia access to documents. It comprises a host of other services, including electronic shopping. The World Wide Web is user-friendly. It is marked up with hypertext (highlighted words and pictures). It employs "point and click" technology for mouse-controlled computers. This allows users to jump from one Web site to another. Electronic mail, or "E-mail," is another attractive aspect of the net. Via E-mail, users can send and receive private messages to and from other Internet users across the globe. The discussion groups, or "newsgroups," located on electronic bulletin board systems (BBSs), provide a public forum for users to express their ideas and opinions. The Internet user also has immediate access to a wealth of timely information such as stock-market ratings, national and international news, and topical research from around the world.

How does one get on the Internet?

One can access the Internet either directly from one's computer or by connecting to a LAN or other computer system that is in turn connected to the Internet. These computers may be mainframes, minicomputers or workstations located at universities and other large institutions, although even stand-alone personal computers may be Internet sites.

How does a home user get an Internet account and address?

One begins with an account. These are obtained through commercial online services, such as DELPHI, CompuServe, Prodigy or GEnie or through public-access service providers, primarily educational or other institutions. Once a user has an Internet account, he or she is given an "Internet Protocol" address. This IP address consists of a user identifier, e.g., the user's first name, followed by the "@" sign and the computer site identifier, a four-part number separated by periods: e.g., elvis_p@123.45.112.15. Strings of numbers tend to be difficult to remember. Therefore each numeric component of the address, e.g., "123," is represented by a corresponding "domain" (e.g., falaw). For example, elvis_p@falaw.mcgill.ca could be the address for Elvis Presley at the Faculty of Law, McGill University, Canada, i.e., user's name, division or department of an organization or institution, institution, country. Often the address begins with the most specific identifier on the left, and ends with the most general identifier on the right. Some addressing choices, however, may be deliberately vague in order to avoid disclosing their location. For example, I_way@zoo.net does not readily reveal the location of the computer system to which comments regarding this book may be sent. The last word in an address is the top-level domain. Generally, a two-letter code is used to designate a country. For example, "ca" indicates Canada. However, the top-level domain may also designate a type of organization: edu = educational, com = commercial, org = (usually nonprofit) organization, gov = government, mil = military, net = network. Each address is separate and distinct from any other address on the network.

How does data reach its ultimate destination?

To the Internet user, the actual functioning of the network remains invisible. The transmission process is often compared to telephone communications. However, this analogy is poor.[13] The phone system functions as a "circuit-switched" network with "dedicated" phone lines. Thus, when a person makes a phone call, a line is dedicated to that phone call, even if the line is not in use, e.g., if the caller is not actually speaking or is put on hold. This results in an inefficient use of a limited phone line resource.

The Internet, by contrast, functions much like Canada Post, although at a much faster pace! Both systems are packet-switched, rather than circuit-switched, networks.[14] A data transmission does not use a dedicated part of the network. Rather, the data is transferred into an Internet Protocol (IP) packet. When information is being routed, the IP packets are coded with the address information, thereby allowing various relay computers to pass on the packets until they reach their final destination. The Internet is connected by a set of computers called "routers." They function like post offices that sort and reroute the mail, moving it closer to its final destination in a period of split seconds rather than days. Each router may choose the cheapest and most accessible route for the next leg of the journey, thus avoiding rush-hour traffic jams. For example, packets may be interspersed into the "silences" of a normal telephone call.

The TCP communications formula manages the transmission

process. It regularizes transmission errors. The Internet Protocol (IP) ensures that the data is forwarded to the computer where the intended recipient has an account. Once the data reaches its intended destination, the packets are reassembled and stored on the computer. The recipient computer then allows the intended recipient user to access it.

Who governs the Internet?

Reconsider the Internet's origins. It was designed to be decentralized and unpredictable in order to withstand a nuclear war.[15] Today, the Internet is a kaleidoscope of computers scattered around the globe. It has no central governing body nor any hierarchical structure. There are, rather, benevolent organizations that establish standards and allocate resources and commercial bodies that administer larger networks.

The most influential organization is the international Internet Society (isoc@isoc.org). It functions as a volunteer advisor, providing assistance and support to groups and organizations using the Internet.[16] Its mandate is to foster global dialogue through the Internet. The Internet Society (ISOC) has a volunteer "council of elders" which meets regularly. The council establishes the network standards. These enable different computers to communicate with one another. It also allocates resources and sets the rules for the allotment of Internet addresses.[17] There are additionally volunteer subgroups which provide opinions and reports to the ISOC council. In the U.S., the National Science Foundation's NSFnet and ISOC have significant influence over the content of and conduct on the Internet. In Canada, CA★net sets similar standards. Despite the existence of these benevolent organizations, the Internet is largely anarchic and essentially self-policing. It relies primarily on the self-control and collective reprimand of its users. To date, there are no official channels through which to complain about or reprimand abuses of Internet ethics and standards.

Consequently, breaches of the Internet ethic are dealt with by collective reprimand. The Internet exemplifies the administration of law and order in an anarchic society. Superfluous and inappropriate communications are confronted harshly. Two typical responses are "flaming" and "spamming" the breacher. To flame a user involves sending nasty messages which express ardent disapproval of the user's conduct. Spamming entails obstructing the breacher's use of the computer. Take one hypothetical case. A lawyer advertises her services on the Internet by E-mailing her advertisements to everyone in the "ca" domain. Offended users react collectively by sending 1,000 copies of the New Testament to the offending user, with particular reference to Jesus throwing the merchants out of the temple. The response floods her electronic mailbox and possibly crashes her system.

Reliance on volunteer organizations and the self-policing method may be adequate when the community of Internet users consists of a relatively homogeneous, self-contained group of academics and computer buffs. But, as the Internet plays an increasingly prominent role and as it becomes more accessible to a wider public, the issue of control will become increasingly meaningful to policy and law makers. The problems of authority and regulation are complicated by the fact that the Internet has no geographical or jurisdictional boundaries. What laws should apply to the Internet? How far should regulations go in restricting the content of and conduct on the Internet? How do you "find" the actual perpetrator? Who should have jurisdiction to govern the Internet? What courts should have jurisdiction to judge? How do we reconcile conflicts in domestic, foreign and international laws? It becomes increasingly urgent that lawmakers address these and other questions.

Are there substantial security concerns?

One must be careful not to embrace this global network blindly. Pitfalls do exist. The legal issues, including security, emerging from the growth of the Internet are unquestionably a concern, particularly when we consider that one needs only a computer, a modem and an account to access the Internet. To drive on traditional transportation systems, one must satisfy certain requirements before obtaining a driver's licence and vehicle registration. Moreover, a driver is subject to provincial and federal laws regulating his or her conduct on the road. Laws prohibit impaired driving and speeding, for example. To date, however, there are no legislated preconditions to access the information highway and no Internet-specific laws governing conduct on the net. Of course, one does not need a licence to make a phone call. Prank phone calls and invading one's voice mail, for example, can be intrusive and potentially harmful. But as we become increasingly dependent on computers for our daily lives, e.g., to store confidential information or engage in commercial transactions, we should consider the implications of this absence of controls.

A more insidious threat lies in the potential for piracy of information. By placing one's research, intellectual property or business intelligence on the Internet, one risks pirating by others who then claim credit for, appropriate, or sell the material. Can conventional laws govern this feature of the international network? Other piracy problems arise where confidential information is stored on an Internet-accessible computer. No security method is foolproof. When the complexity of computer systems far exceeds the ability of a single mind to manage all its parts, a concerted effort to find a chink in a system's armour often results in a serious threat.

There are, additionally, tort law issues (civil as opposed to criminal wrongs) related to privacy rights, and defamation (wrongful injury to the reputation of another). The free flow of information on the network challenges conventional criminal laws, most notably, those respecting pornography and hate literature. The status of an individual's constitutional rights, such as the freedom of expression, must be reconsidered in the context of bulletin board systems (BBSs) and discussion-group communications. Questions of international law, conflict of laws (applicable rules from two or more jurisdictions) and copyright (proprietary rights in the expression of ideas) arise in assessing the legal impact of the Internet and, more generally, the information highway. How can we monitor an international network and control the content and distribution of the information it contains when it is designed to avoid controls by a central authority?[18] If one circuit is shut down, data will find another route on the network, making it extremely difficult to control or block the flow of information on the net.

Will the Internet imitate television to become an advertisers' boon?

Formerly, users banned commercial exploitation of the Internet. It was intended as a source for the exchange of ideas and information after it ceased being a classified military communications network. Commercial opportunists were reviled by other Internet users. Today, however, while the active and intrusive promotion of products and services on the Internet is still opposed, the Internet carries considerable "passive," or noninterventionist, commercial activity, particularly on World Wide Web home pages.

Opening up the Internet to commercial users will fundamentally alter the content and "style" of the Internet. It offers remarkable opportunities for commercial exploitation. It services a huge market and carves out a wide array of well-defined interest groups. Consequently, businesses can target specific consumer markets. Computer imaging technology, e.g., now enables jewellers to market their wares on the information highway. Using digitized camera equipment, a computer and imaging software, one can create almost instantaneously a three-dimensional colour image of a jewel.[19] The Internet is also a vehicle for sound and voice communication. Software companies are developing programs that permit computer users to make long-distance telephone calls over the Internet for the cost of a local call, i.e., free. Early versions are already in use. This sort of technological innovation will make the Internet an increasingly attractive commercial outlet. Inevitably, its days as a bastion of primarily intellectual global discourse are numbered.

II

THE METHODS

3
THE QUALITY OF UNDERSTANDING

"A fact in itself is nothing.
It is valuable only for the idea attached to it,
or for the proof which it furnishes."
— Claude Bernard

What is meant by "information basics" and why are they germane to discussions about the information highway?
By "information basics" we mean the scientific foundation, or groundwork, necessary to understand clearly what the information highway means, at all of its levels. We have split the discussion into two parts. First, in this chapter, we discuss human interaction with the existential environment that surrounds us at a fairly abstract level. We assess the ability of technology to approach human cognition given the state of existing technology. To assist this discussion of "information basics," we employ a model termed *the quality of human understanding.* It presents our best guess as to foreseeable limits of technological development. Second, we discuss "science basics" in the following chapter.

THE QUALITY OF HUMAN UNDERSTANDING

What exactly is this model of human understanding?

Data

Human understanding may be categorized in four discrete components: data, information, knowing, and wisdom. The fundamental component supporting this model is data. These refer to facts. For example, we know that fire is hot and that the earth possesses a gravitational field. These scientific realities underpin our understanding of human existence. For the purposes of a discussion of information technology, data more often consists of nuggets of truth such as a person's name, her height, the colour of her hair, her address, employment or other facts, that in themselves are seldom controversial, and that are demonstrable by the scientific method.

Information

Information stands a rung above data. Information is a collection or compilation of data based on purposeful selection and arrangement. Without further analysis, the assembling of facts based on some criteria does not mean anything or present one with a decided course of action. However, it is only one step away from being placed into action. Individual facts, or data, may be information as well, depending on the context of what is sought. The definition of information as a selection and arrangement of data resembles that of a compilation as found in many copyright statutes including the Canadian Copyright Act (which protects database creations).[1] The conscious selection and arrangement of data are granted a form of proprietary right under these laws. Data combined with other data are information if combined for a conscious purpose. Information takes data one step closer to understanding.

Knowing

True understanding in common parlance is thought to be synonymous with knowing. Knowledge, in everyday usage, relates to perception, and familiarity with fact or truth. It denotes a state of "clear and certain mental apprehension,"[2] and consists of an experiential quality. Knowing has always implied a level of consciousness. However, these definitions suggest that knowing is a range, and not a singular point or threshold. At its lowest level, familiarity with fact could easily be thought of as meaning a pre-existing notion or acquaintance with some truth possibly leading to a response or action. This acquaintance, presumably, arises typically through past experience and learning. For our purposes, this definition can be further distilled to mean the point at which information has been analysed and a course of action has been generated. This course of action may, of course, be to take no action at all. This interpretation is consistent with a "clear and certain mental apprehension."

A commonly used example of the differences between data, information and knowing is a phrase spoken in a foreign tongue. To a person versed only in English, a sentence presented in Arabic will appear as meaningless symbols. It is simply data. To a child who reads Arabic, the words in the sentence may each be familiar. However, the sentence as a whole may not provide a level of knowing that results in action. To an adult who reads Arabic, the sentence will have meaning and may produce an action. Consider, e.g., the sentence "Don't touch hot stove" in each of these cases.

Wisdom

At the high end of the spectrum of knowing lies the notion of consciousness and the beginnings of wisdom. It has long been accepted that wisdom is purely within the province of the human mind. One particularly apt definition refers to wisdom as the "knowledge of what is true or right coupled with just judgment as to action." The complex concept of justice is that quality which is thought to be purely human, although philosophical treatments of justice vary greatly.[3] Wisdom may also be thought of as implying some measure of self-awareness, and using abstraction and experience to look beyond the implications of the information that one is provided with. In this way, wisdom may be thought of as a high level of knowing.

The quality of understanding can therefore be said to increase as one moves through the stages from data to wisdom.

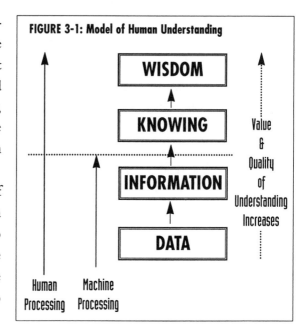

FIGURE 3-1: Model of Human Understanding

WISDOM

KNOWING

INFORMATION

DATA

Value & Quality of Understanding Increases

Human Processing   Machine Processing

How is this model helpful to understanding technology?

It allows us to understand what the current state of technology is capable of achieving relative to human action. It provides a benchmark by which we may separate that which is exclusively within the province of the human mind from that which machines are capable of achieving. At present our technology cannot attain wisdom, nor, according to some, can it even reach the most basic level of knowing. Nonetheless, information technology is useful in assisting us to achieve knowledge and wisdom. As technology moves up the ladder of understanding, this assistance becomes increasingly valuable. Whether machines will ever obtain a level of understanding equal to the highest level obtainable by human beings is not known. Today it remains within the realm of science fiction.

Why should we care about understanding? What is its value?

Understanding is valuable to us for many reasons. In economics, information technology advances have reduced labour content, sped decision-making and work processes and accelerated overall business productivity. These improvements, in turn, drive our modern economies, produce competitive advantages and replace physical products with superior solutions, e.g., fast databases, paperless offices, reductions in storage space. Human labour is gradually being replaced by machine processing at the lower levels of this model of understanding, and being freed to take up jobs that involve more complex, thought-oriented tasks. The nature and pace of this shift is an extraordinarily difficult one for modern economies to understand and manage.

Understanding is also central to human philosophy and self-actualization. Many philosophies and religions stress understanding as the key to attaining a state of bliss. Understanding for such purposes is considered unattainable by most human beings (let alone machines) during their lifetime. In our present state of being, technology may assist the attainment of spiritual nirvana through the widespread communication of ideas and concepts between individuals. Philosophical ideas are given increased currency through the availability of information technology.

Information technology is also valuable for political and social reasons. For us to make informed choices about our lives and the society we live in, understanding and knowledge are crucial. We vote based on what we know and understand about our society, our beliefs, and the persons seeking election. The success of a democracy is a function of an informed population. Similarly, we choose our career paths and make other life-choices based on our knowledge of available options and personal preferences. By increasing the dissemination of information technology, we equip people with more information on which they can base these choices. Information technology and the I-way enhance access to information much as the printing press did in Gutenberg's day.

Where does human intelligence stand on the spectrum of understanding, or what is technology capable of achieving today?

Although we often refer to civilization today as technologically advanced, when put under the microscope of human understanding, information technology is in its infancy. Currently we use computers for the gathering and storage of data. We have the ability to program computers to seek out data given certain criteria. We also use these machines to arrange or collate the data in a meaningful way. As we approach the level of knowing, our information technology lacks the ability to engage in sophisticated decision making based on information and experience. Computers can make decisions based on fixed criteria, and even build past decisions into future decision making. What machine processing currently lacks, however, is the ability to expand, on its own, the criteria that it may take into account without direct intervention by some human force. Human beings, on the other hand, have the potential to expand at will the criteria on which they base decisions. Nevertheless, depending on the scope of knowing, computer processing may be at the lower rungs of the ladder.

Will machine processing ever reach the higher levels of understanding?

It is difficult to predict the limits, if any, of technology. Given the rapidity with which we have attained our present level of development, it is likely that we can go further before reaching any limits. It is natural to expect, however, that as technology marches on we will experience the effect of diminishing advancements. Many of the terms currently used to characterize understanding are defined using the term human. These terms may have to be redefined as we further mimic human thinking using machine processing. Certainly the evolution of technology has allowed us better to understand human thinking processes. Given the characteristics of computer processing and the nature of the distributed network processing of information, it is possible that the I-way may eventually lead to the formation of a sort of consciousness. At present, however, the feasibility of such a conscious network forming is a question left to philosophers and futurists.

4
SCIENCE BASICS

"The science of today
is the technology of tomorrow."
— Edward Teller

This chapter has been designed as a technical primer. It sets out the scientific foundations for the current state of information technology at a very basic level.

What is the science on which the information highway is built?

We use the term "cyberspace" to describe the mysterious realm of the information highway. It evokes imagery of an abstract and intangible universe in which bits of information travel. In reality, communications and data are supported by physical laws that operate both on Earth and in space.

We begin by understanding air, electricity and light. By air, or aether, we mean the clear atmosphere through which electromagnetic waves travel. Electromagnetic waves surround us. They are created by the interaction between electric and magnetic fields. Electromagnetic waves are broken down into classes of waves based on their wavelength or frequency. Examples of electromagnetic waves include radiowaves, microwaves, infrared light, visible light, ultraviolet light, x-rays, and gamma rays. A radiowave is any electromagnetic wave, i.e., propagated by electric or magnetic fields, having a specific radiofrequency. Electricity is a flow of electrons with charges. Harnessed through wires, it can be a beneficial energy source. Unharnessed as lightning through the air, it is sometimes a destructive force. Electrical power, flowing through wires, is measured in volts or voltage and electrical current is measured in amps. More recently, light flowing through fibre-optic cable has become an important communication carrier, partly because of its speed. We shall focus here primarily on radiowaves through the air and electricity through wires.

Data can travel using any of these three signalling techniques, through the air or via wires or cables. There are at least three limitations that affect each type of signal. First, its original strength limits how far it can travel. Second, any interference en route, such as buildings or hills in the case of radiowaves and cuts or poor shielding in the case of wired transmission, will interrupt the signal. Third, the quality of the receiving device limits what is received.

A radiowave is sent from a radio transmission tower located on a prominent height of land. It runs in a straight line over a considerable distance and is picked up by radio receivers located within the receiving range.

A standard telephone communication serves as an example of communication by electricity over electronic circuits. A person makes sound waves while speaking words into a telephone mouthpiece. It converts these sound waves into electronic pulses expressed as voltage. Each sound has a distinctive set of electrical charges. The signals then travel along telephone wires from the point of origin through a series of switching stations before reaching their destination. Once the telephone receiver is raised, the electronic signal is converted from electricity back into a sound wave as words understandable to the human ear and mind.

Telephone communication is also conducted at various points in the network by light-based fibre-optic transmission. Rapid pulses of light are transmitted via fibre-optic cable, imitating the pattern of charges in an electric wire transmission as described, to a receiving device.

Traditionally, electric wire technology was the principal communications transmission medium. Today, microwave transmission and fibre-optic transmission are increasingly important in the building of a global communications infrastructure.

ANALOG AND DIGITAL DATA

How do data and instructions get converted into electromagnetic waves or electronic signals?

To understand how this is achieved, we must first distinguish the concepts of analog and digital data.

What is "analog"?

Analog technology transmits information as continuously varying electrical currents.[1] Analog measurements are referred to as "waves."

An analog device processes data in a continuous form rather than as discrete pulses. By way of illustration, a traditional wristwatch with hands measures time in a continuous, analog form. A computerized digital watch, by contrast, represents time in numerical digits. Although automobiles increasingly are being computer driven, most fuel gauges, tachometers and speedometers are manufactured as analog measuring devices. They are theoretically capable of identifying an infinite number of measurements,[2] because they are continuous.

Because physical quantities are more effectively measured in a continuous manner, analog devices such as thermometers and speedometers, as well as assembly line computers, are more often used for scientific, engineering and process control calculations. They are capable of providing more precise measurement. But highly precise analog measuring devices are very expensive. Thus conventional analog measuring devices are generally less accurate, as they tend to approximate results.[3]

Four technical characteristics of waves should be understood: frequency, amplitude, phase and noise. Figure 4-1 illustrates the first three.

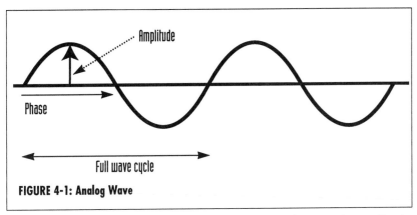

FIGURE 4-1: Analog Wave

A wave can be placed on an imaginary axis. The wave's amplitude is the height of the wave from this axis. The frequency of the wave is the number of times that the wave repeats or re-cycles itself per unit of time (usually one second). The phase of the wave is the point one is at in relation to one full cycle of the wave. Manipulating these characteristics of the wave enables communication.

But how does the communication actually take place?

Once a transmitter and receiver are in contact with one another, a signal known as a carrier, e.g., voltage, is transmitted between the two points. Signals with analog characteristics, such as voltage or radiowaves, may have their characteristics — such as amplitude, frequency or phase — varied according to the message being sent. The message is, in effect, translated into the analog form desired, and is reinterpreted at the other end. "Noise" refers to any features of the wave that are not intentionally encoded with the message.

How does any of this relate to the information highway?

The I-way is about communication. Analog signalling is a commonly used method of communicating through the use of transmission media that carry wave-form signals. For example, our telephone system uses analog signalling to communicate, as do radio and television stations. Although digital communication, discussed below, is favoured for new information technologies, existing communications systems will continue to operate on analog principles for the foreseeable future. Furthermore, analog principles are more reflective of principles found in nature. Understanding their operation will always play a part in the operation of the I-way.

Now what does "digital" mean?

For modern information technology, "digital" refers to a state of information that can be expressed by discrete quantities. Digital data are represented by binary digits ("bits"). Computers today, at their lowest level of operation, function using the binary digit system. All events are understood and manipulated by the computer as 1s and 0s. Binary was used because, at the hardware level, the 1s and 0s work well in representing the voltage-on and voltage-off states. If voltage were in a continuous wave form then it would be analog, as opposed to digital. A digital representation only concerns itself with whether the voltage is present or not — on or off — beyond a given threshold of tolerance.

Digital data are faster and cheaper to process given the current state of technology. Microprocessors which manipulate digital data have, in effect, countless numbers of voltage-controlled switches, which may each be flipped to either an on or off state depending on the digital data that the switch must represent. Digitization is simply the act of putting data into digital form.

What do "bit" and "byte" mean?

People often confuse the terms "bit" and "byte." A bit is a single piece of binary information (either a 0 or a 1). A byte refers to a set of bits that can represent alphanumeric (letters and numbers) characters. *Eight bits make up one byte.* The two terms should not be confused with one another. There are 256 possible characters which may be represented by a byte at any given time (2^8 bits = 256), depending on how you arrange the 0s and 1s. By "at any given time," we mean that different character sets may be used to represent each of the 256 possible characters. Using the scheme of eight bits in a byte, we have 256 discrete combinations to work with. We can use these 256 identifiers to represent whatever items we wish, up to 256 separate items. A character set is a finite group of items that has been designed to work with the byte scheme.

One commonly accepted character set is the American Standard Code for Information Interchange (ASCII). It employs a seven-bit scheme. Consequently there are only 128 characters (2^7 bits = 128). There are many variations of ASCII that use the eighth bit to expand the character set to 256 characters. Consequently, variants of ASCII have 128 common characters and 128 characters that may differ from set to set. In conjunction with seven-bit schemes, the eighth bit is also used by some technologies as a parity bit. Another common character-coding scheme is the Extended Binary Coded Decimal Interchange Code (EBCDIC) developed and popularized by IBM. EBCDIC is an eight-bit coding scheme. It uses all eight bits to represent characters. This all sounds very complicated. But it illustrates how digital technologies "understand" alphanumeric text.

Of course, not all digital (bit) data are meant to represent character data. Digital data may also represent pictures, sounds, animation or any other information. The discussion of Compact Discs below will make this clearer.

You mentioned a "parity bit." What is this parity bit used for?
Parity bit schemes are used to check for errors that may have occurred during the use or transmission of a string of bits. The eighth bit is coded at the beginning of a process, such as transmission over a

network, to reflect certain characteristics of the byte being transmitted. Two common examples of parity-checking techniques are odd and even parity. The even and odd terms refer to the number of 1 bits contained in the byte. Thus under odd parity, if the number of 1s in the seven-bit string is an odd number, the parity bit is a 0. If an even number of 1s are contained in the seven-bit string, the parity bit is set to 1. Upon completion of the process, the parity bit is checked and is compared with the seven-bit string. If the parity bit no longer accurately reflects the number of 1s in the string, then a loss of data has occurred. Parity schemes represent one of the simplest forms of error checking. Many more complex schemes are currently in use.

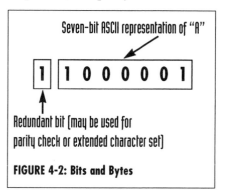

Seven-bit ASCII representation of "A"

| 1 | 1 0 0 0 0 0 1 |

Redundant bit (may be used for parity check or extended character set)

FIGURE 4-2: Bits and Bytes

How do analog and digital data relate to one another?

The term "digital information" refers to data that have been coded into binary digits for base-level processing by some digital processing unit, e.g., a computer. Digital devices, unlike analog devices, are only capable of understanding a finite set of values. Whereas analog signals are continuous and can be represented by waves, digital signals are characterized by pulses or steps, which are transmitted in intervals.

Although digital data exist quite comfortably in the world of today's microprocessors, in actual fact the real world is far more complex. Data in the world we live in, such as sound, usually operate on analog principles. As a result, analog data consisting of wave forms represent the natural world. They must be converted to a digital state to be manipulated by a microprocessor or stored in a digital format. This conversion is effected by analog-digital converters (ADCs). It is reversed by digital-analog converters (DACs). Common popular consumer electronic devices such as Compact Disc players, digital tape recorders and modems must effect these sorts of analog/digital conversions as part of their basic functioning.

How is this analog/digital conversion accomplished?

To convert an analog wave to digital information, one must "slice" the wave into many discrete components. The characteristics of these slices are digitally stored. In Figure 4-3 a graphical curve has many "slices," or rectangles, underneath it. Each rectangle is a certain height and a certain width. If the width of each rectangle were infinitesimally small, one could remove the curve on top and still be able to redraw the curve, based only on the rectangles on the page. If one were then to store the information about the rectangles, such as their height (assuming all were the same width) and the number of slices that had been cut, one could use that information to reconstruct the curve without ever having seen it. In reality, the exactness of the reproduced curve will depend on how finely the curve is sliced. As the number of rectangles increases (and their width decreases), the ability to reconstruct the exact curve will be enhanced.

Digitization of information works in exactly the same way. Analog information is changed from a wave format into numerical characteristics about that analog information by slicing the analog wave forms. The numerical characteristics associated with the slices may then be reduced to binary format and stored for later use.

This wave-slicing technique looks simple in theory. In practice, the amount of digital data that must be stored to represent even the most simple phenomena is extremely large, and is increasing every day.

From the graph in Figure 4-3 at space X, it looks like the digital wave slices miss out parts of the analog wave contained in space X. Does this missing space create a problem?

Correct. Digitization does miss out on recording some of the characteristics of analog data. The slices have a physical width. Therefore there will always be a portion at the point where the slice meets the curve not factored into the digital rendering of the curve.

The width of the slices is vital to the quality of the digital reproduction of the analog data. The number of samples, or slices, per given unit time (e.g., per second) is also known as the frequency or sampling rate, measured in hertz (Hz). For example, today's audio Compact Disc (CD) players, fancy DACs, convert 44,100 sixteen-bit samples of digital data per second into voltage (analog), which is then amplified and converted into sound by speakers. The use of sixteen-bit samples, known as resolution, allows a piece of information that consitutes one of a possible 65,536 (=2^{16}) levels to be stored every 1/44,100 of a second.

The reason 44,100 was chosen as the CD sampling standard was a function of the processing capabilities of the equipment at the time the standard was developed. It was felt that the 44,100 Hz sixteen-bit sampling rate produced sufficient audio reproductions of sufficiently high quality for the human ear. Many feel, however, that digital audio reproductions created at even higher rates sound even closer to the original live performance.

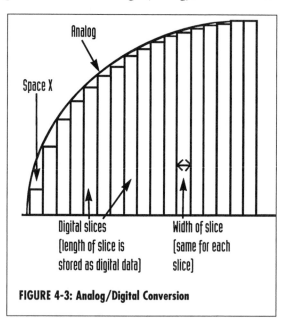

FIGURE 4-3: Analog/Digital Conversion

In sum, the sampling rate is a limit to the quality of the digital reproduction that is made, all having to do with the width of the slice. Depending on what is recorded, and the needs of the application using the digital data, differing sampling rates are required in different contexts.

Is there any way to overcome these limitations of digitization?
Theoretically, no. Even at the highest finite sampling rate technically possible, there will be a loss of the analog data. However, as the sampling rate increases, the loss decreases. Eventually the loss becomes insignificant to the application for which the data is being used. The sampling rate, and hence the quality of the digital data, is directly related to the speed of the processors performing the digitization and reconversion (the ADCs and DACs). The demand for increased clarity and exactness in digital information gives a powerful push to the development of new processor and memory technologies. Adding to the complexity of this explanation is the requirement of memory to store the digital data once produced. Each bit of data must be stored for quick retrieval, especially in real-time applications, to be converted back into analog form.

Memory is required to store the vast amounts of data. Processors are required to convert the digital and analog data back and forth and to manipulate the data in other ways. The greater the demand for clarity, the greater the need for increased memory capacity and the greater the need for processing power. Today, processors are capable of handling data at much quicker rates, and CD-player manufacturers have had to work around the 44,100 sixteen-bit samples/second standard in order to enhance the sound quality. So instead of increasing the sampling rate, today's CD players use alternative methods such as curve-smoothing techniques to enhance the conversion from digital data back to analog data.

How do these curve-smoothing techniques work?
These techniques try mathematically to project the makeup of the analog wave that was digitized. Using the digital data that has already been played and the data that is about to be played, the processor can often provide a better fit to the curve than if only the immediate digital data was used. The processor looks at both the present data it must play and the digital data it will be playing in the near future.

Based on both sets of data, the processor simulates an analog curve. Although the reconstruction may not be exact, each distinct reconstruction represents a very small period of time (in the case of CDs, 1/44,100 of a second). And for the purposes of listening, complete pinpoint accuracy is not necessary. We "hear" over the gaps.

If analog data is perfect and digital imperfect, why don't we use analog data? What's the point of digitization?

Ironically, one of the reasons we use digital data is because of the reproductive quality. By quality, however, we are referring to stability and not merely the faithfulness of the reproduction. A perfect analog reproduction will be closer to the original phenomenon than a digital reproduction. However, it is difficult to achieve a perfect analog reproduction at a relatively low cost because of "stability" problems in the storage of analog data, typically on magnetic media. These are easily corrupted and fade over time. Moreover, analog devices have relatively poor processing capabilities. The precision of high-quality analog reproductions, at high costs, is seldom required. Digital technologies are comparatively stable. They consistently provide high-quality reproductions, even when stored on magnetic media. Digital data based on 0s and 1s can often survive minor deterioration of the media, deterioration that would produce signal loss if the data was analog.

Finally, with digital technology the processing power and memory requirements are easily adapted to the needs and requirements of the application. Other information that may be captured by analog solutions is often considered extraneous. For example, our senses have finite limits as to the level of detail that they can discern. Any information beyond this point is imperceptible and is extraneous. Networking and computing technology in use today is primarily digital.

5
THE INNER WORKINGS OF A COMPUTER

"The march of invention has clothed mankind
with powers of which a century ago
the boldest imagination could not have dreamt."
— Henry George

In this chapter we explore the inner workings of a computer: its processors and instructions, three types of memory, and computer languages. We then consider the application of a computer to the I-way.

In discussing digitization, the term "processor" often appears. What is a processor, and what does it do?
It is a device, usually in the form of a silicon-based microchip known as a microprocessor, that manipulates data based on instructions provided from an external source. Microprocessors are central to computers today. They are its "brains." The main microprocessor that controls a computer's functions is also known as the computer's central processing unit (CPU). The CPU (or CPUs in the case of computers with multiple processors) performs all of the calculations and computing tasks.

Digital computers comprise a majority of computers currently in use. At their lowest level of operation, they function using the binary digit system. Streams of binary digits, represented as voltage in either an on (1) or off (0) state, are fed into the processor as both data and instructions, resulting in a manipulation of electronic gates contained within the processor. The resulting stream of binary data that emerges from the processor, based on where and how it emerges, may be sent to the appropriate peripheral device attached to the computer, such as a screen, printer, disk or network connection, resulting in some real-world event, e.g., the placement of a letter on the screen.

What is the difference between an instruction and pure data?

An instruction tells the processor to do something, to perform a given operation on the data. For example: telling the processor to add two and three. The instruction is to add, whereas the data are the numbers two and three. Conceptually, digital instruction and data work in the same way inside a computer. However, different processors understand digital streams very differently. As both are expressed in binary form (0s and 1s), the sequence and timing of the data as it flows through the processor will dictate how the stream is interpreted. Although the data and instruction quality of digital information differ, the term digital data is often used to refer to both.

How do processor instructions work?

CPUs contain a limited number of instructions. These are activated through electrical impulses that enter the processing chip. The number of instructions will vary with the architecture of each CPU. The effectiveness, largely measured in speed, of reduced instruction set computer (RISC) processors, which contain few simple instructions, and complex instruction set computer (CISC) processors, which contain many instructions at the processor level, has been hotly debated in the popular press over recent releases of Motorola's Power PC (RISC) processor and Intel's Pentium (CISC) processor.

What about memory?

It is central to the use of computers and the I-way.[1] Today's computers use three categories of memory devices to store their programs: internal (primary), external (secondary) and archival (tertiary).[2] Internal memory refers to those memory devices, often built into the structure of the computer, necessary for the computer to operate at its most basic level. External memory consists of devices that provide additional, more permanent, storage at a comparatively cheaper cost than internal memory. While external memory is not essential for the basic operation of the computer, it is required for most practical purposes. Archival memory is more permanent in nature and can be stored away from the computer, often at an offsite location. Information stored in archival storage is typically not accessed with any frequency, hence the term archival.

Examples of these three types of memory?

1. Internal (Primary) Memory

Random-access memory (RAM) refers to silicon-based microchip memory. Also known as volatile or dynamic memory, it is a form of internal memory that stores data as long as electrical impulses are being fed through it. Volatility in the context of microchips refers to a continuous supply of power being required to maintain storage of the information in the chip. A nonvolatile chip maintains its storage without a continuous supply of power. Accordingly, once the power is cut off, the RAM microchip loses all information stored in it. RAM is the functional memory that allows a computer to operate. The programs that the computer processes, or parts thereof, must be stored in RAM during the operation of the computer, with the exception of ROM programs. If programs are otherwise stored on external memory devices, they must be copied into RAM memory to be executed.

Another type of internal memory device is a read-only memory (ROM) microchip. It is a silicon-based chip encoded at the factory, and cannot be written to once encoded. ROM chips store information using a system of microscopic gates. They route electrical impulses to their intended destination based on the chip's programming. Many variants of ROM chips, such as EEPROM (electronically erasable programmable read-only memory) chips, also exist. They support different characteristics including storing nonvolatile data on the chip. ROM chips often contain a host of "service programs." These interact with a computer processor chip's limited instruction set to perform frequently requested tasks such as accepting keystrokes from the keyboard and checking the state of various add-on devices such as external memory devices.

2. External (Secondary) Memory

The most commonly used external memory devices are magnetic tape and disks including both hard disks and floppy diskettes. Disks are magnetic media that hold vast amounts of data relatively inexpensively. Magnetic tape was the storage medium of choice prior to the advent of the disk/ette. Reel-to-reel tape, cassette tapes and their variants all recorded analog information onto the tape by magnetically affecting the tape. Disk/ettes allow random access. Magnetic tape requires sequential access. Disk/ettes, like tapes, vary in their size and storage capacity. The capacity of disk/ettes has steadily improved over the past two decades. The current diskette standard is 3 1/2" in length and width with a storage capacity of two megabytes (one byte = eight bits) of information, although the popular IBM PC standard for this size of diskette is a capacity of 1.44 megabytes per disk. Disks (i.e., hard disks) now vary in storage capacity measured in the hundreds and thousands of megabytes. Disk drives, the devices that connect a diskette with a computer, are capable of reading and writing data to diskettes. The actual magnetic surface of a diskette is often protected by a plastic shell. It is highly susceptible to contamination by foreign elements such as dust. Hard disks, also known as fixed disks, are self-contained units that read and write data onto various disk platters contained in the hard disk unit. Unlike diskettes, hard disks contain multiple magnetic platters or disks. Hard disks are factory-sealed, thereby providing a strong layer of protection against possible harmful contaminants.

2.(a) Floptical Disks

A relatively new disk-storage technology that combines the technologies used in both diskettes and optical disks is entitled floptical disks. They have recently entered the computer world. They are essentially high-capacity diskettes. They store approximately twenty-one megabytes of data. The increase results from using a laser to align and guide the magnetic read/write heads of the disk drive unit. Very fine movements can be achieved. The data may be placed in a relatively more compressed form on the disk.

2.(b) Digital Tape

In the past decade, to compete with the upsurge in digital Compact Discs, tape manufacturers produced a digital tape standard for the home audio market. Two such exist in wide distribution: Digital Audio Tape (DAT) and Digital Compact Cassette (DCC). They record and replay digital data. They may be used and re-used. The clarity of the sound reproduced is identical to that of a Compact Disc. Furthermore, it is easy to convert the digital data contained on one tape to another without loss in quality. Digital tape has the advantage that, at the consumer level, it can be written to and may be re-used countless times. One disadvantage is that when recording and playing there is physical contact with a magnetic head. This causes wear and tear on the tape. Another disadvantage is that, unlike storage media in disk form, the data on the tape must be sequentially, as opposed to randomly, accessed. Thus, to listen to a song at the end of a tape, one must forward through the entire tape. The player cannot instantly play the track one wants. Digital tape recorders are still relatively expensive, starting at $600. DAT recorders are also frequently used for other purposes, such as archiving digital computer and database data. All devices that manipulate and store digital data are unaffected by its ultimate use. Whether it is digital data that recreates a picture on a computer or data that plays back a recorded sound, both are stored as a stream of 1s and 0s, and are indistinguishable to the naked eye.

2.(c) Optical Disks

One of the most popular new technologies is the optical disk, commonly known as a "laser disk" because of the technology it employs. It is better to use the term "optical disk," in order to differentiate between the optical disk standard also known by the name "Laser Disc" and other optical disk standards such as Compact Discs. Examples of optical disks are: Compact Discs, CD-ROMs, MiniDiscs, Laser Discs, and most recently Video Compact Discs.[3] Each type of disk is a variant of the same technology.[4] Digital data are imprinted on the disks by lasers, which imprint the bit information onto the disk surface. Playback, or the reading, of the disk is similarly done by laser. A common misconception about optical disks is that they are all "read-only." Read-only refers to the fact that once the information is stored onto them they can only be used for playback. They cannot be written upon again. In fact, the technology for read/write optical disks does exist. The price for devices that use optical disk technology has dropped substantially in the past five years and units have become more accessible to consumers. Optical disk technology has already proliferated the mass consumer market. Compact Discs were first introduced in Japan in 1982 and in the U.S. in 1983. They have effectively replaced vinyl records, the mainstay of music lovers for decades. Similarly, CD-ROM technology has been standardized. Consequently, CD-ROMs have carved out a niche for themselves in the microcomputer market.

The advantages of optical disks are their durability, their relatively large storage capacity, which allows high-quality information to be stored, and their portability. The size of a CD-ROM (and Compact Disc) is 120 mm in diameter, or about the size of a cardboard-thin doughnut, and is capable of storing 550 to 600 megabytes of digital data, the equivalent of roughly 400 high-density 3 1/2″ IBM-standard computer diskettes. For durability, read-only optical disks are often coated with a protective layer of clear plastic. With some CD-ROMs, as opposed to Compact Discs, a further plastic shell is sometimes used to protect the disk. When the disk is read, there is no physical contact with any part of the reading device. A laser performs the read operation. It scans the disk's surface. Consequently there is no wear and tear on the disk each time it is read.

The newest optical disk technology to appear on the market is Video Compact Discs. Video CDs are a new video optical disk standard developed by Matsushita, Sony, JVC and Philips, four of the world's largest consumer electronics companies. Video CDs can hold up to seventy-four minutes of video images on a conventional CD. The Video CDs can be played on traditional CD players that have a digital output port with the use of a special video adaptor. Because of the Video CD's relatively small size compared to the Laser Disc, the Video Disc can only hold enough digital data to produce a resolution of 300 lines, equivalent to a traditional VHS video cassette. The Laser Disc format produces displays of 430 lines, resulting in a much sharper image. It remains to be seen whether video disks, generally, will eventually supplant videotape, currently the standard.

3. Archival (Tertiary) Memory

Archival memory is used for long-term storage of data. It is usually relatively cheap with slower access speeds than internal or external memory. It is typically tape based. Designating memory as archival depends on the context of each situation. For example, in some cases removable hard disks or diskettes may be used as archival memory. Digital Audio Tape (DAT) archival memory is currently growing fastest, due to large capacity and low cost.

How does memory work with a computer?

Various streams of digital data inputs are sent to a computer's processor. Here they react with each other depending on the characteristics of the processor. An output stream of digital data is generated. They may come from the computer's memory (internal, external or archival) or they may be generated by some peripheral device attached to the computer, such as a keyboard or modem. Data will generally be placed in RAM prior to going through the processor.

Until now, we have used the term digital data broadly to represent both instructions and pure data on which the instructions are to be performed. Both are expressed in digital form and are only discernible as either instructions or data depending on the processor.

COMPUTER LANGUAGES

Computer instructions written down don't appear as 1s and 0s. They more closely resemble human languages. Why?

In fact, instructions represented as binary data are only one type of a computer language. There are many other types as well. Computer programs are written in computer languages which vary in their degree of resemblance to ordinary mathematics and common languages. A higher-level language is said to be closer to common languages, such as English or French, in its vocabulary than a lower-level language. The level, also referred to as the generation, of the language depends "upon the ease with which it can be read" by human beings.

Why don't all languages look like "common languages" then? Why do we use binary notation?

Computers don't actually *understand* higher-level languages. Rather, digital computers are only capable of understanding sets of instructions (programs) represented by 1s and 0s respectively. The instructions expressed as 1s and 0s are referred to as the lowest-level, or first-level, language, or machine language. The reason? The 1s and 0s, or bits, represent on and off states. When converted to on and off voltage states, they trigger countless switches or gates contained in a computer's processor. The triggering of these gates creates a domino effect, with other gates producing an effect that is translated through the computer's hardware into a real-world event, e.g., some form of output or calculation.

The text of a program written in a higher-level language is known as source code. The machine-level translation of the source code is known as object code.

How, then, can a computer understand these higher-level languages?

For a computer to process the instructions of any given language other than machine language, the instructions must first be compiled, or translated, into machine language. These translations are effected by compiler programs, which are also computer programs. Compilers accept source code as data and then generate object code which may be executed, or run, on the computer.

A lesser-used form of higher-level language are interpreted languages. Unlike compiled-language programs, an interpreted-language program is translated as it executes on the computer, line by line. An interpreter program, in machine-language form, must be executed concurrently with the interpreted-language program. This interpreter program accepts the source code and performs the translation as it executes. Interpreted languages are much slower in their execution since the computer must spend time translating the program each time it is executed. To provide for quicker translation, some interpreter programs are hard-coded onto ROM chips. In this way, the computer can access the interpreter program more quickly.

Programs written in machine language can be understood directly by a computer's central processing unit without need of any further translation. But programs are seldom written directly in machine language because of conceptual difficulties.

Why are some higher-level languages more complicated to understand than others, if they all eventually get translated into machine language?

Increased flexibility and speed. As one moves away from machine language, there is a corresponding loss in flexibility and the optimal layout of instructions which affects the speed of execution. Higher languages are more readable because their instructions often represent several machine-language instructions. It is often difficult, if not impossible, when writing in a higher level, to tailor one's instructions so that they will optimally use the processor. Furthermore, compilers and interpreters cannot optimize these instructions fully as they do not know what portions of the compiled higher-level instructions are extraneous to the functioning of the program.

What are some examples of higher levels of computer languages?

Fourth generation languages, or "4GLs," are database languages used primarily by end users rather than professional programmers. 4GL commands often use entire English words and may resemble the following: "ADD SALES UNTIL NUMBER_OF_CUSTOMERS IS 10."

Slightly more cryptic are third generation languages such as C, Pascal, COBOL, BASIC and FORTRAN. These languages are commonly used by programmers. They consist of some English words combined with a greater level of numerically represented computer logic. A 3GL instruction in BASIC similar to the 4GL example above might be: "FOR CUSTOMER = 1 TO 10; TOTAL = TOTAL + SALES; NEXT CUSTOMER."

Second generation languages, also referred to as intermediate-level as opposed to high-level languages, are assembler languages. Assembler language instructions are composed of mnemonic instructions (shortened versions of full-word commands) combined with memory addresses, usually denoted in hexadecimal notation (number system with a numerical base of sixteen, which is conceptually more comfortable to the human eye than binary notation). Programmers use these for performing specialized tasks that require extremely efficient programming. Practically speaking, assembler is the lowest level of language used by programmers, with few exceptions. A typical assembler instruction might be "JMP" followed by a memory address that instructs the computer to branch, or jump, to the instruction indicated by the address.

To summarize, the term "source code" refers to the written form of program that the user physically produces in a given computer language. Programmers today have a wealth of higher languages from which to choose, including Pascal, C, FORTRAN, BASIC, assembler languages, and so on. Once the program's source code has been written, the programmer will generally "compile" the source code into machine-readable object code, using another computer program known as a compiler to perform the conversion. Object code is generally in binary form — a language made up exclusively of 1s and 0s — and is directly usable by the computer. A programmer may, of course, write his program directly in binary form. This is not often done due to obvious conceptual difficulties.

PUTTING IT ALL TOGETHER ON THE INFORMATION HIGHWAY

How does all this technical information tie together on the I-way?

Under the present state of technology, information of all types is being converted into digital form. Whether the information is sound, graphics or text, once in a common digital form it is all 0s and 1s. Until the information is finally presented to the user, the equipment used for its communication, storage and manipulation is the same irrespective of its intended form of output.

Digitization allows many currently disparate networks, including telephone, cable and computer networks, to be interconnected into one virtual communications infrastructure.

How is the computer technology — processing, memory and computer languages — relevant to this communications infrastructure?

Think of a network as a web of nodes connected by wiring. The wiring pipes data from one node to another. Once the data has reached a node, it must be interpreted by some form of computer processor. This computer processor may not appear as a typical computer (with a keyboard or screen), but may be embodied in other devices connected to the network, such as a television, radio or telephone. Currently, these devices generally operate using analog rather than digital signals. However, the conversion of these technologies to a digital format is underway. Furthermore, even if these devices remain analog, analog-to-digital conversion adaptors may be used to render the signal into the appropriate form.

Can you provide a recent example of a digital technology that has come online in Canada?

Digital radio has recently been deployed in Canada. Two companies, Shaw and Cogéco, offer digital radio services. Digital radio consists of the transmission of digital audio signals, which find their way into the subscriber's home via conventional television cable. The data are then converted to analog signals by a decoder box. It also decrypts the signals, which are then sent to the user's audio equipment. The decoder/decryption box is provided by the digital radio service provider. In order to offer this service, both companies have teamed up with American digital radio providers. For programming, the American affiliate sends digital music signals to an American satellite which then get beamed to the Canadian cable company's head ends. The Canadian Radio Service provider, e.g., Shaw, also produces some Canadian programming, which is beamed to TELESAT and then to the Canadian cable company's head ends. The cable company then encrypts the signals and sends them to its users via cable. Because each cable affiliate head end purchases its own cable equipment, the features which users may expect will vary from company to company.

Can you summarize?

At their most basic level, hardware devices connected to digital information networks operate in a fashion similar to the computer processor model presented above. Processors and memory work hand-in-hand to take incoming data and to convert them into some coherent form of output such as text, sound, graphics or mechanical movement. Computer languages are used to design software, the instructions that allow the hardware devices to operate in their intended manner. Software may be contained on removable media or may be hard-coded onto microchips that are part of the hardware.

Data travelling on digital communication networks are in binary form, notwithstanding their real-world representation. This standardization of data allows for the interconnection of networks. Upon receipt, the relevant device will read the data and convert them into their intended output. It is vital that the device used be the same device that the data were intended for, or the output will be meaningless. Data that represent a graphical image in a given graphics format, for example, may be converted into a sound format and the resulting pictorial representation will be meaningless noise.

6

TRANSMISSION METHODS

"The open society, the unrestricted access to knowledge,
the unplanned and uninhibited association of men for its furtherance —
these are what may make a vast, complex, ever growing, ever changing,
ever more specialized and expert technological world,
nevertheless a world of human community."
— J. Robert Oppenheimer

Here we deal with the transmission of data between various points. These telecommunications systems are known as networks. We use telecommunications networks in our everyday lives: e.g., telephone, cable television and computer networks. Each of these operates in similar fashion by taking information, converting it to data, transmitting it and then reconstructing it for use. The discussion will centre around actual methods of digital transmission, currently used standards and their associated costs and benefits.

What is a Basic Communications Model?

The simplest way to understand a digital (or any other communications) model is to think of a communications system as comprising five components: (1) message source, (2) encoding converter, (3) data path or highway (transmission medium), (4) decoding converter and (5) message receiver. The message source and message receiver are self-evident. In a computer network they consist of the processors, such as computers, at either end of the communication. In the case of electronic mail, or electronic chatting, the message source is the user who generates the message. Similarly, in the case of a telephone call, the message source is the person making the telephone call. The message receiver is the person receiving the call. The encoding converter and decoding converter are the components that take the digital or analog data generated by the message source and convert them to and from the form required for transmission over the data path or highway (also referred to as the transmission medium). In a conventional telephone setting, the encoding and decoding converters are the equivalent of the telephones at either end of the connection. The diaphragm in the mouthpiece of each telephone handset converts (encodes) sound vibrations into analog voltage signals, which are transmitted over the telephone highway. At the receiving end, the speaker in the earpiece of the telephone handset converts (decodes) the analog voltage it receives into sound through a similar system of vibrations. Finally, the medium of transmission, often the bottleneck to high transmission speeds, is the physical cabling and switches that route the transmission from sender to receiver.

In Figure 6-1, why do you not distinguish between the message source and receiver?

For two-way communication to take place, often the message source will also be a receiver. There are three ways, or modes, in which two-party communications may take place over a communications link: (1) simplex mode, (2) half-duplex and (3) full-duplex. With a simplex arrangement, there is one sender and one receiver. In other words, the messages flow in one direction only. An obvious simplex example is listening to the radio. The radio station generates a communication signal which the listener eventually hears. The listener, however, does not communicate with the radio station in response.

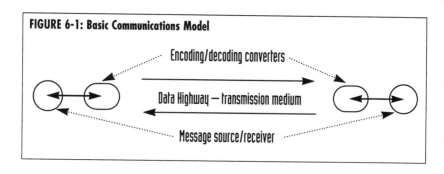

FIGURE 6-1: Basic Communications Model

Half-duplex communication, often denoted by the abbreviation HDX, describes a two-way communications system where only one message may be placed on the data highway in one direction at a time. Once the message has been sent and delivered, the direction of the communications flow may be reversed. Half-duplex examples are walkie-talkie radios and citizen band (CB) radios. Both users can either listen or talk over the radio, but cannot do both at the same time. The final mode of communications is full-duplex (FDX), which allows two-way communications contemporaneously. The most obvious example is the telephone, where users can talk and listen at the same time. Consider a telephone conference call with frequent and heated interruptions. It is interesting to note that human beings generally operate in half-duplex mode — one may speak or listen, but not both simultaneously. Interrupting a person to tell them your own point of view is an example of HDX communication.

The mode of communication used in a given system will depend on a host of factors, including the purposes of the system, the bandwidth (discussed below) of the information highway, the communications protocols used, the type of transmission (digital or analog) and the capabilities of the message source and receiver.

Can you explain transmission speed?

In order to understand transmission speed, we must first introduce several communications concepts. The first is the difference between parallel and serial transmission. Communicating data in parallel involves the transmission of multiple pieces of data simultaneously. Conversely, serial communication involves sending data sequentially, one piece at a time. Clearly, parallel transmission results in faster transmission of data than serial, although it is far more costly to build parallel data highways.

Related to parallel and serial transmission are the (often confused) baud and bit-rate measurements of telecommunications speed. Baud measures the number of discrete signals, e.g., voltage or light, transmitted per unit time, usually seconds. Bit-rate measures the number of bits transmitted per unit time. Bit-rate is often written as bits per second (bps). In order to increase telecommunications speed, one must increase the bit-rate, since it measures the speed of data transmission.

The baud and bit-rate sound like they are the same thing.

They are different. With an uncompressed serial communication, the baud and bit-rate may be the same. If we transmit our data in parallel, however, then the baud will remain the same whereas the number of bits per second will increase. With parallel transmission, the bit-rate is equal to the baud multiplied by the number of data highways. Remember, baud is a measure of the actual signal speed, not the data being communicated. Another example of differences in baud and bit-rate, as will become clearer, occurs where data compression schemes are used.

How does speed relate to bandwidth?

Bandwidth refers to the range of frequencies that can successfully be carried or contained on a given system. Frequencies, as will become clearer, are the carriers of data being transmitted. Therefore, bandwidth denotes the frequency range in hertz (Hz) that can be transmitted on a given data highway. A simple analogy is a water pipe. Bandwidth refers to the maximum amount of water that could be squeezed through the pipe, without considering (yet) the baud at which it travels. By using transmission techniques such as multiplexing, discussed shortly, several bits can be transmitted per unit time using different frequencies in the bandwidth of the data highway. In other words, bandwidth will directly affect the bit-rate.

The term "bandwidth" is often loosely used to mean speed generally. Bit-rate, or bps, is often the more correct term and will often be used in conjunction with bandwidth. For example, coaxial cable has a higher bandwidth than twisted-pair copper wiring and transmits at a higher bit-rate.

What are some of the restrictions on speed and bandwidth?

The factors limiting the speed and bandwidth ("bottlenecks") may occur at any point in a communications system. Traditionally, however, these bottlenecks have largely been a function of the type of cable used. For many years, conventional telecommunications thinking focused on improving the type of wiring and its associated bandwidth. Because of the high cost of rewiring the main telecommunications system, the telephone network, this was an exercise in frustration. In the past fifteen years, however, there has been a marked shift in approach to make do with what we have. New technologies that deal with data transmission and compression are now at the forefront of the technological revolution. Through the development of new methods of switching, compression and multiplexing, it has been possible to increase dramatically the amount of data (bandwidth) that can be sent through traditional wiring systems. To grasp fully the advances in multimedia telecommunications, we must understand the many other underlying concepts of telecommunications technology.

Let's start with cables and wiring.

Note first that communications may be broadcast, using the aether as the medium of transmission. Not all communications systems use wiring. But where wired data highways are used, there are currently several accepted wiring standards used in data transmission: twisted-pair, *baseband* coaxial, *broadband* coaxial and fibre-optic. The first two cable types are often referred to as baseband communication links because of their limited bandwidth. The last two cable types are referred to as broadband communication links because of their relatively high bandwidth. Let's deal with each wiring standard in order, from lowest to highest bandwidth.

1. Twisted–Pair Wiring

Twisted-pair wiring is currently used in traditional telephone systems. It is also the slowest medium in terms of data transmission. Its bandwidth, or frequency range, is extremely limited. The wiring literally consists of several insulated copper wires twisted around one another. One wire serves as the ground whereas the other is live. The great advantage to using twisted-pair wiring has always been its low cost and easy replaceability. Unfortunately, unamplified data sent in digital form (as pulses of electricity) can only travel for about 8,000 feet on twisted pair before dying out. Repeaters, devices that push the data along the cable, as well as amplifiers, must be used to keep the signal alive — at a significant cost. The telephone system was not designed to send digital data, but rather voice data in analog form (as voltages with varying frequencies).

The present telephone network, because of the large number of subscribers, uses complex switching and routing techniques to connect calls. There is only one connection linking each telephone with the circuit switching, routing equipment and trunk lines. A user is not directly connected, by specifically dedicated links, with every other user who has a telephone. This would provide higher transmission rates, but at astronomical costs. The sheer size of the task would render its management physically impossible. As a result of the complex route that a signal must take in order to reach its intended destination, the signal will be slowed down by the slowest cable link in the chain — in this case the twisted-pair wiring that goes into the home.

Copper cabling is also used for geographically limited digital telecommunication, particularly local area (computer) networks as found in offices. In order to increase transmission speed, these cables, such as 10-base-T, have many copper wires to allow for communication in parallel. Copper wire is also being used by telephone companies to provide high-speed digital service through Integrated Services Digital Networks (ISDN) services. ISDN service is an increasingly affordable alternative to using the analog telephone system for digital telecommunications.

2. Baseband Coaxial Cable

Baseband coaxial is a slight step up from twisted-pair wiring and is often used interchangeably with it. Although the cost of the cable is higher, it is more rugged, requires less maintenance and provides increased bandwidth. Baseband coaxial cable is capable of transmitting digital data at speeds of up to twelve megabits per second,[1] without requiring modulation (the digital data is transmitted over the cabling in digital, not analog, form). Baseband coaxial cable is often used as a solid alternative to twisted-pair wiring in local area networks because of the cable's increased shielding and relatively low cost.

3. Broadband Coaxial Cable

Broadband coaxial cable is an upgraded "cousin" to baseband coaxial cable, generally greater in diameter, with increased amounts of insulation, and as a consequence has an increased bandwidth. Most people are familiar with broadband coaxial cable as the core of cable television networks. Because of its increased bandwidth, broadband coaxial cable can carry up to 100 television stations or thousands of voice signals and data at rates up to fifty kilobits per second, with repeater/amplifiers required approximately every 1,000 feet.[2] The ability to squeeze in a great many different types of information is quite attractive, as one only needs one cable for multiple services.

4. Fibre-Optic Cable

The three cable types thus far mentioned all operate based on electrical signals. Fibre-optic cable instead operates on light. Fibre-optic cable is composed of thin strands of glass or plastic fibre bundled together. There is a thin cladding layer between each fibre that essentially insulates and prevents any seepage of signals from surrounding fibres. The bundle of fibres is then insulated as a whole. As with electrical cable, there are many fibre-optic cable types, the most popular of which is graded index fibre-optic cabling.

Because fibre-optic cable is based on the transmission of light signals, they may be digital or analog in nature. The sending encoding converter will transform digital data into light signals — on/off pulses for digital light transmission or varying in intensity for analog light transmission. The receiving decoding converter transforms the light signals back into electrical digital form. Optical-fibre cable offers many advantages compared with electrical wire/cable transmission and surprisingly few disadvantages: bandwidth is dramatically increased; there is no bleeding or leakage of signals causing interference; it is relatively cheap to bundle many fibres together in one cable; and, because light is the carrier, signal loss over distances, requiring the use of repeaters, is significantly reduced.

Broadband coaxial cable can carry several thousand voice communications simultaneously. AT&T's FT3 fibre-optic lightwave system, using a 1/2″-thick fibre-optic cable containing 144 fibre-optic strands, can carry 80,000 voice conversations at ninety megabits per second.[3] Although fibre-optic cabling clearly surpasses other data transmission media in effectiveness, a wholesale rewiring of the telephone system is unlikely within the next few years due to immense costs, called "sunk costs." Instead, key parts of the system, such as long-distance connections and trunk lines, are being replaced with fibre-optic cable to pace technological innovation well into the next century.

What about broadcast communications?

No discussion of transmission media would be complete without covering the most widely used communications media of all, air (also referred to as aether). Broadcast communications using radiowaves over the air may also be used to transmit data. Microwave radio transmission of data is used for television, radio, voice and a host of other signal traffic. For voice traffic, until fibre-optic cable was used for long-distance lines in the mid-1980s, radiowaves were the medium of choice for the telephone companies. The difficulty with using radiowaves is that there is a finite bandwidth for all within the broadcast region to share. With a cable-based system, one can simply lay a cable and create an entirely new and free communications conduit, whereas with radiowaves everyone is using the same conduit. As a result of this difficulty, radiowave frequencies are very strictly regulated, and are often governed by international agreements. Without strict regulation, radiowave communications would overlap and interfere with one another. Another striking difference between wired and broadcast communications is that the former occurs between point-to-point interconnections whereas with the latter, the signal is readily available to all with a receiver within the signal range. The need for encryption is thus increased in a broadcast environment.

For data transmission, most radio data is currently transmitted in analog form. Although digital transmission is possible, the bandwidth required is significantly greater. Since radio-transmission bandwidth is finite, analog radio transmission has evolved as the transmission technique of choice.

With the limited bandwidth capacity of the radio-frequency spectrum, services such as online multimedia databases will within the next few years be distributed to remote locations via telephone or other cable systems and not via radio transmission.

This describes transmission media. But sending the data down this data highway involves an understanding of network topologies and communication protocols as well.

What is a network topology?

This refers to the structure of a network, i.e., how the processors and cabling are interconnected with one another. Topology may be thought of as the "shape" of the network. Some common examples of network topologies are star, bus, tree and ring. One example should suffice. With a star network, all nodes (processing devices) are connected to a central hub — like the spoke and hub scheme used by many airlines. In the case of airlines, planes fly along spokes from various destinations to the hub (a central location). There passengers transfer to other planes which take them to their ultimate destination which may be another hub or the end of a spoke. A star network operates in a similar fashion, transmitting data from each device to a central hub. It then routes the data to its final destination. Other topologies set up the devices and interconnections differently.

What are current limitations on transmission?

There are three important ones: modulation, multiplexing and switching. They limit the physical development of the information highway.

Modulation?

Because conventional telephone technology required repeaters and amplifiers every 8,000 feet when using digital form, the alternative of modulation was developed. This modulates digital data into an analog format and then demodulates it back into a digital state upon reception. The science is this. Sine waves may be used to represent "any series of pulses, sounds, voltages, or similar waves."[4] Modulation of digital data involves representing digital on/off data as a combination of sine waves which can then be sent as voltage over a telephone wire in the same bandwidth as voice communication. Mechanisms that *mo*dulate and *demo*dulate are referred to as "modems." They are familiar to most people who have personal computers. Modems are the most popular means of linking computers from the home to other computers, as they can function using the existing telephone system. But because of the telephone system's limited bandwidth and relatively poor quality of transmission, extremely high rates of data transmission are impossible. One way to boost the information transmitted without necessarily increasing the amount of data transmitted is by using data compression techniques (discussed below).

Multiplexing?

This allows the placement of more than one data signal on the same data highway simultaneously, saving costs associated with laying new cable. Imagine the efficiencies obtainable by sending ten or twenty messages on a cable simultaneously compared with one.

How does it work?

Multiplexing operates by placing different data messages on the same medium by controlling the time (time division multiplexing) and/or frequency (frequency division multiplexing) of the signal that is placed on the data highway.[5]

With frequency division multiplexing, various analog signals are placed on the data highway at different base frequencies next to one another, filling up the bandwidth of the data highway.[6] No signal overlaps the frequencies of any other signal. The signals are then transmitted in parallel to the decoding converter. The broader the bandwidth of the data highway, the greater the number of signals that can be carried.

Time division multiplexing consists of sending data from different sources together in serial form (i.e., one after the other) over the same medium. That is, data travels over the data highway from many different sources piece by piece combined with one another. A time reference is used by both the sending and receiving converters in order to assemble and reassemble the data. The online time is broken up and each sending source is given a block of time within which it can place its signal on the line.[7] For example, assume two data sources, A and B, wish to transmit data over the same data highway using time division multiplexing. A's transmission is the message "howdy" and B's message is "doody." Assume no conversion to binary or further complication. The data is placed on the highway as characters. One form of time division multiplexing could result in a data stream as follows: *hdoowoddyy*. The messages in this case are placed onto the data highway one character at a time. In actual fact, the data stream would probably be broken down into subgroups and sent with some overhead data telling the demultiplexer how to reassemble the data. Overhead refers to extra data that is transmitted, such as error-checking data and start/stop data telling the receiver when to start recording and stop recording the incoming data stream.

What about switching?

Most networks (LANs, WANs and telephone networks) do not directly connect each node or user with every other node or user via dedicated connections. Economically, the costs of such a system would be incredible. Instead, telecommunications networks use extremely creative structures, or topologies, to create the appearance of a virtual connection. With a telephone, there is only one wire going from the telephone to the telephone company's main line. The concept of switching dictates how one's information finds its way through the maze of wires and relays that form the data highway from sender to receiver.

Two switching methods are commonly employed in telecommunications networks: circuit switching and packet switching.

What is circuit switching, and when is it used?

The traditional telephone network uses circuit switching in order to route its messages. Circuit switching involves the tripping, or opening, of a series of the telephone company's circuits,[8] thereby in essence creating a dedicated line between caller and receiver each time one makes a telephone call.[9] Once the circuits are set up between the two parties, the connection is exclusive and is not capable of transmitting data other than between the sender and receiver. Prior to the computer age, circuit switching was the most sensible alternative. However, in an age where transmission time is increasingly valuable, and processing time cheap, circuit switching is unnecessary. Dedicated connections are wasteful because no voice connection nor most data connections are consistently placing information on the line. There are idle times, whether a pause in conversation or being placed on hold, during which the dedicated line stays dedicated but remains unused.

What is packet switching and when is it used?

Packet-switched networks are widely used in data, as opposed to voice, transmission networks (LANs and WANs). Potential uses of packet switching also exist in both voice and videoconferencing applications.[10] Developing and refining packet-switching technologies are considered to be at the cutting edge of telecommunications technology today.

Packet switching involves a multistep process that results in a much greater utilization of network resources. The first step in packet switching involves breaking the information down into blocks or packets. The packets are then attached to some overhead data which contains address information of where the message is to be sent, and may also contain other information such as error-correction information. The address information is much like the address printed on an envelope and put through the mail. It uniquely identifies the person to whom it will be sent. The more information, the greater the overhead, and the larger the size of each data packet that must be sent. After a packet is assembled and sent out over the network, its mission is to find its destination.

Once the packet is on the data highway, it encounters nodes, or relay stations. These decide on the best routing, or path, for the packet to take. These nodes differ from the circuits in the circuit-switching example in that the nodes direct or route the packet traffic as they receive it. Nodes are computers. They have processors and memory that contain instructions and information regarding routing. In complex networks, a packet may encounter many nodes prior to reaching its intended destination. Each node examines the address contained in each packet and chooses which other node with which it is connected is the best route to take. Once the next node is chosen, the information is placed on the connecting data highway and sent to the next node. This process keeps up until the information packet reaches its final destination, where the overhead is removed from the data and the packets are reassembled.

What is fast packet switching?

Fast packet switching is a newly developed variant on packet switching.

The Canadian company Newbridge Networks' fast packet-switching model, entitled asynchronous transfer mode (ATM), uses packets of fifty-three bytes (characters). Only five bytes represent overhead (the address of the recipient). The five-byte address is made up of only the next node and not the ultimate destination, which is often much longer depending on the particular network being used. When the initial connection is made, each node along the way (from caller to receiver) sets up a table with the next node's address. This is referred to as opening up a virtual connection through the network. The packets are then sent to the next node, which replaces the five-byte address with the next node's address, and so on. No error-correction overhead is used due to the high quality of the equipment, and the address overhead is relatively small. As a result, more information may be squeezed through the network, thereby increasing the speed of the overall transmission.[11]

By providing increases in the amount of data that may be transmitted, technologies such as fast packet switching are providing the means by which multimedia solutions such as videoconferencing can operate on existing equipment (i.e., circuit-switched twisted-pair wiring).[12] The technology is here, whereas the uses are yet to be discovered. With the ability to transmit real-time images over conventional telephone equipment, multimedia databases can now provide users with not only text but real-time audio and video information as well. While the equipment controlling these technologies remains relatively high priced to the home market, as with all innovation, the price will drop to manageable levels within a short period of time if demand develops and economies of scale set in.

What about compression?

Digital compression is the act of encoding the digital data so that more data can be squeezed onto a given storage device or onto a data highway. The digital information is sent through a computer which looks for trends in the data, e.g., consecutive strings of either 1s or 0s. Once a trend, understood as such by the compression algorithm, is identified, it is removed from the data and replaced by a new string of data (bits) meant to symbolize the trend. The newly inserted bits are, of course, much shorter than the original string of data and consequently the total amount of data is reduced, or compressed. Once compressed, the data can be transmitted more quickly or stored using less storage space. Once the storage or transmission operation is complete, the compressed data must be reconstructed, or decompressed, by a computer before it can be used.

Decompression is simply the reverse of compression: the symbolic data are replaced by the trends of original data that they represented. Both the compressor and decompressor must work with the same symbol and trend sets in order for the operation to be successful. Many different types of digital compression exist today and, as processing speed increases and processing cost decreases relative to storage and transmission costs, compression will remain a vital part of digital technology.

What are protocols?

Protocols are the rules by which the transmission of data takes place. Both the sender and receiver of the data must agree on these rules. While the transmission techniques, topology and transmission medium allow the data to move from the sender to receiver, the protocols —

existing at both ends of the communication — allow the encoding and decoding of the data into a form that can be understood by both processors. A good example — a complete communications model illustrating all the concepts we've discussed — is human communication, one person speaking to another. The message sender and receiver are both human beings. The transmission medium is the aether (air). The transmission of the data is analog, encoded through sound waves generated by the sender's vocal chords and received by the receiving party's eardrum. It picks up the vibrations of the sound waves within a given range and interprets them. The protocol used is the physics of sound waves. Its limits are dictated by nature. Both parties to the communication must be able to properly construct the sound waves into their intended frequencies. A damaged eardrum may result in a garbling of the intended message. If this happens, there will be no comprehension of its content. In the same way, a processing device cannot, without understanding the appropriate protocol, understand the contents of a data message. Protocols will vary depending on a host of factors including specifications of the network, the message and equipment used. With more complex networks, the protocol will also contain information that allows addressing of the message so that the intervening devices will deliver it to the appropriate destination.

The costs of wiring everyone to the I-way seem extremely high.

This is a commonly expressed concern. Cost has often been perceived as the steepest hurdle preventing the deployment of a nationwide high-speed communications infrastructure. It is true that the costs associated with laying high-bandwidth, such as fibre-optic, cable to every home and business from scratch are fantastic. Although twisted-pair copper wiring has been around for more than half a century, it was thought that to achieve high rates of transmission a rewiring would be necessary. In reality, both cable and telephone companies have already upgraded much of their equipment and cabling to allow high-bandwidth transmission. The bottleneck therefore rests primarily in the connection to the home.

Currently, most (99 percent) of Canadian homes have a telephone connection and a majority (estimated at 75 percent penetration) of Canadian homes have cable connections. With the development of new transmission data compression technologies, current wiring may prove to be sufficient. Furthermore, as the main lines have been redeployed as high-speed links, the cost of rewiring the end links into the home is relatively low.

7
STANDARDS

"The greatest invention of the nineteenth century
was the invention of the method of invention."
— Alfred North Whitehead

What are standards?

A standard is defined as: "something considered by an authority or
general consent as a basis of comparison; an approved mode."[1]
Standards exist to some degree in everything we do. They ensure the
orderly functioning of society. Consider four examples. First, the
North American electrical current standard is 120 volts (120V). The
European standard is a much higher 240V. Our electrical wires trans-
port 120V alternating current. Therefore, North American electrical
appliances are designed for the 120V standard. Voltage converters must
be used in countries where the 240V standard exists. A North
American–made hair dryer plugged in without a voltage converter in
France burns out because the 240V power surge is too high.
Conversely, a French-made 240V hair dryer gets insufficient power to
heat up in Canada because of the lower 120V standard. Second,
Canada recently adopted the metric system (metres, grams, litres . . .)

as a measurement standard, emulating European and, increasingly, international practice. However, the U.S. did not follow its declared intent to move from the imperial to the metric system. Thus, Canada and the U.S. are "out of sync" with respect to these measurement standards. Road signs indicate maximum speeds in miles in the U.S. and in kilometres in Canada. Readily available conversion tables exist to translate nonmetric into metric standards, e.g., on vehicle speedometers. Third, S. F. B. Morse developed a system of telegraphic signals composed of dots and dashes and short and long flashes corresponding to letters of the alphabet and numbers. Morse Code evolved as an internationally accepted standard for the transmission of telegraphic messages. Finally, languages are, in essence, communication standards.

For the information highway, standards provide a common "language." They enable hardware, software and data to interact. They permit interconnectivity and interoperability of networks and equipment.[2] Standards bring the I-way to life as a virtual network of networks tying together existing disparate networks. Since different I-way components, such as cable, broadcast and telephone, currently have different transmission capabilities and modes of operation, they require a common standard to interconnect and operate seamlessly. Just as two people need to speak the same language to understand one another, communications systems require standardized methods "to talk" intelligently.

Standardization occurs at all levels of the I-way. At a "micro" level, standards apply to its inner workings, such as computer hardware or the style of computer program writing. Incompatibility at this stage is not fatal to interoperability because "macro"-level standards enable different systems to interact. Standards may also be "proprietary" or "open." Often corporations will formulate standards for their own products. These proprietary standards are associated with individual manufacturers. They may be protected against unauthorized use by intellectual property laws. Open standards, by contrast, are ownerless. Any producer can adopt them. As a result, they tend to prevail in the industry.

What are examples of I-way standards?

Consider three. Data communications standards, or "protocols," govern how computer systems interact to send and receive data. Standard protocols enable computers from different manufacturers to speak the same language during data transmission. Computers can use completely different software if the programs in the sending and receiving computers agree on what the data mean. At the receiving end, data must be translated into a readable format. Standardized schemes, such as ASCII and EBCDIC, exist for the digital coding and decoding of text. They function much like Morse Code, using standardized symbols to transmit a message or data.

Second, digital compression is the process of digitizing, and thereby shrinking, analog video or audio signals into 1s and 0s. Digital video compression standards (discussed later) are used to transmit video signals via satellite.

Third, the federal government announced in August 1995 that it will adopt the Eureka 147 system as the digital radio broadcasting standard when digital radio is introduced.[3]

How are I-way standards developed or established?

Standards may be informally (de facto) or formally set. Initially, many standards are adopted in a piecemeal manner through use or practice. They develop largely through industry and market groups. The standards development process in information technology fields has transformed substantially over the past decade. Through traditional mechanisms, a select group of independent international, national, regional and subject-matter standards-making bodies follows a gradual and deliberate well-established process. Standards professionals administer it. In the past ten years, new bodies with diverse constituencies and jurisdictions have emerged. They include both industry-based and ad hoc global groups.

Because standards may be slow to develop through formal channels, many bigger industry players create their own "proprietary" standards.

Often, smaller industry players adopt these standards (if they are not sheltered by intellectual property protection). IBM, for example, developed a standards architecture called the Systems Network Architecture (SNA). Other computer manufacturers subsequently appropriated it. Through this informal process, standards are determined by which products prevail in the market. The most popular and most widely used technology becomes the "standard" in a particular industry. Ad hoc standards development forums have blossomed in Canada. Through them, standards develop faster but tend to be more national or regional, rather than international, in scope.

With globalization, uniform worldwide standards have become increasingly important to communications; so have more formal standards development channels. There are numerous players collectively responsible for the definition and deployment of technical standards, in particular, international standard-setting bodies. The International Telecommunications Union (ITU), over 100 years old, is the oldest of the standards organizations. It was originally responsible for setting international standards for telephone communication between countries. The International Consultative Committee on Telephone and Telegraphy (CCITT) traditionally sets communications standards. It operates in concert with the Geneva-based International Standards Organization (ISO) and the International Electrotechnical Commission (IEC). Committees of each handle standards adoption for particular sectors of the communications industry.

At a national level, the Canadian Standards Association (CSA) and the New York–based American National Standards Institute (ANSI) are actively involved in setting international standards for existing and emerging technologies. While their standards development processes are usually lengthier than that of ad hoc groups, they develop standards at an international level.[4] As well, standards development organizations that represent different sectors of the industry (manufacturers, telecommunications enterprises, financiers . . .) have a stake in the outcome. They are key participants in the definition of standards.

In Canada, a governmental/industry body, the Telecommunications Standards Advisory Council, oversees the process and provides national coordination.

Where standards are determined by market forces, standards development can be complicated by the fact that industry players are often reluctant to adopt standards compatible with their potential competitors.[5] They frequently disagree on choice of standards. This often causes confusion and higher prices, at least in the short term. It raises the question of whether standards set by a regulatory body constitute a better system.

For example, digital video compression (DVC) technology is used to shrink or compress satellite signals so they take up less space on satellite transponders that send and receive signals. Because the transmission spectrum is finite and because there is a growing demand for this space, signal compression is clearly needed to satisfy this demand. As a result, broadcasting, cable and satellite companies have been trying to agree upon the adoption of a single DVC standard. Without a common standard, these technologies cannot communicate. Yet, the rivals have been unable to reach a consensus. This confusion has stalled the introduction of direct-to-home (DTH) satellite. The Canadian satellite distributor Expressvu Inc. announced in August 1995 that it would be unable to launch DTH service in Canada as planned in September 1995.[6]

What role, if any, should government play in developing standards?

Three broad options exist for government involvement. It could impose technical standards upon the information technology industries. It could leave the adoption of standards entirely to the marketplace. Or, government could foster a nurturing environment for industry-developed standards. We prefer the third avenue.

Government-controlled standards have a number of disadvantages. First, government cannot finance all standards research and regulation.

Second, telecommunications and information markets are very competitive and continually and rapidly evolving. There is a risk that government-imposed standards could stifle innovation by freezing existing standards or by imposing a rigid, constraining philosophy. Third, government may not have as much expertise and experience as the private sector in standards evaluation. Fourth, the increasingly global nature of competition in these industries precludes a particular country or government from imposing specific standards that are incompatible with the international marketplace. Such attempts would put that country at a disadvantage by limiting the quality and performance of available services and products.[7]

Microsoft President Bill Gates opposes the imposition of government-formed technical standards.[8] He argues that consumers will benefit more from market-driven standards, using the computer and software manufacturing industries as examples. They have flourished over the past two decades because of the minimal regulation of technical standards. "The competition drove incredible innovation. The market drove standards, which provided practical interoperability of computers without standing in the way of fast-paced evolution." Bill Gates has become the richest person in the world in less than two decades. In this context, international and industry-wide guidelines outlining common and interoperable standards become desirable. The PC industry illustrates how the lack of regulation can deliver more innovative technology, more efficient standards, more consumer choice and lower prices. However, market-driven standards can also result in the development of standards monopolies, although competition law helps limit the occurrence. And special efforts to ensure that competitive forces prevail may also be salutary. More than fifty of the world's largest computer firms have joined together to fight Microsoft's relentless advance into the business software market. They have agreed to adopt a common standard for the next generation of UNIX software aimed primarily at large office computers.[9]

If government is not directly and actively involved in standards development, what role should it play?

It should foster research and encourage collaboration and the development of open standards. It should disseminate information and promote technology transfer. It should oversee the standards development process to ensure the public's best interests are being served.

Won't bigger firms dominate smaller ones in the development of standards because of economies of scale?

Probably not. Even if new market players do not possess an absolute advantage over existing firms, they may possess a comparative advantage through specialization. This allows more efficient allocation of resources, resulting in lower prices. Big players will have more lucrative alternatives for their resources. This leaves smaller players with opportunities. All of this happens if barriers to entry are reduced as a result of open, as opposed to proprietary, standards being adopted. Because the Canadian economy is driven primarily by small- and medium-sized enterprises, open standards are especially beneficial here.

How are uniform standards beneficial?

First, interoperability of communications systems is the foremost benefit. Interoperability is the ability for users of different hardware, software and network components to communicate effectively. It is essential to the information highway's growth. The DVC standards confusion has held up the implementation of DTH satellite service due to the inability to interact. Second, incompatible standards impede competition within the information technology industry. Once consumers select their initial merchandise, their ability to mix and match products is hindered by the fact that other brand-name technology cannot interact with the initial product purchased. Third, a standardized environment saves scarce resources because technology developers need not reinvent the wheel each time they create. This results in lower R&D costs and, ultimately, lower product prices.

Cheaper costs to producers usually result in greater savings to the consumer. Additional consumer savings result from less training and retraining of users and fewer errors from unfamiliarity in a non-standardized environment. Fourth, standardized environments are more user-friendly, resulting in lower training costs.

How so?

Take the example of standardized user interfaces. These are features, such as keystroke commands, that allow users to interact with a computer program. Over time, users become adept at running programs largely because they become familiar with how the user interface functions. If the program's interface is altered, even if the underlying function of the program remains unchanged, a user may be unable to use the software. Imagine if the location of the steering wheel and gear shift of an automobile were switched. Drivers would have difficulty driving the automobile. The number of accidents would increase dramatically. These accidents produce real costs. To reduce these costs, users retrain themselves. This also involves direct costs for retraining and indirect costs for lost time.

Why do we need international standards?

Because uniformity is vital to the stable operation of a worldwide communications infrastructure. With the proliferation of new communications technologies and globalization of human interaction, internationally recognized standards have become increasingly important. They remove barriers to the international transmission and reception of information and data. The I-way is a global animal. It does not confine itself to state borders. That is its strength.

By way of illustration, the international community is attempting to implement a universally recognized standard for digital radios.[10] The development of such a standard would result in digital radios being produced and sold to a worldwide market. With the exception of the United States, every country has accepted as a uniform standard a "wide-band" system, Eureka 147, for digital radio. The United States, by contrast, is researching a carriage system that would transmit digital programming along conventional AM and FM analog bands rather than along the proposed wide-band carriageway. These two systems transmit radiowaves at different frequencies. Consequently, if and when Canada, and not the United States, adopts the Eureka 147 standard, we could not use our digital car radios across the border without some sort of a converter.

What are pitfalls of adopting standards?

Three should be noted: (1) "going down the wrong path," (2) technological myopia and (3) monopoly development.

1) "Going down the wrong path"

Developing appropriate technological standards is a costly and sometimes risky process. To compete effectively in information technology markets, entrepreneurs must launch new products early.[11] Innovation typically occurs several years before the adoption of standards. Consequently, many new products and systems are incompatible. This becomes costly and wasteful. Businesses must redesign their products in accordance with standards. A related problem is that many multinational or large corporations adopt unique standards compatible only within their organizations.

Much can be spent "going down the wrong path" before discovering the error. The transaction costs required to start over and find the superior path may be prohibitive. This can result in a less efficient technological standard and consequent opportunity costs relative to the better technology. Because this risk is not quantifiable, it cannot easily be weighed against the associated advantage of a standardized environment. The selection of a particular standard is tied to a host of factors including initial cost, availability, ease of use, flexibility and marketing.

The extinction of the home-use Betamax videotape standard illustrates this calculated risk. The Betamax standard was abandoned in favour of the VHS standard. The former was originally patented and obtainable via licence from Sony Corp. It was clearly the technologically and functionally superior videotape format relative to the competing VHS standard developed primarily by JVC Corp. However, because the VHS standard was an open standard, universally accessible, it gained widespread acceptance over the Betamax format, which was difficult and expensive to license. Consequently, home-use Betamax videotapes and recorders have largely faded from existence.

Another example is the IBM PC architecture for personal computers, developed in the late 1970s. At the time, computer engineers did not foresee the dramatic improvements in processing and memory technology from rapid scientific leaps and dropping computer chip prices. The adoption of the IBM standard through the distribution of PC "clones" limited memory accessing abilities to 640 kilobytes (kB). Generations of PC-technology computers following the hugely successful PC were also forced into the 640kB yoke for reasons of compatibility. Despite acknowledgement of the 640kB standard's weaknesses, manufacturers and users continued to use it. Compatibility, cost, marketing and availability of alternative software were underlying reasons. The 640kB barrier hampered software development over numerous years. This caused substantial inefficiencies and economic opportunity loss to the computer software industry and to consumers.

2) Technological myopia

Where a standard becomes pervasive, it can foster industry technological myopia. It may forestall or at least hinder new technological approaches to problems. Taken to the extreme, every problem is formulated only in terms of existing technology, thus precluding creative research into alternative solutions. For example, many currently believe that advances in technology will be digital in nature, driven by microchip. This has created a certain myopia, in that universities are training their students and encouraging researchers to work within the limits of this environment. Both funding and research into alternatives to digitally based chip technologies have waned. Who is to say that a more effective analog technology or a biologically based digital technology would not have developed had more universities and researchers not shifted to the digital chip standard?

3) Development of industry monopolies

Standards development in the computer industry is a naturally occurring phenomenon. Users often need to share computer data files with one another. Data files are typically generated by various application programs. Software developers themselves are often the greatest proponents of a standardized environment. One of the most effective ways of marketing a computer program is to make it compatible with as many existing programs as possible. Newer programs often incorporate existing technologies. This allows users of existing programs to switch easily to the new software. Once the software developer has captured the market it seeks, and developed a standard of its own, it often changes its tune and demands that its standards be protected. This enables it to exercise monopoly power over its users, thereby obtaining a greater level of profits. Two often-cited computer industry examples are the Apple Macintosh and Lotus user interface standards. Both companies based their own products on existing technology.[12]

In sum, a standardized computing environment has both economic benefits and costs. The costs tend to be less quantifiable than the benefits. While standards are essential to the growth of the information highway, we must be aware of and attempt to overcome the weaknesses of standardization in the development process.

III

THE PLAYERS
AND THE CONTROLS

8

THE CARRIERS

"Competition is the keen cutting edge of business,
always shaving away at costs."
— Henry Ford II

The purpose of this chapter is to identify the players responsible for carriage on the information highway, to analyse how their role is changing and to identify the principal challenges for public policy and the private sector in that change. A leading theme is that the enormity of change and competition from new technology and the new economics creates great tension for old law and existing institutions and ways of doing business.

Who are the players?

It is hard to draw a definitive list. It depends partly on how early one starts. Gutenberg's printing press in the fifteenth century is a clear point of departure. Looking over the past century, one can identify the telegraph, telephone, radio (both broadcast and two-way communication), television (both over the air and cable), satellite and computer companies, including Internet access providers. Simply put, carriers are the entities that build the networks and transmit signals over them. Suppliers, by contrast, are those who create and place content in those wires and air waves.

How do these carriers function?

Currently, each carrier has a distinct technology or mode of transmission used to transport its content. Mobile or cellular telephone services, for example, employ a switching system to transfer calls between radio channels or radio towers as a vehicle moves from one area, or "cell," to another. Consequently, scarce radio frequencies can be reused and mobile services can be provided to many more people in urban areas.[1]

Traditionally, each carrier, with the exception of computer networks, has had its own regulatory framework, giving it a monopoly. In turn, the state has imposed certain performance requirements such as universal and minimum levels of service, regulated prices and rates of return on investment, or state ownership, regulation of foreign ownership and subsidization of nonprofit services and supplies. It has used comprehensive and detailed regulation to accomplish this. A good example is Canada's 99 percent telephone penetration of good quality at comparatively low rates, partly due to cross-subsidies from long-distance to local service. This becomes more difficult to sustain when other international carriers can provide cheaper long-distance service to Canadian customers.

How is the information highway affecting the carriage industry structure?

The information highway is eroding two principal defining characteristics in the telecommunications and broadcasting industries: first, the traditional monopolies, and second, the historical division between the two. Both were dictated by government. Technological change and market forces, not the regulatory or legal environment, are the driving forces behind this shift.[2] But, technology and the market are forcing shifts and creating powerful tensions.

What are the tensions?

The core tensions are convergence, competition and their regulatory and economic implications. Technological advances are blurring the traditional distinctions between telephone, cable and computer communications systems and between telecommunications, broadcasting, entertainment, computing and data information industries. Convergence is a function of cost, coverage and capability or capacity. The new wine of technology, however, flows poorly into the old bottles of law and monopoly institutions. Compression of time and space, led by digitization and convergence, has destroyed the tidy traditional compartmentalization of distinct carriage technologies and industries on the information highway. This change in function has led to change in form: privatization, deregulation and extensive competition, the disappearance of natural monopolies and the creation of new ones. Canada's current long-distance phone wars resulted from two regulatory directives which opened up the long-distance telephone service market and ended Bell Canada's seventy-year monopoly.[3] New long-distance competitors have been undercutting Bell's prices drastically in order to lure clients away. Bell has fought back with its own price cutting and aggressive advertising. Long-distance rates have dropped by half since 1987. It is presently unclear which companies and industries are profitable.[4]

This phenomenon is increasingly global because traditional nation-state boundaries have eroded. As a result, regional and national regulation has lost some of its potency. A useful way to look at this is to consider the technological developments outlined in the earlier chapters placed against the rules and regulatory institutions analysed in this and subsequent chapters. We sail in a turbulent technological sea of change with less secure navigational bearings.

What are the principal laws governing carriers in Canada?

Three federal acts form the regulatory core. The Telecommunications Act[5] is the principal statute. It sets out the CRTC's broad supervisory and regulatory powers over federal telecommunications carriers. They are concentrated primarily on rate and tariff control. The Act encompasses the major telcos such as Bell, Unitel, and Sprint, as well as cable companies' telecommunications services. This Act expressly excludes regulation of broadcasting facilities. With convergence, however, telecommunications facilities are providing increasing amounts of cultural products and services. It will be interesting to see how this affects their characterization as carriers.

The Radiocommunication Act's[6] scope includes the allocation, authorization and technical regulation of all public and private radio spectrum users. This encompasses everything from telecom carriers to radio stations to ambulances. The CRTC has no specific supervisory role under this Act. This is performed by the Department of Communications within the Ministry of Industry.

The current Broadcasting Act[7] dates from 1991. Its predecessor was enacted in 1968. It governs the powers and functions of the CRTC that pertain to broadcasting and the operations of the Canadian Broadcasting Corporation (CBC). The Act applies to three categories of broadcasting activities: programming, distribution and networks. It does not cover telecommunications carriers and nonprogram activities.[8] Very generally, its emphasis is on content rather than rates, culture rather than economics.

Have these Acts been reformed to reflect the carriers' changing role?

Yes. Within the past six years, each of them has undergone fundamental change. This gives Canada a competitive advantage. Yet, much of this reform is already somewhat dated. Other jurisdictions are wrestling with outdated legislation. The U.S. is attempting to reform legislation from the 1930s. It is also undergoing substantial deregulation dramatized by the divestiture of the AT&T telephone monopoly in the 1980s. Because of the gridlock between the executive (a Democratic president) and the legislative (a Republican majority) branches of government, and the many checks and balances in the U.S. system, legislative reform has not been achieved.

In Europe, tensions exist between the European Commission and individual nation-states, with the further complication that much of the information highway is cloistered in government departments or state-run crown corporations — ministries of post, telephone and telecommunications. But this too is rapidly changing.

Canada's parliamentary system of fused executive-legislative functions is advantageous. So is the fact that telecommunications and broadcasting are fields of federal jurisdiction. In the U.S. federal system, individual states have much more jurisdictional authority, thus complicating the regulatory terrain.

What about foreign ownership?

Like most jurisdictions, Canada considers telecommunications and broadcasting, but not computers, to be "essential" industries from a domestic ownership perspective. Thus, legislation closely controls these two industries and regulates their ownership. The Telecommunications Act limits foreign ownership to 20 percent of the voting shares of facilities companies and one third of telecommunications holding companies. The Broadcasting Act limits foreign ownership to 20 percent in both cases. But the Minister of Heritage Canada, responsible for broadcasting, has given notice of an intention to harmonize the broadcasting limitations with the less restrictive telecommunications framework. The IHAC has recommended harmonization to the less restrictive threshold for all regulated communication entities.

Should the government go further to reduce or eliminate altogether foreign ownership controls?

Again a balance is to be struck. On the one hand, nation-states wish to control instruments as vital to their society as communications. They also want to ensure these instruments adhere to national objectives. Finally, they wish to see the profitability from what traditionally have been "monopoly rents" and related economic activities remain in the country.

On the other hand, increasingly large sums of capital are necessary to build telecommunications infrastructures. Moreover, it is not so much the ownership, as the behaviour of capital, that is to be influenced if national objectives are to be met. This may be accomplished without ownership controls. Innovation occurs best with the free flow of ideas and better technology and practices across national borders. Spreading the risk of large and precarious R&D often lies beyond the financial resources present in one nation-state, particularly a smaller one like Canada. Issues of reciprocity across national borders arise, including those concerning satellite usage and the terrestrial "footprint" of its signals. Finally, if competition drives innovation, there are strong arguments to allow international competitive forces as well as domestic ones.

How do we strike a "right" balance?

Partly, it depends on the place of the particular nation-state in its international context. For Canada, there is the reality of the mouse and the elephant. We are a relatively small industrial state, one tenth the size of the U.S., sharing the longest undefended border with the world's largest industrial and cultural power. We are also the world's largest trader on a per capita basis in an age where intensive bilateral, regional and world efforts are being made to reduce barriers to capital flows and trade.

Thus, one must consider international reciprocity. For example, at the G-7 meeting specially convened on the information society in Brussels in February 1995, U.S. Vice-President Al Gore outlined the American Global Information Infrastructure (GII) policy. The U.S. currently requires 80 percent American ownership of telecommunications and broadcasting. He proposed these barriers be relaxed to zero with any country that allowed equal penetration by U.S. ownership of its domestic communications infrastructure.

The General Agreement on Trade and Tariffs (GATT) trade negotiations completed the Uruguay Round in 1994 but postponed further negotiations of free trade in communications infrastructures and services for the next round convened by the World Trade Organization (WTO). There will be increased pressures, led by the Americans with dominant positions both in carriage and content on the information highway, to reduce ownership and trade barriers. There are suggestions that the U.S. is seeking modification to NAFTA's telecommunications and intellectual property provisions in the discussions to bring Chile in as the fourth partner.[9]

Canada will have to tack to these international winds while charting its own domestic communications policy course. IHAC recommended that competition in international services should be permitted as soon as such competition is viable and sustainable and does not eliminate domestic players. Its determination should be part of a public proceeding that examines international business issues, use of Canadian facilities, international treaty and trade obligations and foreign ownership caps.[10] And on one particular policy, global mobile satellites with an international "footprint," the Canadian government introduced a new reciprocal policy in November 1994 stipulating that Canadian satellite service providers must hold an equity share at least proportional to the expected Canadian usage of a system.[11] This policy recognizes that, because of their vast international operating areas and the large number of satellites and their costs, the satellite systems are usually owned by international consortia.

What are the regulatory models?

There are many. But three, in particular, merit careful study because they are the foundation for the current Canadian situation. Each has taken a different approach to one of the three key industries that create the information highway. For seventy years in Canada and the U.S., telecommunications followed the path of a government-conferred monopoly franchise over a geographical area to one private-sector company. In return, that company provided basic universal service at regulated rates and regulated returns on capital.

Broadcasting, for almost that same time period, has followed a parallel but distinct path. Government has allocated monopoly space on the radiocommunication spectrum to radio and television broadcasters and, more recently, cable television and cellular phone services. In return, as conditions of the licence, the service providers have agreed to specified Canadian content requirements, price regulation, balance in programs, financial and in-kind contributions to domestic production, controls over offensive content and advertising. The CRTC administers both regulatory models.

In the case of computer hardware and software manufacturers and distributors, there has been little such regulation, though recently the U.S. Department of Justice has shown increasing concerns about monopoly practices developing through mergers and alliances. It intervened to prevent Microsoft's acquisition of Intuit, which has a dominant market share in a personal finances software management system. As this is being written, the Department is reviewing Microsoft's Windows 95 comprehensive software introduction in late August 1995, with a view to intervening after the fact. The software includes an operating system for the Internet. Comprehensive market coverage by one supplier with proprietary software protection threatens to create a near monopoly situation in a rapidly growing market. Stay tuned!

A major reason for the lack of regulation of computers has been the technological dynamism and rapid pace of the industry, springing initially from World War II and postwar defence R&D. Since the end of the Cold War in the early 1990s, the hardware and software industry has taken on its own surging life.

For Canada and the U.S., telecommunications and broadcasting regulation has satisfied national objectives of universal service and coverage. Arguably, however, innovation and the development of new markets and products have suffered. The computer industry has been the dynamic leader in this respect. To what extent this is cause and effect from the absence of regulation is largely conjecture. But, competition has led undeniably to the information revolution. It has also produced the somewhat chaotic situation of many unique standards and the difficulty of manufacturers' systems interconnecting as proprietary standards carve out large profits.

The first two traditional models are under great tension. Digitization, convergence and competition are forcing change. A sensible way to analyse this is simply to trace the crescendo of regulatory change in Canada over the past decade:

(1) the 1984 licensing of competitive cellular services;

(2) the 1989 Supreme Court decision recognizing federal jurisdiction over all Canada's major telephone companies;

(3) the 1989 Canada-U.S. Free Trade Agreement opening the Canadian market for competition in enhanced telecommunications services;

(4) the privatization of Teleglobe (overseas telecommunications), TELESAT (satellite communications) and Canadian National's telecom holdings;

(5) from 1989 to 1993, the revision of the three major framework Acts — telecommunications, broadcasting and radiocommunications — giving new scope to competition as the driving force for innovation;

(6) the 1992 licensing of competitive public cordless telephone services;

(7) the 1992 CRTC 92-12 decision opening facilities-based competition in long-distance voice telecommunications. A number of new players entered, featuring Canadian companies such as CN-CP Telecommunications (the old railway telegraph operators combined) with Rogers Communications and the largest U.S. telecommunications operator, AT&T, in a consortium. Significant rate reduction

ensued and this marketing intensity has reached red-hot levels. Whether this competition is sustainable is yet undetermined with Bell maintaining a 80–85 percent market share and the new players some distance from sustained profitability;

(8) the September 1994 CRTC framework decision[12] which split the rate base into regulated (local telephony) and competitive (long-distance equipment supply) segments; proposed price caps for rate of return regulation effective January 1998 for the regulated segment; removed earnings regulation of the competitive segment; proposed a carrier access tariff to encourage interconnection by rival suppliers; proposed rate rebalancing to reduce the cross-subsidy from profitable long-distance to local services, thus anticipating price increases for local services; proposed competition in local telephone service, allowing telephone companies to penetrate the broadband video market through a video dial tone which would permit movies on demand. Most of these changes will require further detailed hearings to take place over the next several years;

(9) the May 1995 CRTC's Convergence Report which provided more detail on ending barriers to telephone companies (telcos) providing cable television and related cable services and vice versa, and identified a number of barriers to be eliminated before each would be allowed into the other's domain to ensure that the dominant telco position would not jeopardize fair and sustainable competition. At present, each has difficulty providing competitive services at similar costs. Cable, on the one hand, has the advantage of high bandwidth capacity, particularly because video requires broadband. But, it is largely one-way. Telcos, on the other hand, have the advantage of switched two-way communication and vastly superior financial and

R&D resources.[13] Both have significant residential market penetration (telcos at 99 percent and cablecos at 75 percent), but with huge "sunk" costs: telco's copper pair wiring and cable's coaxial. How much new technology can convert these two "sunk" systems into crossover services is a major and risky decision.

This is a dizzying pace of change. What are the principal policy objectives that should guide government?
IHAC summarized these as follows:

> The primary role of the government, in respect of the issue of competitiveness, is to foster a dynamic and progressive policy, and a regulatory and legislative framework within which firms and entrepreneurs can flourish and expand employment. All levels of government should examine legislation, regulation and policies in order to eliminate unnecessary barriers and promote the use and development of the information highway by individuals and firms. Areas of priority attention are teleworking and home-based businesses, consumer protection and the encouragement of financing.[14]

The revised framework legislation is consistent with this philosophy. The 1993 Telecommunications Act sets out nine policy objectives:

(1) orderly development of a Canadian telecommunications system that serves to strengthen the social and economic fabric of Canada and its regions;

(2) access to affordable and reliable services in both urban and rural areas in all regions;

(3) enhanced efficiency and competitiveness of Canadian industry;

(4) Canadian ownership of the infrastructure;

(5)   promote the use of Canadian transmission facilities;

(6)   increased reliance on market forces and efficient, effective regulation where required;

(7)   stimulate R&D and encourage innovation;

(8)   responsiveness to users' needs;

(9)   protection of privacy.

But, most of all, the Act places increased reliance on competitive forces. It enables the CRTC to exempt classes of carriers from regulation or forbear from regulating services when competition is sufficient. The Government may issue policy directives to the CRTC and review its decision.

This evolution raises an interesting question of regulatory roles. The Competition Act is a federal law of general application substantially different from industry-specific legislation. Its Competition Bureau may conduct inquiries, appear before regulatory boards or bring matters before the courts or to the Competition Tribunal. The Bureau has long been interested in telecommunications, frequently intervening in CRTC hearings and encouraging discussions which stimulate greater competition. The telecommunications industry is not exempt from the Competition Act but benefits from "the regulated conduct defence"— recognizing that industry behaviour approved by a regulatory authority is in the public interest. The CRTC's implementation of the new Telecommunications Act will alter this, particularly through exemption and forbearance which will not necessarily constitute "deregulation." This may be a new more penetrating role for the Competition Bureau.

Are there any emerging carrier technologies which illustrate some of these principles in action?

Yes, several. First, personal communications services (PCS) use wireless technologies on the radio spectrum through mobile or portable terminals. Compression of signals has made it possible for a much smaller portion of the radio spectrum to support a much larger amount of data and encourage new value-added communications services from pagers to remote sensing. It is expected that wireless technologies will grow rapidly as their range of use multiplies and as costs diminish rapidly. However, because the radio spectrum for these services is presently licensed to carriers with fewer services and cannot be displaced for at least two years and, given the challenges putting new equipment into place, PCS will not be significantly competitive for another eight to ten years. In June 1995, the Industry Ministry finalized a PCS policy framework and called for tenders from service providers with emphasis on:

- balancing abilities of large proven companies with new providers to ensure sustainable competition;
- ensuring the greatest possible choice;
- nondiscriminatory access and nonproprietary standards supporting interconnectivity and interoperability;
- universal access at affordable cost;
- privacy and security;
- rapid development;
- value-added service and opportunities for small and medium-sized enterprises;
- research and development;
- international trade possibilities;
- right to interconnect with telcos, cellulars, telephone networks and other inter-exchange carriers on a fair, reasonable and reciprocal basis as all carriers.

Are there other examples?
Direct-to-Home (DTH) Satellite. It has dominated policy discussions in Canada in the last year. DTH television opens up the possibilities of first 100 channels and subsequently 500 channels of television, including pay-per-view movies, due to the compression of signal

capacity on satellites in the sky. It requires a consortium of a telecommunications carrier, a satellite owner and a broadcaster. At present, an estimated 500,000 Canadian homes "illegally" subscribe to American DTH services by installing one-metre-diameter dishes outside their homes in Canada and paying subscriber fees through a U.S. address. They are illegal because the CRTC has not licensed them. Thus, they do not meet the minimum Canadian content requirements and other domestic licensing conditions.

In response to this growing grey market, in the fall of 1994, Expressvu, a consortium of Canadian cablecos, telcos and program producers, was exempted by the CRTC from the Broadcasting Act's requirements, though required to meet most of the standard licensing conditions. Its service is scheduled for October 1995 in Canada. Subscribers must purchase a pizza-sized external dish and a TV-top decoder box costing approximately $1,000. They will pay monthly subscribers' fees of approximately $30 for basic television service.

Once the exemption order was issued, protests arose over the granting of the monopoly and doing so by exemption order rather than by following regular CRTC licensing procedures. Power Direct TV led the protests. It is a competing consortium led by Canada's Power Corp., with substantial newspaper publishing interests and 20 percent participation (the maximum under Canadian foreign-ownership laws) by Hughes U.S., which owns the U.S. satellite. As a result of the protests, the federal government appointed an ad hoc panel of three.[15] It recommended that DTH be opened to competitive services on application for licensing — and not by way of exemption. The government issued a policy directive to the CRTC applying these recommendations. It has granted a licence to Expressvu. Power Direct has applied for a licence as well, though the hearings will not be completed for several months after Expressvu's start-up date.

Expressvu will use Canadian satellites for transmission, thus permitting its signals to cover virtually 100 percent of Canadian territory.

Power Direct will use U.S. satellites servicing only 90 percent of the Canadian population. It has a competitive advantage in that it can purchase North American rights to U.S.-made programs and the Canadian-use segment is only a small portion of the total cost. The much larger U.S. advertising and subscriber base ensures a much lower unit cost. Expressvu must negotiate with U.S. program suppliers to purchase separate Canadian distribution rights at probably higher rates. This led IHAC to make the following recommendation respecting the protection of ownership of program rights:

> Government policies should continue to enforce a discrete Canadian marketplace for program rights and to discourage the continentalization of such rights. New measures need to be developed to offset the economic harm to Canadian broadcasters . . . [losing] the economic value of their program rights through the prior exhibition of programs by United States rights holders on Canadian distribution systems.[16]

IHAC also recommended regulatory measures to fully support programming rights licensed to Canadian individuals and organizations.[17]

But are there larger policy questions about the intensive mergers and acquisition activity as carriage and content players on the information highway combine?
This is business convergence. Here, the operation of the marketplace and capital flows produce different — and larger — corporate forms. And again, this "feeding frenzy" challenges existing regulation. Examples of convergence across the carrier, computer, broadcaster, information and entertainment industries abound in the financial newspapers. Telcos' acquisition of cablecos, publishing and entertainment companies' acquisition of broadcasters and cablecos, computer software and hardware manufacturers' alliances, all present enormously difficult regulatory problems. These fall within the specific domain of

communications regulatory tribunals such as the CRTC in Canada and the Federal Communications Commission in the U.S., and more generally competition regulation administrative agencies such as the Anti-Trust Division of the Department of Justice in the U.S. and the Competition Bureau of the Canadian Justice Department. New regulatory patterns have not clearly emerged and reforms to telecommunications legislation currently before the U.S. Congress are beset by partisan politics. In Canada, deregulation is allowing many more combinations than were possible several years ago but the patterns are still unclear.

IHAC, amidst a more generalized philosophy to allow the marketplace to dominate, suggested caution with respect to carriage/content separation. It observed:

> The *Broadcasting Act* calls for programming that is varied and comprehensive, expressing a range of different views on matters of public concern; indeed, the promotion of diversity has been a tradition in Canadian broadcasting policy and regulation. As companies merge to face global competition, maximize competitive advantage and enjoy the benefits of vertical interpretation, maintaining this goal of diversity will require structural measures that discourage preferential treatment based on ownership interests.
>
> The principle of carriage/content separation should be maintained at a minimum, through the requirement of structural separation between programming and distribution undertakings and with reasonable safeguards.[18]

What is happening in other jurisdictions?

In the landmark 1982 decision, AT&T lost its monopoly over long-distance and local telephone services.[19] The implementation, overseen by Judge Green, continues through a series of "modified consent" decrees. Five separately owned Bell companies provide local telephone service with FCC and state regulatory authorized monopolies. AT&T and a new group of players compete to provide long-distance services. Cablecos enjoy regional monopolies with price regulation determined by the FCC. Long-distance service, particularly data transmission, is cheaper than in Canada due to economies of scale but cable and telephone penetration are less. Bills currently before Congress are intended to reform the 1933 Telecommunications Act. They failed in the 1994 session due to Republican-Democratic party conflict. In the fall of 1995, the Democratic President Clinton has threatened a veto over the Republican-sponsored House and Senate bills which would deregulate substantially, in particular allowing the local Bell companies into long distance.

But, the major U.S. development is business convergence and merger of content and carriage providers. A few names in the news illustrate. Disney Corporation acquired Capital Cities and broadcaster ABC (entertainment and broadcasting). Appliance manufacturer and television and radio station owner Westinghouse acquired the broadcaster CBS. IBM acquired Lotus (computer hardware and software). Rupert Murdoch acquired Fox (publisher and broadcaster/entertainer). Seagram's purchased 14 percent of Time Warner and then 80 percent of MCA-Universal Studios (publisher and entertainer). Viacom and Paramount merged (cable and film). Turner Broadcasting (content and cable and network broadcaster) allied with McCaw and MCI (cable and long-distance telephone service). In Canada, where mega-mergers have been fewer, the example gaining the most recent attention was Rogers (cableco, cellular phones and 29.5 percent stake in long-distance carrier Unitel) acquiring Maclean-Hunter (publishing and cable), permitted by the CRTC.

In Europe, the British experiment is the most interesting. In the latter part of Mrs. Thatcher's revolution, telephone service was privatized. Two major players, British Telecom and Monarch, compete in long distance. They and a number of smaller players including cablecos compete for local phone services. Foreign ownership restrictions have been abolished. An interesting Canadian consortium of Bell (phone) and Videotron (cable) provides unified local phone and cable service in several municipalities including the borough of Westminster, seat of the Mother of Parliament. In television broadcasting, two state-owned networks compete with two private ones. But, proposals, including a Canadian-sponsored one by Winnipeg's Can-West Global, are being considered by the U.K. government for a fifth one. On the continent, the state-owned Post, Telephone and Telegraph (PTT) continues to dominate in local and long-distance service. But a European Union Report, authored by Communication Commissioner Bangemann, proposed deregulation and inter-European competition by 1997.

Singapore and New Zealand are the most interesting smaller countries to watch. New Zealand completed deregulation in the late 1980s in response to its fiscal crisis. It relies largely on market forces including open foreign investment to build its information highway. Singapore has maintained closer state control but has driven technological innovation in a bid to be the communications centre for the East. For example, it is now considerably cheaper to route a long-distance call south from India to Singapore and north to England than to go directly north from New Delhi to London. And so much of the rest of the world is just beginning the series of experiments in a virtual global village.

9
CONTENT AND CULTURE

"Television is now so desperately hungry for material
that they're scraping the top of the barrel."
— Gore Vidal

In the previous chapter, we discussed the carriers on the information highway. Now we turn to the content suppliers and the fate of Canadian culture in the electronic era. This chapter discusses two topics concurrently — content and culture — because, especially in the Canadian context, they are inextricably intertwined. This is a traditional Canadian theme. As deregulation, globalization and new technologies heighten competition, transcend national borders and vastly increase consumer choice, and as we gaze into the "500-channel universe," whether a distinctive Canadian culture will exist and whether we will see and hear ourselves are key concerns. Reinforcement of Canadian cultural identity and sovereignty was one of the three objectives (with job creation and accessibility) which the federal government referred to IHAC in May 1994.

There are three fundamental questions of content on the information highway:

(1)   Should the state regulate content?
(2)   If so, should the state regulate to protect and promote Canadian content and cultural identity?
(3)   If the state should, can it?

We answer yes to the first of these questions, though many will disagree. In fact, a more detailed affirmative, but qualified, answer appears in relation to cultural content. This chapter discusses the second of these questions, largely in the affirmative. This chapter also suggests that advancing technology, led by digitization and convergence, makes an affirmative answer to the third question increasingly problematic, but not impossible.

On what foundation is Canadian content regulation built?

Traditionally, we have distinguished between (i) broadcasting and telecommunications, (ii) public and private communications networks and (iii) carriage and content. Traditionally, telephone, cable,[1] computer hardware and software suppliers and now wireless services have been the carriers; broadcasting enterprises provided the content. Broadcasting constitutes the electronic transmission of entertainment and information programs for reception by the public. Traditionally, it is a public, one-way communication from broadcaster to viewer or listener. Irrespective of the mode of reception (television, radio, computer, film, etc.), irrespective of the mode of transmission (air or wire) and irrespective of the audience size, what is key in broadcasting is the message or the content which is transmitted to the "public."[2] Canadians have access to Canadian programming through several channels: public broadcasters, local private television stations, national private broadcasting networks, cable TV, specialty and pay TV programming and, soon, direct-to-home (DTH) satellite TV.[3] By contrast, telecommunications are essentially private, two-way connections between individuals via voice, data, text or video. Our national telecommunications infrastructure enables Canadians to communicate with one another and with the rest of the world. The apparatus includes telephone, fax, computer networks and now video phones.

Why is this distinction important?

Because the state chose to regulate the information highway from its earliest days — at least as early as the printing press. In so doing, it has regulated the carriageway in one manner, and the content providers in another, to reflect their different objectives. As the carriageway rolls out the national communications network, a central policy goal is *accessibility* for all Canadians. Broadcast programming, on the other hand, is "the primary source of information and entertainment for the great majority of Canadians" and therefore a "key cultural medium of our time."[4] Consequently, the primary regulatory objective is to *protect and promote cultural values*. This content/carriage distinction is reflected in the allocation of ministerial responsibility for the governing Acts. Whereas the Minister of Industry is responsible for the Telecommunications Act,[5] the Minister of Canadian Heritage oversees the Broadcasting Act.[6] Unfortunately for the sake of clarity, the carrier/content distinction is blurring and merging or, to use a "familiar" term, converging!

How is the broadcasting/telecommunications distinction eroding?

Consider one example: television. It is no longer simply an instrument for one-way transmission of entertainment and information to a passive public. With the advent of interactive television, it can serve as a medium for private, two-way communications between the viewer and the broadcaster, e.g., for home shopping or video-on-demand. Consider another example: the personal computer or, more particularly, the Internet. It is viewed traditionally as a carrier of digital signals. Accordingly, it is not subject to the cultural policies imposed upon broadcasters. As it expands in scope, however, it exceeds its function as a worldwide private communications network. Increasingly, the Internet is becoming a medium to broadcast content publicly. As a result, we have to reconsider the content/carriage characterization.

While this traditional distinction has been blurred, the essential differentiation prevails in the two fundamental regulatory regimes: the Broadcasting Act and Telecommunications Act and their administration by the CRTC.[7] It regulates the public and private use of radio waves, as the radio spectrum is a finite public resource.[8] The following table contrasts their objectives.

BROADCASTING ACT	TELECOMMUNICATIONS ACT
s.3(1)(d)(iii) & (g)	s.7(a) & (f)
Cultural orientation	*Socio-economic orientation*
"The Canadian broadcasting system should encourage the development of Canadian expression by providing a wide range of programming that reflects Canadian attitudes, opionions, ideas, values and artistic creativity, by displaying Canadian talent in entertainment programming and by offering information and analysis concerning Canada and other countries from a Canadian point of view . . . the programming originated by broadcasting undertakings should be of high standard . . ."	". . . Canadian telecommunications policy has as its objectives . . . to facilitate the orderly development throughout Canada of a telecommunications system that serves to safeguard, enrich and strengthen the social and economic fabric of Canada and its regions [and] to foster increased reliance on market forces for the provision of telecommunications services and to ensure that regulation, where required, is efficient and effective . . ."

Why do we need regulation?

Because Canadians, throughout their history, have not been content to let the marketplace determine cultural identity. The state has intervened in a variety of ways to protect and promote Canadian culture. This becomes more difficult in an era of convergence and globalization, e.g., where satellite transmission ignores national boundaries. Briefly, the motivation for state intervention is twofold:

(1) It permits Canadians to see and hear themselves on the airways, and

(2) It helps Canadians keep and enhance jobs in the culture industry, estimated to represent 4 percent of GDP, or roughly $24 billion, in 1992.[9]

One Canadian writer, John Gray, author of *Billy Bishop Goes to War*,[10] dramatizes this motivation in colourful images. He recalls Frankenstein and Dracula as two powerful allegories of the nineteenth century. He evokes their return in sinister form as a warning on the eve of the twenty-first century. Frankenstein's monster represents science gone amuck, an invention that has exceeded the control of and eventually destroys its creator. Dracula is a vampire who has no soul. He lives by drinking the lifeblood of others. Dracula is destroyed by a mirror — seeing his reflection and realizing he lacks substance. Similarly, a nation that lives off the culture of others and develops no identity of its own is doomed.

Why is culture so important?

Culture defines nations. "[C]ulture is not only a product for consumption and export: it is also our national mirror. Just as we look into the mirror to assess our condition as individuals . . . as a society we look to our cultural products as a means of assessing *who and where we are now*."[11] Few countries strive for national identity as much as Canada. Perhaps, few have had to struggle as hard to realize it. Cultural insecurities flow, in part, from our heterogeneous roots and in larger part, from our proximity to the United States, the world's biggest exporter of entertainment. Canada's more patchwork culture subsists in the shadow of the American "big screen." In dealing with our chronic identity crisis, we constantly try to distinguish ourselves from Americans. This is, in part, a function of size. When the American elephant sneezes, the Canadian mouse catches a cold.

But, it is also, in part, a product of different political philosophies.

First, the U.S. is a melting pot — a more homogeneous, pride-instilling, embracing culture with a fierce sense of nationhood, born out of revolution. Canada is the tossed salad or mosaic — a more heterogeneous mix symbolized by understated tolerance and encouragement of differences and preservation of heritage. Second, the U.S. is more individualistic; Canada puts more emphasis on the collective and the community. The fundamental precept of the American Constitution is Lockean: life, liberty and the pursuit of happiness and private property and a caution towards government. The underlying theme in the Canadian Constitution, as expressed in the 1867 British North America Act, is "peace, order and good government" and a (perhaps excessive) reliance on and trust in government. Consider three issues of recent public debate which highlight the different philosophies: (1) freedom of speech and content control on the information highway, (2) freedom to bear arms and gun control, and (3) free markets for health care and universal public health administration. These contrasting schools of thought will clash increasingly, although, for the moment, they are exempt from the liberalizing provisions of the North American Free Trade Agreement.

Is the question of culture only about national identity?

No. Culture also has significant economic importance. Canadian culture, manifested in entertainment, information and education, creates jobs and wealth. To enhance wealth, Canadians must be not only consumers of culture but also producers and exporters. Yet, Canadians live with a cultural and economic paradox. On the one hand, producing Canadian culture and entertainment is expensive, due principally to the small domestic market. It is cheaper to import from the entertainment giant across the border. On the other hand, by purchasing American entertainment products, Canada contributes to job growth in the United States rather than employment and economic growth at home.

What about the francophone market?

An intrinsic concern for Canada is language on the information highway. Consider the economic and cultural ramifications of the Canadian market's small size. The dilemma is magnified in the domestic francophone market. Due to the even smaller size of the French-speaking market and consequent lower economic return, the vast majority of Internet services and products are available and affordable in English only. This creates a linguistic and psychological barrier to many Francophones wishing to hook on to the network. A recent Andersen survey indicated that 3.5 million Canadians (almost 15 percent of eligible Canadians) but only 5 percent of Québécois have used the Internet.[12]

French-content producers find financing difficult due to their small audience. Just as American entertainment eclipses Canadian cultural content, French content lives in the shadow of English content. This concern is mitigated in the realm of broadcasting through the CBC's French counterpart, Radio-Canada. French CBC has a much higher audience penetration than English CBC. If we are to cultivate and nourish the French language in all facets of the I-way, approaches similar to the broadcasting guidelines should be taken on new communications avenues.

What regulatory mechanisms exist to promote Canadian cultural sovereignty on the information highway?

A substantial array. Canadian book publishers and film producers receive direct financial assistance from organizations such as Telefilm Canada and the Canada Council. Rules for the broadcasting industry and for cable companies providing broadcasting services[13] combine licensing preconditions, content controls, promotion through public institutions such as the CBC, various forms of mandatory and voluntary subsidization and restrictions upon foreign ownership to foster an environment that promotes Canadian culture. A listing and individual analysis follows:

(1) Regulatory and licensing measures such as the require-
     ment of a CRTC licence subject to fulfillment of certain
     conditions, Canadian-content air time and channel quotas,
     Canadian-content access and foreign access restrictions;

(2) Public institutions such as the CBC and national museums
     to produce and display Canadian culture;

(3) Direct and indirect industry funding through avenues such
     as broadcasters' mandatory contributions to "Can-con"
     development funds, taxation of foreign entertainment
     products, tax incentives and investment opportunities;

(4) Foreign ownership rules.

The May 1995 CRTC Convergence Report, "Competition and
Culture on Canada's Information Highway: Managing the Realities of
Transition,"[14] perceptively described the Canadian framework:

> The Canadian broadcasting system, as it exists today, is the prod-
> uct of more than five decades of cooperation between public and
> private elements; compromise between idealism and pragmatism;
> balance between national identity and continentalist market
> forces; and concentration on the principles in section 3 of the
> *Broadcasting Act.*[15]

(1) Regulatory framework

The Broadcasting, Radiocommunication and Telecommunications
Acts, administered through the CRTC, provide a regulatory framework from which to influence cultural content. The licensing and
regulatory powers of the CRTC are designed to uphold the cultural
objectives of the Broadcasting Act. The CRTC controls entry into
the Canadian telecommunications and broadcasting systems. Each
broadcaster requires a licence to operate in Canada. To obtain a
licence, a prospective broadcaster must satisfy certain prerequisites and
must agree to fulfill certain requirements. These directives establish

priority carriage for Canadian content. Through licensing fees, the CRTC generates revenue for Canadian programming. The Convergence Report outlined the delicate balance between social and cultural goals, on the one hand, and market forces, on the other hand:

> The obligations placed on Canadian licensees by the CRTC and its predecessors flow from the broadcasting legislation and are designed to ensure that the broadcasting system is owned and controlled by Canadians; that licensees offer the public appropriate amounts of Canadian programs and services; that licensees take responsibility for their programming; that all such programming be of high standard; and, that licensees play effective roles in addressing issues of concern to our society.
>
> In exchange for their meeting these obligations, the Canadian system has developed various measures to support and protect licensees. These measures include carriage rules for distribution systems, public support for the production of Canadian programs, and a licensing system designed to ensure that adequate resources are available in the market to permit licensees to fulfill their obligations.[16]

The intent and effect of this regulation is to enhance, and not to restrict, consumer choice. Canada's broadcasting policies blend the goals of satisfying individual consumer choice, on the one hand, and reflecting broader Canadian values, on the other hand. As a result, Canadian programming showcases a wider selection of content than any other country.[17]

(2) Public institutions

Both the federal and provincial governments support public bodies designed to produce and distribute Canadian cultural content to the public. The CBC and Radio-Canada are prime examples. Similarly, provincial governments fund public broadcasting enterprises, e.g.,

Radio-Quebec. There is some movement away from state-owned broadcasting corporations, however. The Alberta government privatized TV Alberta in January 1995, selling it for $1 to Toronto-based Moses Znaimer's CITY-TV. He intends to double "public interest" programming hours and function without government subsidy. Privatization of TVOntario is under consideration.

Should the state intervene directly with a publicly funded broadcasting system?

The U.S. has answered largely in the negative. This is consistent with the U.S. tradition of (i) individualism, (ii) a reserved view of government, particularly in cultural or religious matters, and (iii) reliance on market forces. Nevertheless, Congress has provided moderate federal government subsidies for television and radio to the Public Broadcasting System (PBS) whose broad mandate is to portray American culture and history. It is more largely dependent on voluntary charitable contributions from the private sector — individuals, corporations and philanthropic foundations.

Adopting the British model of the British Broadcasting Corporation (BBC), Canada created and federally supported the CBC as a Crown corporation in the early days of radio. This state initiative is consistent with the Canadian tradition of (i) emphasis on the collectivity and community, (ii) reliance on government, and (iii) government intervention in the market place. Today, the CBC receives $1.1 billion support. This will shrink to $700 million over the next three years as the Canadian government questions the *degree* of subsidy from the Canadian taxpayer at a time of high deficits. The issue of whether to subsidize state broadcasting at all has not been raised squarely.

Supporters argue that the Canadian broadcasting system is a fundamental communication component, a vehicle for "the creation and delivery of Canadian stories and ideas along the information highway."[18] If we are to "keep Canada on its own airwaves," we must rely on "reasonable forms of Canadian public intervention" to counterbalance the U.S.-dominated market forces.[19] "Like Canada itself, our national broadcasting system is not an accident of the market; it is an act of will."[20] Detractors contend that the state has little place in the marketplace of ideas.

(3) Industry funding

Direct subsidies are allocated to high-cost, high-demand Canadian entertainment programming that would otherwise be prohibitively expensive to produce. These range across a spectrum from the National Film Board and Telefilm Canada, at a federal level, to provincial educational television broadcasters who create or distribute programs, to the Canada Council which makes grants to artists, writers and other creators, to CRTC conditions of licensing which currently require all cable operators to provide 5 percent of basic service revenues to the production of community programming and also may require contributions to a fund to assist in producing Canadian content.

(4) Foreign ownership rules

Both the Telecommunications Act and the Broadcasting Act limit foreign ownership of operating companies in these industries to 20 percent. The Minister for Canadian Heritage has recommended that the Telecommunications Act allowance of one-third foreign ownership for holding companies with a telephone operating subsidy be extended to broadcasting. Combined with the content regulations, these caps provide some protection for Canadian culture on the air waves. There have been suggestions, however, to loosen foreign ownership rules in broadcasting to permit up to 49 percent foreign ownership, thereby increasing voting rights and, hence, control. U.S. cable networks, critical of the Canadian broadcasting restrictions on U.S. entertainment products, claim that these restrictions give Canadian broadcasters an unfair edge in the international market. Addressing these complaints, the *Globe and Mail* columnist Jeffrey

Simpson wrote: "From the U.S. entertainment giants that dominate the entire world comes the complaint that 'protectionism' gives Canadian producers and channels an unfair edge in international competition. Some edge, when Canadians struggle to be heard even in their own country."[21]

Consider Canada's movie theatre industry. Canada does not regulate ownership of its movie theatres. Consequently, 98 percent of our cinemas are foreign owned. Canadian film occupies only 6 percent of screen time. A somewhat similar situation exists with our book publishing industry. Book publishers do not receive the same protections as Canadian broadcasting and telecommunications companies. There are no tax incentives, no ownership restrictions, no licensing requirements, no governing regulatory body such as the CRTC. Book publishing is an open market, subject only to Investment Canada (formerly the Foreign Investment Review Agency) guidelines. How has this affected Canadian content in print? At present, 75 percent of book sales in our country are non-Canadian.[22] Moreover, the February 1995 federal budget cut by 55 percent ($25 million) book publishers' subsidies. Publishers predict that these cutbacks will result in a 20 percent drop in the number of Canadian titles and layoffs of 20 percent in the publishing industry. The Association of Canadian Publishers warns that the hardest hit will be "culturally significant" literature.[23] Yet, books are germane to the I-way because books *begin* the content which goes onto the highway. Moreover, book publishers are at the forefront of I-way developments, particularly in the realm of CD-ROMs. This reality moved the IHAC to recommend that the federal government put in place fiscal measures that support this industry's financial viability until longer-term measures emerge. The Council also recommended that the long-term structural policies include investment incentives and access to public funds designated for multimedia purposes.[24]

Nonetheless, globalization is rendering the question of "national" ownership in the information era less and less relevant. On this point, the IHAC commented:

Retaining national control over the Information Highway is partly about ownership but it is increasingly about ensuring that firms operate in a manner that is consistent with Canadian economic, social and cultural objectives. Our concern is more with capital's behaviour than its source.[25]

How does the production of Canadian content fare?

Surprisingly, to some, it has fared relatively well. Canada is the second largest exporter of television and film entertainment, next to the U.S. Toronto is now the second largest North American movie and television production site, after Los Angeles and surpassing New York. The cultural industry contributed approximately $24 billion to Canada's GDP in 1992. It generated 660,000 jobs. French and English Canadian musicians increasingly are penetrating the international market. A growing number of Canadian authors are winning international literary awards such as the Pulitzer, Booker, Goncourt and Feminina prizes.

Have these control mechanisms worked?

This is a matter of much controversy, beginning with bilateral and multilateral trade negotiations. Moreover, in the face of vanishing frontiers and rising costs to protect and promote culture, it has become increasingly difficult to safeguard. An evaluation of these measures may be best achieved by analysing examples. To take one, the CBC has clearly imparted a Canadian face and voice to radio and television. It has furnished career starts and many permanent jobs for Canadian-content providers. But, this has been accomplished at a cost to the taxpayer. This subsidy will be reduced from $1.1 billion to $700 million over the next three years. Beyond these cuts, there are searching questions where state broadcasting fits with other priorities competing for a share of the public purse in an era of deficit reduction. And how effective and efficient has the CBC been in its use of public moneys? And what is the role of the federal government amidst assertions by some that culture, education and entertainment are provincial prerogatives and responsibilities?

Much of the international and domestic success of Canada's cultural industries is attributable to the federal broadcast policy fleshed out in the Broadcasting Act. Canadian-content regulations in radio and television broadcasting have contributed to the growth of both those industries. Canadian television is flourishing. The diversity of Canadian television programming is heartening. If one compares this to the country's feature film industry and the dismal status of Canadian feature films both domestically and abroad, where no such protection and little promotion exists, one would conclude that the foreign ownership restrictions and Canadian-content requirements in broadcasting have been successful.

Yet a paradox exists. In the spring of 1995, Rogers Cablesystems, and other smaller cablecos, attempted to bundle new specialty channels featuring Canadian content with more popular American shows. This was an attempt to respond faithfully to the Broadcasting Act's cultural imperatives. Yet, this negative option selling produced a massive public backlash. The paradox: offering consumer choice while maintaining domestic cultural content on the air. This raises the question, who are the cablecos' customers and who must they seek most strenuously to please?

Isn't the CRTC's cultural policy antithetical to the new competitive environment?

Somewhat. It is bureaucratic. It constrains competition. However, Canada cannot consider competition in a vacuum. Increased competition may be appropriate for the telecommunications industry where there is no cultural imperative. Even here, "fair and sustainable" competition is sought, not wide-open "free" competition. In the context of broadcasting and the I-way, competition must be balanced with considerations of culture and Canadian content. With culture, unlike trade in other goods and services, the American poet, Robert

Frost's observations may be apt: "Good fences make good neighbors." As one IHAC advisory group remarked, "In international terms, recognizing and protecting cultural differences is an expression of good will, not ill-will. It is not about creating barriers — it is about tolerance."[26] Moreover, this is not a uniquely Canadian preoccupation. A former CRTC chair, André Bureau, observed: "There is only one country in the world that doesn't have to concern itself with cultural objectives and national identity — the U.S."[27]

How does the I-way affect Canadian culture?

The information highway is an excellent tool to market Canadian culture worldwide. It collapses national borders by providing closer communications links between states. We must remember, however, that it carries *two-way* traffic. Just as it opens up new avenues for exporting Canadian culture, it creates new opportunities for the introduction of foreign cultural products into Canada. Additionally, producers of Canadian content are confronted with the new challenge of unfettered international competition. Formal economic and political associations such as the North American Free Trade Agreement (NAFTA), the General Agreement on Trade and Tariffs (GATT), the World Trade Organization (WTO) and the European Union (EU) are contributing to the extinction of trade barriers and to more open trade relations. This is a particularly daunting reality considering the proximity of the United States (only a satellite dish away) and the fact that the U.S. leads the entertainment industry globally. Unlike traditional transportation routes, there are no border crossings or toll booths to control the import and export of information. This is an important consideration, particularly when more populated countries can produce entertainment cheaply. There is a concern that, rather than exploiting the I-way to market Canadian content, Canada will become a passive recipient of foreign culture.[28] The Canadian entertainment market, including online services, could be swamped with less expensive foreign products whose production costs have been covered already by sales in their domestic markets.[29]

Is this behaviour not considered dumping and is it not illegal?

The answer is difficult. First, satellite technology and computer networks are particularly difficult to monitor and regulate. In some industries, foreign competitors sell their products in foreign markets at lower prices than at home, usually lower than the prevailing price in the foreign market. This practice is "dumping." A topical Canadian example is steelmaking. Canada has charged others, and been charged, with steel dumping at different periods in recent history. There are a few possible outcomes from this type of price discrimination. First, it can force the complaining enterprises to become more competitive. Second, it can put the complaining participants out of business. Third, domestic authorities can invoke anti-dumping laws and end the dumping practice at least temporarily, thus protecting the complaining industry. In the Canadian cultural and entertainment industries, all three outcomes occur. Canadian culture producers cater to a small market. Consequently, in some areas, it is difficult to improve efficiency. If left unregulated, Canadian buyers will be swayed by the cheaper foreign material. Anti-dumping laws exist to prevent this behaviour in some business sectors. But note that the foreign producer may sell into the foreign market at the same price as its domestic market and at prices considerably lower than those prevailing in the foreign market, due to economies of scale. This is not dumping.

So what's the solution?

Very generally, we need to find an appropriate balance between a pure economic or market analysis and a countervailing emphasis on cultural sovereignty. We must inject the purely market-driven determinants with cultural considerations. This approach traditionally has shaped Canadian broadcasting policy. It underlies the wide variety of television programming available in Canada today.[30] Multilingual and multicultural (French, English, aboriginal, foreign), educational, public or private, specialty television, pay-per-view, etc. — Canadians have access to these options via cable at a lower cost than in the United States.[31] A key question is how satellite technology will alter this. The important point is to enter into this process with our collective eyes open, to protect Canadian cultural sovereignty and promote Canadian content worldwide.

How do we do this?

We already have to an extent, both internationally and domestically. Canada has defended cultural sovereignty internationally through GATT and the G-7. It has exempted culture from the provisions of NAFTA, thereby removing entertainment from the normal free trade rules. The current tripartite domestic protections — regulation, public institutions and funding — will continue to play an important role.

The IHAC emphasizes four premises from which to evaluate these policies in the context of the I-way. First, the I-way is a natural extension of the current broadcasting and telecommunications environments. It is a change in degree and not in kind. Second, the current cultural and broadcasting policies have been essential to the survival of Canadian content "in the face of ferocious competition from numerically superior foreign sources."[32] Third, cultural policies must adapt to the changing relationship between consumer and producer. Fourth, diminishing national borders, particularly through satellite transmissions, increasingly put into question the effectiveness of traditional regulatory instruments.

Will new content providers be subject to the cultural objectives and regulations of the Broadcasting Act?

The answer is not yet clear. There are many new services: near or true video-on-demand, interactive television, new forms of television programming such as video games, home shopping and distance learning. Whether a new service will be regulated under the Broadcasting

Act will depend on whether it constitutes "broadcasting" within the meaning of the Broadcasting Act. The CRTC tackled this issue in its May 1995 Convergence Report. The Commission concluded that, if a new scheduled programming and distribution service constitutes "broadcasting" and contributes materially to the cultural objectives of the Broadcasting Act, then the Canadian content regulations and spending requirements should apply in the same manner as existing programming services. These will not always be straightforward inquiries. In its review of the CRTC Report, the IHAC recommended the CRTC provide a more detailed definition of broadcasting and the guidelines appropriate to its interpretation.[33]

The purest example of confusion is video-on-demand, or "VOD." The CRTC noted that "[i]n a bi-directional, broadband universe, Canadian consumers will have just as ready access to video libraries elsewhere in the world as they will have to those in Canada. Multimedia applications will transcend borders, creating global villages bound by common interest, not just heritage and geography."[34] Is this "public broadcasting" or is it a private contract between the video supplier and the viewing consumer? According to the latter characterization, the cable, telephone or satellite company suppliers merely replace the neighbourhood video rental store. To answer this question, the CRTC report distinguished between "true VOD services" and "programming offered in a scheduled sequence" or "near VOD services."[35] True VOD is not scheduled. Rather, the viewer selects his or her own programming. The CRTC explained that "these services will be akin to a book store or library, where individual programs are stored on electronic shelves and customers access the titles they want by navigating through a series of menus."[36] Near-VOD services, on the other hand, schedule their programming sequentially. Pay-per-view, e.g., offers different but specific movies at set times, e.g., each half hour. While a viewer may deem this to be programming on demand, the CRTC contends that, due to this prearranged sequential format, programmers are capable of offering a set quantity of Canadian programs in their schedules. This mechanism has ensured that pay-per-view services respect Canadian cultural objectives.

True video-on-demand is still in the experimental stages. However, because its arrival is imminent, we must consider to what extent it can and should be licensed and regulated. Would it be subject to current Canadian broadcasting laws? If not, should we devise new regulatory schemes to cover new cultural outlets, requiring licences? Even if we require new services to provide Canadian content, how can we ensure that they advertise their existence to consumers?

So much for broadcasting. What about computer networks? Can you regulate content on the Internet?

This is a complex issue. It involves a multitude of policy choices and value judgments. Originally, the Internet was a vehicle for private communication between people. In this sense, it is no different than telephone or regular mail. Accordingly, it would be absurd, from this perspective, to regulate its content, just as it would be folly or worse to regulate the content of telephone conversations. Increasingly, however, the Internet is becoming a medium for public communication and entertainment. It is penetrating deeper and deeper into the lives of Canadians. There is a concern that cheaper foreign materials will flood the Canadian core of the Internet at the expense of domestic content. If online services are exempt from content regulation, they may forgo potentially more expensive Canadian content.[37] This scenario is analogous to that of video-on-demand. At what point does the state draw the line and declare that the Internet is not just a carrier of information but also a content provider or "broadcaster" and thus subject to cultural regulation?

Who is responsible for the protection of Canadian cultural sovereignty on the information highway?

At least two predominant views exist. At one end of the spectrum, some argue that the state must protect Canadian culture. At the opposite end, others conclude that protecting Canada's cultural sovereignty is entirely the choice of individual citizens. Interestingly, a recently commissioned Andersen Consulting survey found that 62 percent of Canadians believe that government should be responsible for protecting our cultural identity. Presumably, the same majority would agree with regulation of Canadian content and, perhaps increased, subsidization. Currently, 2 percent of federal spending and 1 percent of provincial spending is allotted to culture. With massive budgetary constraints, culture is an easy target for cuts.

As Canada grapples with large debt, the role of government is changing. In this era of tight fiscal restraint, governments cannot fund Canadian content and all other public programs at traditional levels. As federal and provincial governments gradually chop away at the debt, public funding for Canadian culture may go onto the woodchip pile.

10

SECURITY ON THE INFORMATION HIGHWAY

"The only fence against the world
is a thorough knowledge of it."
— John Locke

The I-way plays a central role in the social and economic lives of Canadians. The quantity of information and services available in electronic form multiplies daily with rapid digitization. Much of it is intended to be confidential or is more valuable if kept private. Thus, security is a key concern. Managing it is critical to the I-way's growth. Without reasonable security guarantees, individuals, organizations and corporations will be reluctant to use it. In fact, to date, many businesses and individuals hesitate to join the Internet for fear of security violations.

Why is electronic information particularly vulnerable?
It is stored digitally — in binary strings of 1s and 0s. This storage method has numerous advantages. However, it is exceedingly easy to manipulate, reproduce, change or transfer information between computers. One can reproduce or digitally alter copies of a song, movie

or novel with alarming efficiency.[1] Of course, virtually all information is vulnerable to security violations. One can access illicitly documents stored in an office's filing cabinet. But this requires more effort. One must know where to find the files. Then, one must break into the office, spring the filing cabinet and exit the office without being detected. It is easier and much faster to obtain electronically stored confidential information such as credit card numbers or medical histories. One need only know the digital database and ascertain how to breach the electronic security system. Moreover, greater quantities of information are stored in one electronic database. A recurring theme is the law's difficulty keeping pace with technology. Electronic security is a classic case. Not surprisingly, computer security is a booming industry.

What is an "electronic" security breach?

"Electronic" crime is actually quite familiar: theft, fraud, vandalism, invasion of privacy[2] and copyright infringement.[3] What distinguishes them on the I-way is technology. Technology is the felon's tool, the hacker today's artful dodger.

What are the most prevalent security abuses on the I-way?

Two technologies are particularly vulnerable to security breaches: computers and telecommunications. Common examples of computer abuse are "hacking," intentional infliction of computer viruses, password theft and software piracy. Telecommunications theft and fraud are also quite prevalent. The widest concern is security abuse on the Internet, particularly computer hacking.

Why?

Principally, because the Internet is the I-way's backbone. Enforcement is especially difficult. Six interrelated factors hinder enforcement in cyberspace. First is the absence of an "official" legal structure governing the Internet. The law of the electronic jungle is characterized by a state of virtual anarchy, mediated, or perhaps exacerbated, by vigilante justice. Second is the Internet's exponential growth. Presently, 30 million users in seventy-five countries have access to the Internet. This number is growing by 20 percent every month and the spectrum of users is expanding. Third, detection is difficult and often slow. Fourth, the Internet is like quicksilver. Fresh security problems arise daily, staying one jump ahead of prevention and sanctions. Fifth, most network security is poor. Hackers can breach many systems with relative ease and efficiency. Because hackers usually possess an intimate understanding of the systems they breach, they are quick to erase their tracks. Hackers keep pace with technological innovations designed to prevent hacking. As new prevention and detection mechanisms are developed, they devise new ways of beating the system. Sixth, cracking tools are widely available, largely through Internet newsgroups. Here, hackers exchange secret information or passwords. The extensive availability of hacking instructions on the Internet attracts many novice hackers. Additionally, hacking software exists which is designed specifically to detect flaws in computer networks and systems. These applications provide step-by-step guidelines for cracking computer systems.

Isn't this software illegal and therefore inaccessible?

There are two complicating factors. First, rather than being sold in stores, this software may be available on the net as freeware, i.e., accessible to anyone free of charge. Second, a hacking program actually may have a lawful *purpose* but produce an unlawful *effect*. Consider the recently produced and ingeniously named security probing program SATAN (Security Administrator Tool for Analysing Networks) — one of the most lethal and controversial cracking tools available. It is especially potent because its inventors (modern-day Robin Hoods?) released SATAN to the general public as freeware. SATAN functions much like a human hacker. It was designed by former employees of the California-based Silicon Graphics Inc. to provide system administrators with a high-powered and efficient tool for evaluating a computer's security. A disconcerting side-effect of SATAN is that it enables hackers to detect security flaws in a computer system. SATAN illustrates how security is a constant challenge.

What is the profile of a hacker?

Surprisingly uniform. They tend to be male, young, well-educated, university-student computer junkies. Hacking is a white-collar crime. It is seductive: hackers derive pleasure from "breaking" a secured system. It represents a challenge: acquiring the ability to understand and "conquer" the systems. Consider the following examples: Kevin Mitnick, a thirty-one-year-old American cybernaut using the code name "Condor," misappropriated more than $1 million of data and over 20,000 credit card numbers. Mitnick managed to elude authorities during a seven-year investigation. After a drawn-out virtual "cops and robbers" chase and stakeout, he was arrested by the FBI in February 1995. Mitnick, dubbed the world's most wanted computer criminal, was charged among other things with computer fraud carrying a maximum sentence of twenty years' imprisonment and a fine of $250,000. Mitnick had been convicted of computer-related theft in 1988 and sentenced to one year in jail. On the Canadian front, a Vancouver teenager, a young offender, broke into the University of British Columbia computer network of 4,000 computers two years ago. He was arrested recently by the RCMP and charged with unauthorized use of a computer and mischief to data.

Clifford Stoll, author of *Silicon Snake Oil*, rejects the popular image of hackers as unruly and ingenious technical prodigies. Hackers are not technically creative, he asserts. "Like other thieves, they steal through lies and deception. They just phone a corporation, claim to be from the computer department, and ask the secretary for the password. Sometimes they reach a smart person who hangs up and reports the conversation. Other times, well, Guss Gullible answers."[4] Understanding the profile and motivation of hackers will be instructive in devising preventative security mechanisms.

What is the motivation to hack?

Motivations are multifarious: fun, greed, curiosity, power, egotism, glamour, malice. Most computer junkies break into computer systems for fun. Additionally, some "Robin Hood-esque" computer hackers crack systems to draw attention to their security flaws or to circulate to the public valuable services and information they feel should be free. Finally, some have a criminal design — intending to cause damage, to commit computer fraud, theft or data mischief or to plant computer viruses. Interestingly, a recent survey of New York hackers revealed that most had been approached by corporations requesting industrial espionage.[5]

What is the cyberpunk movement?

It is a product of pop culture. Its source, cyberpunk literature, focuses on marginalized people living on the fringes of a technologically advanced society. The stories tend to have urban settings and tend to be pessimistic and sombre in tone. Inspired by this literature, the cyberpunk movement sprouted up in the mid-1980s. Certain groups, identifying with these cyberpunk characters and stories, adopted the name. There are three primary types. "Hackers" are the computer geniuses who understand the inner workings of computers and can manipulate them to their advantage. "Crackers" break into computer systems for a variety of illicit reasons. "Phreaks" break into telephone systems. These groups are united by the common desire to manipulate emerging technology for their individual and personal satisfaction or gain. Hacking is viewed as a manifestation of "freedom of expression." It is a form of rebellion where the electronic sphere is the battleground between freedom and repression.

Where do computer viruses fit in?

They are the anarchist's extension of this freedom. They destroy other people's order. Computer viruses can be especially lethal, when one considers society's growing dependence on computers. Moreover, interconnectivity facilitates the spread of viruses. For the first time ever, in February 1995, the text of the annual federal budget speech was made available electronically. A computer virus injected into the digital version of the federal budget almost brought down the computer systems of Canada's banks and investment and accounting firms. Just one hour before the diskettes were to be shipped off to these major financial institutions, the virus was discovered in a final virus-detection scan of the electronic version of the budget. The celebrated August 1995 debut of Windows 95 was marred by a virus attending its birth.

What is password theft?

There are many types. Originally, the use in network systems of one common default password, usually left on by systems developers for "first-time" entries, was unsafe. It enabled anyone who knew the default passwords to log on. A more recent development is "password sniffer" or "packet sniffer" software. It monitors network activity. It divulges every keystroke on every computer, thereby allowing hackers to identify what users are doing on the network. The program can capture packets of data — including passwords and user IDs — that travel between multiple computer sites on the network. The hacker can then use the password to access the user's account or retrieve confidential files or even input viruses into the network. The most frequent password theft, however, results from careless storage of one's password or from the use of easily identifiable passwords such as one's phone number or last name.

What is telecommunications crime?

Security concerns on the information highway began long before the Internet. Telephone "tapping" originated with the use of the telephone itself. In fact, in the early days of the human switchboard and party lines, all conversations were easily intercepted. Is it any surprise that the village telephone operator was the best source of gossip?

Mechanical and, later, electronic switching and the phasing out of party lines reduced these "passive purloin opportunities." But, as telecommunications play a greater role in our business and personal lives and with innovative new services, telephone fraud is on the rise. Many corporate phone systems, e.g., have a "remote access" feature. This enables employees to make long-distance business-related calls off-site and bill them to their employer by using a security code. Thieves can gain unauthorized access to these phone systems by cracking the employee passwords. Moreover, unscrupulous employees can use "their" password for non-business related calls. Telephone fraud costs Canadians approximately $300 million annually.[6]

Telecommunications hackers are assisted by Internet access. Some Internet newsgroups, such as the alt.2600 USENET group, provide instructions on how to break into the phone system to get "free" long-distance phone calls from pay phones. A device called a "red box" can mimic the tones that tell a pay phone that money has been deposited. The instruments for a red box are available at hardware stores.

Credit card and voice mail fraud have become a lucrative business. So much so that organized crime has now infiltrated the long-distance piracy racket. Hackers, who can crack voice mail passwords and have reasonable knowledge of the telephone system, can rack up enormous long-distance bills at someone else's expense. An eighteen-year-old in Ontario was arrested recently for breaking into someone's voice mail, changing the greeting to "Yes operator, I will accept the charges," and then posting the phone number on electronic bulletin boards across North America.

How do you prevent computer and telecommunications misuse?

Given the skill and/or determination of some hackers, intricate and continually updated forms of protection must be devised to prevent widespread security breaches on the I-way. This resembles other forms of property protection, such as the burglar-proof home and automobile security systems. What distinguishes security systems on the I-way, however, is the speed with which they can be decoded and the resulting need continually to evolve techniques. There are many ways to safeguard against security breaches on the I-way. The data security industry has flourished developing new security mechanisms. Consider the primary security methods currently employed.

(1) Innovative user identification techniques

Researchers are developing innovative user identification and password systems. Human identifiers such as digital signatures (i.e., thumbprints), voice recognition and retinal scanners will replace the ubiquitous multiple-digit password and will greatly reduce the ability to forge identification. Canadian-based Northern Telecom markets a program called Meridian Safe. It identifies users by their voiceprint. This helps to prevent theft of long-distance communication.

(2) Encryption

As a result of the sensitive nature of much information travelling on the I-way, data are often encrypted before being sent. Encryption transforms the information into unintelligible coded signals prior to transmission. They are converted back to their original readable format upon receipt by reversing the coding. In the case of data transmission, e.g., from a database to a remote computer site, the actual characters of the outgoing message will be converted, based on some encryption algorithm. Upon receipt, the receiving computer applies the algorithm in reverse to reconvert the data. While the information travels over the data highway, it cannot be readily understood if intercepted. Only those who know the encryption algorithm can "crack the code" and understand the data as intelligent information. While it is not infallible, encryption foils hackers. The ease with which a communication can be cracked depends on the sophistication of the encryption technique employed.

Public key encryption is used in some software programs. It enables software developers to employ a standard encryption coding method. This technology scrambles messages and data so that only the intended recipient, i.e., the authorized owner, with the decoder key can recognize them. IHAC recommended the rapid development of Public Key Infrastructure (PKI) technology.[7] Under this scheme, enterprises would rely on an independent and trustworthy third party, a Certification Authority, to verify the electronic identity of persons accessing their system. A "certification network," known as the PKI, would link these Certification Authorities. This technology would harmonize security standards and enhance their reliability.

Encryption and decryption is a time-consuming process. Hence, not all data is encrypted. It should be noted that cryptography functions for the storage of data as well as its transmission. IBM has developed a set of guidelines known as the Data Encryption Standard (DES) for formulating encryption algorithms. While these standards do not dictate the algorithms themselves, they provide checklist guidelines by which software engineers may develop encryption formulae. These have become the accepted standard.

(3) Modes of transmission

Security considerations should influence new carriers' selection of modes of transmission, whether wire or wireless. Depending on the cable's insulation, cable communications are relatively harder to tap and to intercept than wireless communications.[8] By contrast, transmissions via radio signals are easily intercepted. Radio signals travel through the air and can be picked up by any radio receiver within the signal's range. Thus, one simply requires a receiver with the ability to intercept the radio signals being broadcast.

Cellular phones operate on radio signals. Transmitter/receiver "cells" broadcast these signals through the air. These are connected to a central switching system which, in turn, is connected to the public telephone system.[9] The vulnerability of cellular transmissions has caused national scandals. During the 1992 Charlottetown Accord constitutional negotiations, Diana Wilhelmy, a constitutional advisor to former premier Robert Bourassa, disparaged him in suggesting he defended Quebec with insufficient vigour. Her cellular phone conversation was intercepted and publicized widely in the media. Likewise, Prince Charles's notorious declarations of love to his lady friend, Camilla Parker Bowles, via cellular phone made international headlines.[10]

(4) Human intervention

Finally, one cannot forget the human element and the need for detection. Systems administrators, such as bulletin board operators, supervise online activity to detect any irregularities in use patterns. A sudden surge of users on an electronic bulletin board may indicate illegal activity. A user's repeated attempts to access a sensitive database at odd hours also may flag the presence of a hacker. Often hackers are caught when they are careless.

In addition to pragmatic solutions to security concerns, legal recourse exists to proscribe computer and telecommunications crime.

What is computer crime?

The term "computer abuse" identifies all forms of unethical computer-related conduct. Computer crime is a subset of computer abuse constituting legally recognized criminal offences. It comprises many forms of conduct. The computer may be the object of, or the medium for, the crime. A non-exhaustive list of types of computer abuse follows. Where this conduct falls within the legally recognized offences, it constitutes computer crime:

- Unauthorized access or use of a computer, service or data;
- Unauthorized reproduction of a computer program or data;
- Manipulation or alteration of data, programs or a computer system's hardware;
- Spreading a computer virus;

- Misappropriation of information via a computer or telecommunications system.

How is the criminal law applied to handle computer and telecommunications crime?

Under Canadian law, no criminal offence exists unless it is found in the Criminal Code.[11] Many federal and provincial statutes also contain quasi-criminal offences. In Canada, making criminal law lies exclusively in the federal government's jurisdiction to ensure uniformity across the nation. The criminal law attempts to safeguard computer systems, programs and data in three ways. First, generic offences such as theft, mischief and fraud are used to prosecute computer and telecommunications-related crime. Second, Parliament has enacted a limited number of specific computer and telecommunications-related offences. They have only been in effect for a decade — a relatively short period for a century-old statute. Third, copyright infringement may be prosecuted under the Copyright Act.[12]

Prosecuting computer and telecommunications crime under the Criminal Code has been problematic, primarily because computer technology — data and programs — are new to the criminal justice system. Criminal Code provisions reflect nineteenth century and earlier conceptions of property. They are often inadequate to prosecute new intellectual property offences. Intellectual property rights concern intangibles. Consider a computer program contained on a diskette. It is really no more than a set of coded instructions that process data or information when inserted into a computer. The diskette has no significant real value. Theft of the physical material of the *diskette* involves an economic loss of roughly $1. It is the intangible *information* contained on the diskette that is most valuable, theft of which may cause substantial economic loss.

What specific computer crimes does the Criminal Code contain?

Parliament added two new offences to the Criminal Code in 1985 to penalize computer crime. Section 430(1.1) of the Criminal Code creates the offence of willful mischief in relation to computer data and computer programs. It penalizes (a) the destruction or alteration of data, (b) rendering data meaningless, useless or ineffective, (c) the obstruction, interference or interruption of data or programs or (d) of the persons using the data. In some cases, computer virus contamination could be prosecuted under s.430(1.1) where it has one of the effects described in (a) to (d). Section 342.1 criminalizes the unauthorized and fraudulent use of a computer system or computer service. Both are hybrid offences, i.e., they can be prosecuted by indictment or summarily.[13] Both provisions carry a maximum sentence of ten years of imprisonment for an indictable offence and six months for a summary conviction. However, most offenders receive only a fine, which may be combined with community service and probation.

How is telecommunications crime treated under the Criminal Code?

It was incorporated into the Criminal Code long before the computer crime legislation. Section 326 of the Criminal Code targets the theft of a telecommunications service and the unauthorized use of a telecommunications facility. "Telecommunication" is defined as "any transmission, emission or reception of signs, signals, writing, images, sounds or intelligence of any nature by radio, visual, electronic or other electromagnetic system." This would capture theft of cable, telephone (wired and cellular), satellite, radio and facsimile services. Theft may be an indictable offence or an offence punishable on summary conviction.[14] The maximum penalties are ten years' imprisonment for an indictable offence where the value of the stolen matter exceeds $1,000, two years' imprisonment where the value is less than $1,000, and six months' imprisonment or a $2,000 fine for summary offences.

What about theft of computer services over a network such as the Internet?

The Supreme Court of Canada considered this question in a 1984 case, *R. v. McLaughlin.*[15] It concluded that the unauthorized use and alteration of data and programs from a remote terminal in a university's local area network could not be prosecuted under s.326. The Court reasoned that the local area network was a "computer facility" and not a "telecommunications facility" within the meaning of s.326. This decision reflects a "pre-convergence" characterization of technology where telecommunications and computer technologies were identified as two solitudes serving distinct functions. The convergence of telecommunications and computer technology has eroded that distinction. Consider the current function of computers. By combining a computer with a modem and appropriate communications software, the computer becomes a telecommunications medium. Using a computer to access the Internet constitutes a telecommunications facility.

Parliament responded to the *McLaughlin* decision by enacting section 342.1 of the Criminal Code which criminalized theft of computer services.

What about telecommunications fraud and mischief?

Section 326(1) of the Criminal Code targets only telecommunications theft. Hence, it would appear that telecommunications-related fraud and mischief, if they do not include the misappropriation of services or technology, must be prosecuted under the generic fraud and mischief provisions in the Criminal Code.

Which is more effective to enforce security on the information highway — technology or the law?

Both. It is necessary to combine enhanced security measures with legal sanctions. Technology should be developed as a preventative mechanism to create roadblocks to potential computer and telecommunications criminals. Legal sanctions act as a deterrent and as "after-the-fact" punishment. The creation of preventative mechanisms is vital to a more secure information highway because detection is so difficult.

How so?

There are several impediments. First is the ephemeral and intangible quality of computer crime. Often, there is no lingering physical evidence. Second is the speed with which one can commit computer-related crime. Traditional fraud or theft-related crime may require months, days, hours, or occasionally minutes of effort.[16] By contrast, computer pirates may wreak tremendous havoc in a span of seconds. They can widely disseminate illegal material such as credit card numbers and other confidential information with relative ease. Finally, technology and telecommunications ignore borders. Combined, these impeding forces create an awesome barrier to the prevention and detection of computer crime.

How significant is the global village, the absence of national borders, to computer crime?

Computer and also telecommunications crime is proliferating geographically and interjurisdictionally. As this chapter's lead caption[17] observed, "Digital 1's and 0's have no respect for national laws, national borders and national controls."[18] A computer hacker can initiate an offence in one country while the victim may reside in an entirely different country. As an ominous example, American authorities discovered in August 1995 that Russian computer hackers broke into a Citibank electronic money-transfer system and stole over $10 million. They wired it to accounts around the world before being caught. As this book is being written, the head Russian hacker is fighting American attempts to have him extradited to the U.S. to face criminal charges, arguing that there was no evidence that American computers were used to commit the fraud. The limitless nature of the cyberspace frontier impedes detection and enforcement of security breaches. These international dimensions also raise numerous legal issues. If the offender is in one jurisdiction and the victim in another, whose laws apply? Whose law enforcement officials should be involved? What if the offender's country does not prohibit the conduct? Can the offender be extradited? There is urgent need for more effective international cooperation in this domain.

Because this is an international problem, enforcement must be at an international level. Yet, many countries, particularly developing countries such as Russia and China, that may have less at stake with lax rules, hold different perspectives on the appropriate level of security and enforcement on the information highway, and perhaps on the underlying property values to be protected. A good illustration was the U.S.-Chinese trade battle in late 1994. The U.S. threatened to bar Chinese membership in the new World Trade Organization and most favoured nation trade status unless China enacted and enforced laws prohibiting intellectual property piracy. American computer software and Compact Discs were routinely copied in China without payment of royalties. They were massively sold domestically and for export. In part, different conceptions of private property in China blurred the sense of wrongdoing. And the Chinese desire to catch up with Western technological and economic advantage blinded its will to emulate American law. In the end, the Chinese capitulated, at least on paper. But, it remains to be seen how thorough and effective will be their legal regime to protect Western intellectual property.

11

CONTROLLING CONTENT

"The basic test of freedom is perhaps less in
what we are free to do than in
what we are free not to do."
— Eric Hoffer

INTRODUCTION

New technology poses significant challenges for existing law. The
rapidly evolving information highway has many illustrations. One
such challenge is the ability and desirability of the state to control
dissemination of offensive material or control offensive conduct on the
I-way and its most ubiquitous manifestation, the Internet. This chapter
deals with freedom and control, rights and responsibilities on the Internet
because it is a microcosm of the information highway and because it
evokes the most widespread and heated debate on content controls.

How does modern information technology affect this age-old debate?

Technologically innovative communications systems provide increasingly larger amounts of information at faster speeds to rapidly swelling

audiences. Users can upload files from their personal computers onto the network. Posting illegal or offensive material on the Internet is particularly vexatious because it is easy to obtain, difficult to monitor, and pervasive. While it still constitutes a small fraction of the information available on the Net,[1] what is most alarming is the rate at which it is growing.

This chapter explores content controls and freedom of expression in three stages. First, we outline the problem. Second, we consider the law — the sanctions and enforcement tools used to constrain offensive conduct. Third, we probe the related policy issues and some reform initiatives. The underlying questions throughout the chapter are if, why and how the state should exercise control in a society which prizes individual freedom of expression.

THE PROBLEM

From World Wide Web sites to USENET discussion groups to electronic bulletin boards, the Internet is the easiest, cheapest and quickest way to disseminate information to wide audiences. Hate and violence mongers can reach millions of people within seconds. Moreover, digital technology permits users to circumvent national boundaries and laws. Users need only address their message through a foreign user for rebroadcast on the Internet to avoid local laws. With its millions of users and the almost total absence of regulation and screening, it offers a wealth of opportunities for propagandists and violence. Furthermore, the bulk of network users are young and often more impressionable than adults. Many have not had the same experience as the "reading," "viewing" and "listening" population in general, and do not have an extensive knowledge of history and its lessons.[2] If left unregulated, censorship proponents argue, false or objectionable material may acquire validity bred by frequency and familiarity.[3]

The Internet challenges existing law. It can present offensive material in a substantially different form. "[It] has stretched the concept of what the law means, where it applies, and to whom it applies. Copyright law, privacy law, broadcasting law, the law against spreading hate, rules governing fair trials: all are running up against the technology of the Internet."[4]

What type of offensive material circulates on the Internet?

Hate-motivated, racist, sexist and illegal material are the most prominent manifestations. Most of this already circulates in print and/or broadcast form through other communications channels. Computer networks have the added dimensions of worldwide pervasiveness, speed, an almost total absence of regulation and user anonymity. Consider five general categories traditionally viewed as offensive.

1) Pornography

Hardcore pornography on the Internet attracts the most controversy. Pornographic magazines and amateur pornography portraying virtually every form of sexual activity are now displayed online. Child pornography, illegal in Canada, is common. To many, the extent of violence and sexism on the Internet is disturbing. A user can create pornographic computer images with the help of devices such as scanners or digital cameras and image-altering software. The scanner converts photographic images and text into digital representations. Applying this technique, a recently convicted eighteen-year-old computer pornographer, Pecciarich, who lived with his parents in Toronto, scanned catalogue photos of children into his computer.[5] Using imaging software, he removed the clothing from the bodies and drew in genitalia. He then manipulated the images to cause these children to engage in bizarre sexual acts with one another, with adults and with animals. He uploaded these pictures from his computer to an electronic bulletin board. He took special pains to conceal his computer as the source of the upload. Through some imaginative "cyber-detective" investigation, the police established a probability that he was the source, obtained a warrant to search his home and there discovered the incriminating pornographic material. The prosecution was successful in convicting him of disseminating child pornography through a controversial reliance on this circumstantial evidence. They could not establish through direct evidence that he uploaded the pornographic material. As he was a youthful first offender, he was sentenced to 150 hours of community service and two years' probation.[6]

Because of the Internet's interactive quality, one of the primary parental concerns is the ability of pedophiles to solicit young users. This fear materialized for a New York mother whose ten-year-old son received an E-mail message from a stranger containing pictures of sodomy, heterosexual and homosexual sex. Additional concerns are the embarrassment caused to the persons unwittingly portrayed in the material and the encouragement it may give to the perpetrator and viewers to act on fantasies generated by these images.

2) Hate crime

Affordable technology and computer networking help hate groups communicate and coordinate. Newsgroups such as alt.skinhead help disseminate their message to recruit new members. One white supremacist posted the following:

> I do hate. I hate what is happening to my people, white people.
> I hate the fact that we forgot the laws of nature. The laws of
> nature dictate that you must look after your own kind. The laws
> of nature dictate that any living thing that becomes apathetic to
> its own fate will perish.

This is particularly appealing to these groups because most of their recruits are white males in their teens and twenties.[7] This is also the largest category of Internet users. Hence, they can easily target their main constituency.

Hate propaganda can be uploaded onto the Internet from jurisdictions where it is lawful. The Toronto neo-Nazi publisher Ernst

Zundel has a homepage on the World Wide Web. It contains, among other anti-Semitic messages, his assertion that the Holocaust never happened. He bases himself out of the U.S. This places him outside the reach of Canadian hate crime laws under which he has already been convicted. He can also circumvent a new German law prohibiting Holocaust denials. The Toronto-based white supremacist group Heritage Front also has an online magazine located on the Web.

3) Gambling

Gambling is legal in some jurisdictions and banned in others. Virtual casinos are sprouting up on the Net. Internet Casinos Inc., based in the Caribbean island of St. Martin, serves gamblers anywhere the Internet is available. Yet, it is technically illegal to access this cyber-casino from jurisdictions where gambling is prohibited.[8] Presumably, the opposite would also be true: Internet casinos would commit the offence of unauthorized gambling in the prohibited jurisdictions by making casino games accessible in those prohibiting jurisdictions.[9]

4) Advocating illicit activity

Anyone with a computer, modem and Internet account can get step-by-step instructions on anything from building a bomb to committing suicide. The American-based Right to Die Society sponsors a newsgroup on euthanasia and suicide called DeathNet. Among other functions, it disseminates materials on how to commit suicide. Teenagers constitute a large portion of Internet users and tend to be more prone to commit suicide. Emphasizing this fact, DeathNet opponents argue that it should be banned or restricted.

5) Breach of court-ordered publication bans

In 1993, Karla Homolka pleaded guilty to manslaughter in the tragic deaths of Leslie Mahaffy and Kristen French. The court ordered a publication ban on the testimony at Homolka's sentencing proceedings in which she revealed graphic details of the case. From a legal standpoint, the ban was imposed to ensure the fairness of the subsequent trial of her co-accused ex-husband, Paul Bernardo, which took place in the summer of 1995. By withholding Homolka's testimony from the public, potential jurors would not prejudge the issue of Bernardo's guilt. Fairness of the trial process is a constitutionally protected fundamental tenet of our criminal justice system.[10]

Despite the publication ban, various Internet newsgroups posted details of the case. The number of Internet users in Canada in 1993 and, more importantly, the number of people who accessed those newsgroups, were still relatively insignificant. As a result, the effect of the ban violation was not considered to be prejudicial. If, however, the electronic communications had threatened the fairness of Paul Bernardo's trial, i.e., the jury's objectivity, then a mistrial could have been declared. This example raises the question of how far a state can or should go in suppressing information from an entire population (Canada) to ensure that twelve individuals from that population can be subsequently empanelled to bring fresh minds to an individual's innocence or guilt. This is complicated by the fact that the information was freely circulated in the U.S. and found its way back north of the border electronically. Additionally, this example exposed a legal quandary: whether "posting" on the Internet constitutes "publishing." Did users who posted details of Homolka's testimony violate the "publication" ban? This issue has yet to be resolved legislatively or judicially.

THE LAW

How does the state regulate this type of content?

In Canada, each level of government has distinct responsibilities related to content control.[11] The federal government enacts national legislation. This includes the Criminal Code[12] and the Canadian Charter of Rights and Freedoms,[13] the Broadcasting Act,[14] Telecommunications Act,[15] the Canadian Human Rights Act[16] and the

Customs and Excise Act.[17] Provincial legislatures enact consumer protection legislation. This covers labelling and display requirements to protect children from violent and sexually explicit material and film and video review boards which set certain limitations upon content and viewership.[18] Finally, municipal authorities are responsible for zoning and licensing by-laws that may control the location and distribution of "adult entertainment" such as video sex boutiques.

What are the principal statutory tools used to control content on the I-way?

Let's examine three: the Canadian Human Rights Act, Broadcasting Act and Criminal Code.

The Human Rights Act prohibits the use of telecommunications equipment to transmit hate messages or to promote hatred[19] towards groups discriminated against on the grounds of race, religion, gender, national or ethnic origin, age, marital status, family status, disability or criminal conviction where a pardon has been granted.[20] The Act provides for various recourses ranging from investigations of complaints to compensation to prohibitions. However, the Act applies only to areas of federal jurisdiction, e.g., the federal civil service and telecommunications facilities. As the issue of formal jurisdiction over the Internet has not yet been resolved, it is questionable whether this Act would apply to discrimination via the Internet. The issue is whether the Internet constitutes a telecommunications facility.

The Broadcasting Act regulates radio and television transmissions to the public. Content controls on television exist by virtue of this Act. The Internet plays an increasingly prominent role in the lives and education of young people. At this early stage, we do not know how pervasive computer network communications will become and what effect their content will have on Canadian youth. However, the Internet will probably become at least as significant an influence on our lives as television. The Internet introduces hate propaganda, pornography and other offensive or illegal material into Canadian homes and schools with higher speed and quantity than other media forms. Yet, currently, there is no federal broadcasting or other legislation tailored to regulate the Internet. If the Internet begins to influence people as much as television, we should assess the psychological and societal impact of illegal and offensive content in evaluating the need for controls.

As well, the Customs and Excise Act stipulates certain restrictions on and establishes penalties for importing obscene or illegal materials.

If the Internet is an instrument for public communication, should it not be subject to broadcasting laws and regulated by the CRTC?

The Simon Weisenthal Center, among others, advocates this view.[21] One must bear in mind, however, that the Internet differs substantially from television, especially in one respect: interactivity. Television broadcasts unidirectionally to a "passive" public audience. There is no dialogue between broadcaster and viewer. The viewer merely absorbs the information. By contrast, while it originated primarily as a medium for private communications, the Internet now features a vast and diverse array of activities. These include private E-mailing, contractual relations through home shopping services, public dissemination of news, information, entertainment and opinions. In many respects, the Internet resembles the telephone more than the television.

At present, it is unclear whether and when computer network communications constitute "broadcasting" within the definition of the Broadcasting Act. Broadcasting is defined as "any transmission of programs, whether or not encrypted, by radio waves or other means of telecommunication for reception by the public by means of broadcasting receiving apparatus, but does not include any such transmission of programs that is made solely for performance or display in a public place . . ." Because its functions are diverse, the Internet does not fall clearly and completely within the broadcasting laws. Many Internet users argue that the Broadcasting Act is not the appropriate vehicle for regulating the Net. Under the Broadcasting Act, commercial online-service providers would become cyberspace gatekeepers of electronic information. This would be tantamount to holding Bell Canada responsible for the content of its customers' telephone conversations.[22]

On the flip side, interactivity extends television beyond the traditional realm of public broadcasting. Television is also becoming a medium for private interchange. This exceeds the scope of the Act. This is one more example of convergence: the merging of technologies. The IHAC considered the meaning of "broadcasting" within the Broadcasting Act. It recommended that the CRTC review the definition of "broadcasting" and publish clear guidelines with interpretive and illustrative examples.[23]

What makes "offensive" content "criminal"?

This is a very important distinction because not all "offensive" material is illegal. It deals with a twofold problem: political pluralism and degree of harm. First, there is a wide range of views or "sensibilities" among different people as to what is offensive. This is particularly true in a society as heterogeneous as Canada, contrasted with a more homogeneous society such as Japan. Second, even if the vast majority of people agree that certain material is quite offensive, before the state intervenes to disturb individual freedom and control, it must be satisfied that some significant harm is likely to occur without control mechanisms such as criminalization. This harm threshold often depends on what is done with the offensive material. Hate literature, e.g., is offensive to most but not illegal. Hate propaganda — "the spreading of ideas, information, or rumor for the purposes of helping or injuring an institution, a cause or a person"[24] — is prohibited. Most of the content-related crimes in cyberspace are familiar: obscenity, child pornography, hate propaganda, counselling or aiding illegal activity, harassment and defamation. They are not peculiar to the Internet.

The Criminal Code establishes the boundary between "offensive" and "criminal" content and conduct. It attempts to strike a balance between freedom of expression and preventing harm to individuals or groups. The Criminal Code targets distributors and not possessors of prohibited materials.[25] Generally, it is not the content per se that is illegal but rather, what one does with it, specifically whether one disseminates it publicly. None of these provisions were drafted with the Internet specifically in mind. Consequently, with much of this material, we are in a "legal grey zone." Is it subject to existing laws or not? This also raises the broader issue of whether our courts should extend general criminal provisions to new technological realities (judge-made law) or whether it is preferable that elected representatives enact tailor-made laws appropriate to these new realities.

What does the Criminal Code proscribe?
Examine three of the above examples:

1) Obscenity
It is a Criminal Code offence to make, print, publish, distribute, circulate or possess for those purposes obscene materials.[26] This section is located in Part V of the Criminal Code dealing with sexual offences. It is the communication of obscene materials and not their possession that is the focus of the crime. The act of uploading files onto bulletin boards, which are publicly accessible through an application process, constitutes "distribution."[27] A rather specific provision[28] deems obscene "any publication a dominant characteristic of which is the undue exploitation of sex, or of sex and any one or more of the following subjects, namely crime, horror, cruelty and violence."

So, pornography, per se, is legal in Canada. Where is the illegality?
Where pornography is considered to be "obscene" within the meaning of s.163(8), its publication is illegal. Child pornography of any type is proscribed by s.163.1 of the Code. The 1992 Supreme Court of Canada in *R. v. Butler*[29] explained the test for obscenity. The court

delineated a two-step inquiry:

(1) Does the material in question involve the "undue exploitation of sex"?

(2) If so, is it the dominant theme in the material or is it essential to a wider artistic, literary or other purpose?[30]

Thus, criminal "obscenity" involves the "undue exploitation of sex." To determine whether sexual exploitation is "undue," courts apply a "community standards" test — what the community would tolerate others being exposed to on the basis of the degree of harm that such exposure may cause. Harm, in this context, is defined as antisocial behaviour.[31] The greater the risk of harm, the lesser the degree of community tolerance. The Supreme Court in *Butler* identified three categories of pornography, ranging from the most to the least obscene:

(1) explicit sex with violence;

(2) explicit sex without violence but which subjects people to degrading or dehumanizing treatment;

(3) explicit sex without violence that is neither degrading nor dehumanizing.

Violence, in this context, includes actual and threatened physical violence. The first category is almost always "undue" and therefore obscene. The second is "undue" where the risk of harm is substantial. The third rarely constitutes undue exploitation of sex. If the court concludes that the impugned material is obscene, it must then examine it in context. The court must determine whether, within the entire work or communication, it plays a dominant or subsidiary but essential role. If it is both obscene and dominant, its publication is unlawful.

2) Hate crime

The Criminal Code prohibits certain targeted "hate."[32] It establishes two offences: (1) inciting and (2) intentionally promoting hatred against an identifiable group by communicating statements in a public forum. Another separate offence prohibits advocating or promoting genocide.[33] An "identifiable group" constitutes "any section of the public distinguished by colour, race, religion or ethnic origin."[34] Interestingly, gender is not included as a ground for discrimination. "Communicating" is defined expansively to include communications by telephone, broadcasting or "other audible or visible means." Presumably, this comprises digital transmissions. "Public place" includes "any place to which the public have access as of right or by express or implied invitation."[35] How does one characterize public access to the Internet? As of right? By implied invitation? Typically, users will apply for access, i.e., an account with an Internet-service provider. Canada's anti-hate laws have not yet been applied to Internet materials.[36] Hence, these issues have yet to be clarified.

3) Counselling suicide

It is a Criminal Code offence to "counsel" or "aid" a person to commit suicide, irrespective of whether suicide actually ensues.[37] The maximum penalty is fourteen years' imprisonment. To date, this section has rarely been invoked for charges of counselling suicide. It is extremely difficult to prove in a court of law that someone was "counselled" in committing suicide when a "successful" attempt eliminates the key witness. Moreover, the subject matter of this section is controversial. Consider the public debate surrounding the 1993 suicide of Sue Rodriguez and the rumour that her friend, New Democratic M.P. Svend Robinson, "aided" her in the final act.

Although some may view it as offensive and immoral, "instructing" people on how to commit suicide is not a crime in Canada. Hence, setting up a suicide newsgroup, such as DeathNet, is not illegal. If it was shown, however, that the "instruction" in any way encouraged a specific suicide, those associated with the newsgroup could be charged with "counselling" a person to commit suicide. Exactly who would be charged is unclear: those who post the materials, those who administer the networks, or those who own the networks. It will be interesting to see whether this provision gains prominence in view of emerging electronic suicide newsgroups that provide "how to" suicide instructions to the general public. Could this constitute "counselling"? The Criminal Code provides a non-exhaustive definition of "counsel" including procure, incite and solicit.[38] Parliament or our courts could conceivably extend this definition to include "instruct" or "advertise."

What about freedom of expression?

As a democracy, Canada cherishes free expression. The Canadian Charter of Rights and Freedoms,[39] adopted as part of the 1982 Constitution Act, guarantees certain fundamental rights and freedoms, including freedom of expression. It applies to the federal, territorial and provincial governments of Canada. Freedom of expression is not absolute. The Charter attempts a delicate balance between individual rights, on the one hand, and collective rights to equality and cultural identity and dignity, on the other hand.[40] Subsection 2(b) guarantees the fundamental "freedom of thought, belief, opinion and expression, including the freedom of the press and other media of communication."

What "expression" does this provision protect?

It protects all forms of expression, whether oral, written, pictorial, commercial or artistic irrespective of how offensive, odious or disdainful the message may be.[41] The words "other media of communication" extend the protection to electronic and digital expression. This means that the state must justify in a court of law regulation of any form that is constitutionally challenged.

How are these rights tempered?

Section 1 of the Charter qualifies them. It sets out the general formula for balancing individual rights against collective rights and state interests.[42] It authorizes the imposition of reasonable limits on these rights provided the limits are sanctioned by law and "can be demonstrably justified in a free and democratic society." Justification depends on the presence of two central conditions.[43] First, the restriction must be of sufficient importance to justify overriding a constitutionally protected right or freedom. It must relate to a pressing and substantial societal concern. Second, the means chosen to limit the right must be reasonable and proportionate to the objective sought.

Parliament can enact a law that, on its face, infringes the freedom of expression enshrined in s.2(b) of the Charter. If challenged, this law would be upheld by the courts only if the proponents of the law (the state) demonstrated that this infringement is justified in a free and democratic society in accordance with the "section 1 test." Both the obscenity and hate provisions of the Criminal Code survived this process of constitutional validation. Both provisions violate the constitutionally guaranteed freedom of expression. However, the Supreme Court of Canada concluded that they were reasonable limits on that freedom.[44]

The Canadian judiciary generally safeguards an individual's freedom of expression from government encroachment. Laws encroaching upon this right must be narrowly tailored. A sweeping ban on a particular form of expression would certainly meet its demise before Canadian courts.

Do other jurisdictions limit freedom of expression?

It is interesting to compare the Canadian Charter's guarantee to that of the European Convention for the Protection of Human Rights and Fundamental Freedoms,[45] ratified by all members of the now European Union states in 1950. Article 10 of the Convention outlines much more explicitly the balance between freedom of expression and community interests and values. It reads:

(1) Everyone has the right to freedom of expression. This right shall include freedom to hold opinions and to receive and impart information and ideas without interference by public authority and regardless of frontiers. The Article shall not prevent States from requiring the licensing of broadcasting, television or cinema enterprises.

(2) The exercise of these freedoms, since it carries with it duties and responsibilities, may be subject to such formalities, conditions, restrictions or penalties as are prescribed by law and are necessary in a democratic society, in the interests of national security, territorial integrity or public safety, for the prevention of disorder or crime, for the protection of health or morals, for the protection of the reputation or rights of others, for preventing the disclosure of information received in confidence, or for maintaining the authority and impartiality of the judiciary.

The First Amendment of the U.S. Constitution guarantees the freedom of speech. It reads:

Congress shall make no law respecting an establishment of religion, or prohibiting the free exercise thereof; or abridging the freedom of speech, or of the press; or the right of the people peaceably to assemble and to petition the Government for a redress of grievances.[46]

As in the Canadian Charter, the U.S. free-speech guarantee is not absolute. However, unlike the Charter, there is no constitutional balancing provision similar to section 1. Rather, American courts are responsible for limiting free speech where it is deemed necessary. In practice, the American free-speech guarantee has a much broader scope. This approach reflects the American tradition of individual rights and suspicion of government. In fact, it was a direct response to eighteenth-century British sedition laws which prohibited public criticism of government. Legislative and judicial bodies in the U.S. are much more tolerant of racist, violent or hate speech than their Canadian counterparts.

Canada, by contrast, strives to achieve a "healthy" balance between individual and collective rights. This path is rooted in our emphasis on pluralism and cultural diversity — the cultural mosaic — and general willingness to accept controls. In light of the different guarantees of free speech, it is interesting to contrast the Canadian approach in the *Pecciarich* case with the American approach illustrated in the prosecution of Jake Baker, a University of Michigan student. Baker composed an article about the fictitious rape and torture of a woman whom he named after one of his classmates. He then posted this article on the Internet. He was arrested in 1995 on charges of threatening a fellow student. Pecciarich was convicted, with no discussion of freedom of expression in the judgment. Baker was acquitted on appeal on the grounds that his expression was constitutionally protected under the First Amendment.

Should freedom of expression in cyberspace be interpreted in the same way as for traditional types of media?

Conventional forms of news media such as newspapers, magazines, television and radio rely on editors to screen the information being transmitted to the public and to ensure its legality, accuracy and credibility.[47] They also are bound by ethics codes. By contrast, the Internet lacks any formal checks or controls. It has no universal "official" code of ethics. Rather, it relies primarily on bulletin board operator and network administrator monitoring and on its users' self-restraint and self-policing. It permits unbridled expression. As a result, more controversial topics surface. In view of the lack of formal "quality controls," censorship proponents, such as anti-racist groups, argue that the constitutional guarantee of free "digital" expression should be interpreted more restrictively or cautiously than traditional forms of media.[48]

On the other hand, as many free-speech proponents argue, the Net is not only a "broadcasting" or "publication" tool. Internet technology allows instantaneous dialogue, principally through electronic discussion groups. People can challenge and ridicule racist, misogynist or other discriminatory views and discredit unfounded assertions, such as Holocaust denials. In this sense, uncensored communications may serve society in the long run by discrediting these hate groups in an open forum. There is an inherent value in having an informed citizenry.

Are there other civil recourses for "victims" of harmful or offensive communications?

A victim can sue for defamation where a statement is made which causes harm to that individual. Defamation has two elements: (1) slander, which encompasses any communication that is temporary and audible only, and (2) libel, constituting permanent communication which is visible to the eye.[49] However, proof of the statement's truth is a complete defence. Audio (slander) and video (libel) electronic communications of defamatory statements may give rise to a claim for monetary damages.

DEVISING CONTENT-CONTROL POLICIES

The issue of censorship on the I-way raises fundamental policy questions. It obliges us to define and rank collective values. It is central to the classic tension between two competing values: protection of the individual's freedom of expression and protection of the collective right to equality, cultural diversity and dignity and freedom from hateful or harmful conduct.

There are three principal approaches to monitoring and controlling offensive material on the Internet: state regulation and censorship; technological mechanisms such as filtering software; and private, as opposed to state, intervention at public, community and individual levels. No one approach is a panacea.

What role, if any, should the state play in cyberspace?

Three relevant inquiries help shape the direction for state intervention: Should the state regulate and censor offensive and illegal content on the information highway (Internet)? If yes, can it enforce these laws on a system that was designed to be evasive? If so, how does it censor and regulate it? How do we establish what should be forbidden, and who should be liable? Let's examine each question in turn.

Should the state control expression on the Internet?

This is a long-standing debate. It boils down to what society will tolerate and what limits it is willing to place on freedom of expression.[50] Many Internet users argue that censorship and regulation proponents just don't understand the Net. One American technology researcher explained: "It is well-intentioned but wrong-headed, applying an old broadcast mentality of regulation to an entirely different technology."[51] Television programming is administered by central broadcasters, such as CBC and CTV. Computer networks, by contrast, are displayed throughout the world. Also, the nature of television (one-way) and computer network (both one-way and two-way) communication differs. The Internet permits users to challenge one another's views.

State censorship in the home is socially and legally unacceptable and practically impossible. It fundamentally erodes freedom of expression and contravenes the values of a democratic society. Free-speech advocates advance the argument that once we allow state censorship we start down a slippery slope. Moreover, at a practical level, government cannot control the flow of electronic information into the home. There is an additional concern that state censorship merely abdicates to the government parental responsibility for childrearing. Is it not the parents' role to decide what their children will or will not be exposed to? Technology may offer a partial solution. Parents can purchase filtering software that allows them to block access to designated Internet sites.

At present, the state partially subsidizes the Internet. If there are no content restrictions on offensive and illegal material, must we consider whether government should continue to subsidize it?

Is it practicable to enforce censorship laws on the Internet?

Some argue that if we can create a global computer network of databanks we can implement control mechanisms. But, can we enforce these laws on a system that was developed originally to withstand nuclear destruction? The Internet was designed to be elusive. No one owns or controls the Internet. Computer and legal experts agree that enforcement is difficult.[52] One industry executive explained that: "The Internet regards censorship as a hardware failure and just works around it."[53]

Enforcement is further impeded by the speed of communication on the Net and by its global dimensions. It transcends national boundaries and laws. It is very difficult, therefore, to enforce breaches that originate in a jurisdiction where the content is lawful or law enforcement is lax. Foreign authorities are reluctant or unwilling to participate or assist in the investigations. A more insidious fear is that some smaller countries will find data havens profitable, just as they profit as money-laundering havens.[54] Harmonizing laws presents a nearly insurmountable task.

What are alternatives to state intervention?

Many people argue that the best method of control is simply to let the Internet develop its own checks and balances. Accordingly, community intervention through public-interest groups, self-policing, established codes of ethics and public education will provide the "healthy" balance between free expression and community interests. Another effective preventative mechanism is to develop software that protects users from receiving hateful and offensive materials. To this end, software companies are now designing programs that alert users to certain types of Internet material or that filter the material.[55]

IHAC advocated a multi-level approach to content controls on the information highway. The Council concluded that regulatory and technological measures should be combined with the public's and information providers' involvement. The Council recommended the following:[56]

- Fine-tune current laws to make them more responsive to digital information and the global nature of communication today.
- Encourage information providers to develop voluntary codes of ethics and lawful practices. The federal government should develop a model code of ethics and practices reflecting community standards.
- Educate the public on the rule of law as applied to computer technologies.
- Publicly support community organizations actively fighting hate and violence mongering.
- Encourage R&D investment in technical solutions such as filtering software, law enforcement techniques.

Who is liable for infringement?

At present, it is unclear whether liability extends to owners, users and/or computer network operators. Computer network operators argue: "Don't shoot the messenger."[57] It is not up to computer networks to police users and information online. Presently, bulletin board operators in one jurisdiction may be held liable in another jurisdiction. They are thus bound to know the laws and thus community standards of other jurisdictions.

How do we ascertain whether the electronic communication is "private" or intended for distribution to the public?

The state draws an important distinction between private communication, e.g., between two consenting adults, and public communication, particularly when it covers the entire spectrum of the population, e.g., including children. Thus, for example, as the Internet has moved from its traditional role as a means for private communication between specialized researchers to a series of bulletin boards and freenets used worldwide, it presents different challenges. This requires clarification of the meaning of the "public."[58]

What American efforts have been made?

Most of the cybercrime cases we read about arise in the United States.[59] In June 1995, the U.S. Senate approved a proposal to ban obscenity in cyberspace as part of a plan to overhaul American communications legislation. This Communications Decency Act, sponsored by a Democrat senator, would impose fines as high as $100,000 and jail sentences up to two years on people who transmit material that is found to be "obscene, lewd, lascivious, filthy or indecent." While the amendment is aimed principally at outlawing child pornography, it could have a much wider reach in view of the vague and sweeping wording. In its present form, it would not likely survive the strict First Amendment test.

The question of content controls on the I-way or, more specifically, the Internet, is both fascinating and perplexing. It forces us to define our collective values. Nevertheless, deciding whether and how to regulate the Internet may be defeatist because the Internet is a global phenomenon. At the very least, international collaboration must be sought to achieve any sort of effective regulation. Because this question is so fundamentally rooted in a society's values, is this even feasible? This question is particularly germane to Canada, where newsgroups can base themselves south of the border where the free speech guarantee is more expansive and speech controls more lax.

12

INTELLECTUAL PROPERTY

"Nothing can with greater propriety be called a man's property
than the fruit of his brains. The property in any article or substance
accruing to him by reason of his own mechanical labour is never denied him:
the labour of his mind is no less arduous and consequently no less worthy
of the protection of the law."
— Copinger and Skone James on Copyright

This chapter deals with intellectual property (IP) and, more specifically, copyright protection of works that are placed on the information highway. Copyright is currently the primary, and often sole, form of statutory protection granted to authors over their works. Unless a radical redefinition of those rights takes place, copyright will also serve as the principal scheme of control of economic property rights in the developing information economy. In that economy, copyright laws will define property rights in the same way as traditional property laws provided the legal framework for earlier agricultural and industrial economies.

What does "IP" mean?
IP, unlike traditional concepts of property, such as real property (e.g., land or buildings) and personal property (e.g., clothes or cash), refers to informational creations such as ideas, their expression, formulas,

trademarks, trade names, goodwill, and other intangible creations of the intellect. While not occupying physical space, these are the product of some input or work process. Not all intangible human creations are protected as IP. Rather, IP is a catch-all phrase. It refers to the wide range of laws from statute and court decisions that protect these products. Examples of statutory laws dedicated to protecting IP rights include acts bearing these titles: Copyright, Trade-Marks, Patent, Integrated Circuit Topography, Industrial Design, and Plant Breeder's Rights. IP rights are also mentioned in other statutes including the Criminal Code and the Competition Act. Finally, certain forms of IP also derive protection from the common law (i.e., case law evolving over the decades from judges' decisions). Some IP examples of common law include trade secrets, trademarks (which may also be protected by statute) and unfair competition.

So IP is not really property per se?

Yes and no. Philosophically, intellectual creations may be deserving of proprietary protection. It depends on how broad one's definition of property is. In a Canadian context, IP is not considered property in the traditional, strictly legal sense. It lacks physical presence. It displays characteristics synonymous with public goods: IP does not garner protection from traditional laws that protect tangibles.

Can you illustrate?

Yes. In the case of R. v. Stewart,[1] the accused, without permission, obtained a list of names and addresses of a hotel's employees in order to establish a unionized bargaining unit. The hotel considered the information confidential. It was not publicly available. Stewart was charged with counselling the commission of the indictable offences of theft, fraud and mischief. The issue was whether confidential information, the list, was property and could be the subject matter of theft. The Supreme Court of Canada held that for the purposes of the theft provisions under the criminal law, information was not considered property. The lack of a physical deprivation of the owner's rights to the information was central to the Court's decision, notwithstanding the economic deprivation that was suffered.

The *Stewart* decision is a good example of the malleable nature of property in common-law jurisdictions such as Canada. Property is often referred to as a bundle of rights. That is not a helpful definition. There are no hard and fast rules as to what is property. Instead, for the purposes of law, property is that which it has been for centuries: real and personal property — both tangible. This definition may yet change over time. But currently, IP does not fit the prevailing definition.

What is a public good?

This is a product characterized by non-exclusive and non-rivalrous use. Non-exclusive use means that once the good is created, everyone is free to use it regardless of her contribution to creating the good. Non-rivalrous use occurs when one person's use of the good does not affect another's use of that good. The air we breathe and the roads we drive on are public goods. My car is a private good. The public transit bus for which I pay a dollar to go to work shares public and private good characteristics. Much of the wealth of the new information economy based on ideas and innovation comes from using IP to protect private goods and prevent the ideas from becoming public goods.

Putting time, energy and effort into the creation of an IP product in no way guarantees control over that product or remuneration for its creation. The laws governing traditional property do not take into account these public goods characteristics. They cannot effectively apply to IP. Thus legislatures have created IP laws.

Why do we need to exercise control over IP in the first place?

This is a tough question: space constrains a thorough answer, and views on this issue are many. The debate has raged for centuries.

Some argue that to use what one has not created (expended labour) or paid for (through indirect labour) is tantamount to theft. But increasingly the dominant reason to protect intellectual creations in the western economies is to encourage further creation. As a society, we find IP creations, whether they be artistic or utilitarian in nature, immensely useful and desire more. Economic realities of life, however, impose a cost for this creation. Generally, creators will not create if not assured payment for their efforts. If the copying and public good nature of IP are not controlled, this funding will likely not come from the private sector. This leaves the public sector to fund creators, such as artists, scientists, engineers, computer programmers and all others who expend their labour creating IP. We have not chosen this state route. Rather, we have chosen, by the use of laws, to constrain the public-good aspects of IP so that it is more readily controlled, adaptable to the existing economic environment which grew out of tangible non-public goods, and largely governed by private transactions.

Other explanations?

Others argue that certain IP creations, such as literature and art, are properly thought of as an extension of one's personality and being. Natural law dictates their protection. Just as we protect our physical bodies, we should also protect the intangible nature of our person which exists as expression. Another basis of protection is a first occupancy argument, often used in support of tangible property laws: we protect the first one to do something because to do otherwise potentially leads to conflict and even violence. This also supports the idea that we must give something to the discoverers/inventors of new things whether land or intellectual creations. Human beings should be encouraged to reveal as much as possible of their universe. Another common justification is attainment of economic efficiency (maximization of wealth) regarding the allocation of scarce societal resources (including human capital).

Each society, depending on its political philosophy, will apply these arguments in varying degrees. For example, a Marxist regime may decide that IP creations must be freely available for use by all members of the society ("From each according to his abilities; to each according to his needs"). The artist is supported by the state in the same manner as all other members of the society. Conversely, in a free-market system, private ownership and transferability of ownership encourage private investment and the optimal allocation of human resources. Generally, IP laws reflect not one, but a combination of these theories. In the fall of 1994, the trade dispute over "pirated" computer software, Compact Discs, and videos between China and the U.S. was rooted in two different conceptions of property and political philosophy: the Chinese "socialist market" economy and the U.S. free-enterprise private property system.

How are IP theories relevant to the information highway?

The existing system of copyright is most applicable to data — whether it be film, music, art, information or other forms of intangible good — available on the I-way. The existing Canadian copyright regime has a complex history, supporting a utilitarian and even economic view of the rights it creates. The I-way roll out, and rapid moves towards an information economy, will require amendment to existing law, if we continue to support those utilitarian objectives. The need to amend will require Canadians to reassess the value of informational products and their desired treatment of them. We may find that existing laws no longer meet today's political-philosophical realities.

COPYRIGHT

What does existing copyright law protect?

Copyright, a branch of IP law, originally protected published literary works. Then, a literary work only consisted of printed matter. Copyright laws have since considerably expanded their scope. In addition to protecting unpublished literary works against unauthorized copying, the Copyright Act[2] currently protects a range of works including dramatic, musical and artistic. The definition of literary works has also been expanded: e.g., computer programs are literary works. Examples of works protected by copyright include tables, compilations, photographs, engravings, sculptures, maps, plans, computer programs and databases.[3]

Copyright is important for the I-way because it protects the software technology that allows it to operate and much of its content. Copyright is also the IP regime most applicable to data travelling on the I-way.

How does copyright protect these works?

Simply put, copyright protection gives the copyright holder a time-limited exclusive right to make copies of the work, and to prohibit others from making copies of the work, or a substantial part thereof. Copyright protects the author's original expression. It does not protect the idea(s) underlying the expression. Copyright has never granted protection over ideas, only over the form in which ideas are expressed — the idea/expression dichotomy. Finding the line that delineates idea from expression is not an easy task. It is more difficult when dealing with utilitarian works, such as computer programs and databases. These are often intertwined with the ideas they seek to express.

Copyright protects two distinct sets of rights: economic and moral. Economic rights are those rights that protect the economic interests of the copyright holder. The copyright holder may charge users for the authorization to buy or license copies of a work. Moral rights, more commonly found in civil law jurisdictions, protect the right of the author to be associated with the work, remain anonymous, not have the work mutilated or distorted, and not have the work associated with any product, service, cause or institution.[4] Moral rights were added to the Copyright Act in 1931. Sanctions associated with an infringement of moral rights were enhanced considerably through

1988 amendments. The ease with which digitized works can be manipulated and disseminated by users on the I-way has given moral rights new importance.

So once a work is created, the copyright holder has a complete monopoly over the work?

Not quite. Although copyright grants the copyright holder the right to prevent copying of her work, it does not grant a monopoly in the work preventing another person from producing the same work if it is independently created.

How does Crown copyright fit in?

These are rights held by government in works that it generates, including legislation, case law, reports and any other government-generated material. The Crown owns the copyright. This copyright ownership is not problematic where the government willingly releases material for public consumption, referred to as placing material in the public domain. Where private individuals wish to reproduce government materials, however, Crown permission is required. This permission is not given in a consistent manner, or through a single body. Obtaining permission to reproduce government materials can be a costly and often frustrating process. With the increased ability to disseminate information via the I-way, maintaining Crown copyright is problematic. Various recommendations, from abolishing Crown copyright to maintaining it in a modified or clarified form, have been issued.[5] To replenish diminishing treasuries, various government departments have implemented cost recovery schemes whereby they license their copyrighted materials to the private sector for a fee. This practice hampers the flow of information to the public. Only those who can afford it will get access. There is also a more profound concern that this practice violates democratic principles. The U.S. Copyright Act expressly states that copyright protection does not apply to works generated by the United States government, although provision is made for ownership of copyright in works where the copyright has been transferred to the government by others.[6]

Copyright protects only the expression of an idea. Does this expression have to be tangible? Isn't the purpose of IP to protect intangibles?

To qualify for copyright protection, a work must be fixed, or stored, in some manner. The "fixation" requirement has developed largely through copyright case law. It is statutorily based only for dramatic works, musical works, and most recently for computer programs. For works where fixation is not explicitly required by the Copyright Act, the courts have required it.[7] The U.S. Copyright Act is slightly more specific. It requires that a work be expressed in a form which is sufficiently permanent and stable so that it may be "fixed in any tangible medium of expression, now known or later developed, from which they can be perceived, reproduced, or otherwise communicated, either directly or with the aid of a machine or device."[8]

For computer programs, in Canada, the Copyright Act requires that a computer program be "expressed, fixed, embodied or stored in any manner" in order for copyright protection to apply.[9]

Issues of fixation on the I-way are many. Without further guidance from law-makers and the courts, uncertainty will persist.

Examples of fixation problems?

A typical example for computer technology is this. Are literary and artistic works, such as text and graphic output screens, which can only be displayed during program execution, "fixed" in the memory devices containing the computer programs and data? Recent jurisprudence suggests that fixation in volatile memory devices such as video interface RAM is sufficient to meet the fixation requirement. For screens generated by a computer program, the protection exists because the screens are said to exist under the umbrella of the underlying computer program's copyright. However, Canadian law has held that a fleeting image of broadcast on television does not fulfill fixation requirements. If the television program is otherwise fixed, such as on some form of videotape, even if done simultaneously with the broadcast, the fleeting image described may be protected as part of the underlying copyright of the fixed program.

An especially relevant I-way question is whether transitory combinations of data, such as the results of a database search conducted at the direction of a user, are sufficiently fixed for copyright. These results are often only stored in volatile memory. They cannot be said to be part of the underlying search engine (the computer program that performs the search) as the user's search criteria is entered only upon use. Only if it is established that such combinations are indeed copyrightable, would one move to the next step and decide who rightly owns the copyright. A related problem is raised by the I-way's interactive capacity. We are witnessing the birth of "you program it" interactive entertainment systems. If a user programs a selection of programming that suits her tastes, one wonders if the user has a copyright in that selection of programming.

A fundamental problem related to the issue of transitory combinations of data is whether "browsing" works on the information highway results in copyright infringement. Browsing refers to the downloading of a work, or part of a work, to scan its contents to see if it suits one's purposes. Some liken this practice to browsing through books in libraries or bookstores, with the important exception that in a networked environment browsing potentially results in copyright infringement. Browsing is a hot topic with copyright scholars. Most propose some legal reform.

Is browsing an infringement of copyright, and how does it relate to fixation?

When browsing through a work located on a network, you must first demand that the work be transmitted to you by the server on which it is housed. Once the work travels over the network wiring, it may come to sit on your local machine, usually a computer with memory, or be directly played for you, on a television for example. In both cases, a copy of the work has been made. It may, especially in the former case where disk storage has resulted, be sufficiently fixed to result in an infringement of copyright. A finding of infringement, of course, requires that a substantial portion of the work be copied.

At present, it is unclear whether browsing is in fact a violation of copyright law, especially where the copy made resides in volatile memory, e.g., a computer's RAM. This uncertainty has prompted policy makers to consider the browsing problem with respect to copyright reform. We set out at some length the recommendations and rationale of IHAC:

> If the Information Highway is to be truly viable and sustainable, creators must be assured of continued protection of their works. At the same time users must be assured of fair and reasonable access to those works.
>
> In its final report, the Copyright Subcommittee [of IHAC] had concluded that "the art of browsing a work in a digital environment should be considered an act of reproduction." In other words, browsing a work could mean either accessing a work, even if it is temporary or ephemeral in nature, as the making of a copy. In some countries, accessing a work in a digital environment is considered a reproduction, even where the work is temporarily stored in the random access memory of a computer.
>
> There was general agreement that copyright owners must be able to determine whether and when browsing should be permitted on the I-way. However, Council members were cognizant of the need to strike a balance between the interest of creators and users.
>
> Some Council members were concerned that broad interpretation of "browsing" would limit users' ability to access works. They felt that browsing a work simply for the purpose of deter-

mining whether they would like to use it could mean users would be unwittingly liable for copyright infringement.

Other Council members felt that users' ability to access works should not be a concern because copyright owners would authorize, in advance, the use of their works before the work is made available. Such is the case now, e.g., with respect to the right to communicate to the public; the television viewer is not liable for copyright infringement since the use of the program in respect of this right has already been negotiated between the copyright owner and the broadcaster.

At the end of the day, to assist both users and creators in the new digital environment, Council recommends that the Copyright Act be amended to provide clarification of what constitutes "browsing" and what works are "publicly available."

Recommendation:

6.4 It should be left to the copyright owner to determine whether and when browsing should be permitted on the Information Highway; the owner should identify what part of their work is appropriate for browsing.

The Copyright Act should be amended to provide a definition of "browse" along the following lines:

"browse" means a temporary materialization of a work on a video screen, television monitor or a similar device, or the performance of the audio portion of such a work on a speaker or similar device, by a user but which does not include the making of a permanent reproduction of the work in any material form.

In addition, the Copyright Act should provide a definition of "publicly available work."

For copyright to apply, the work must be "original." How does one gauge what is "original"?

Copyright protects the expression of an idea. It does not protect the idea itself. However, merely expressing oneself in one of the protected forms set out in the Copyright Act is not in itself sufficient to obtain protection. Protectable works, at a minimum, must demonstrate a modicum of originality.[10] Under Canadian law, to demonstrate originality, one need only show that the work originated from the author and was not a copy of an existing work. Originality under Canadian law has a comparatively low threshold compared to continental droit d'auteur jurisdictions such as Germany or France. Under German copyright, a work must display a high degree of creativity (*Gestaltunghöhe*) and individuality (*Individualität*). The French regime uses a lesser degree of originality, amounting to "the evidence of an intellectual contribution of the author" and novelty as compared with existing works.[11]

The person who creates the work owns the copyright?

Generally, yes. There are exceptions, however. For example, the author of a work is presumed to be the first owner of the copyright in the work, except where a work is created under a contract of service. Then the employer is presumed to be the first owner of the work. A "contract of service" refers to an employment relationship in the traditional sense, described in somewhat arcane language as a "master/servant relationship." Contrast it with a "contract for services." This refers to a situation where an independent contractor arranges to produce a work under a specific contract as opposed to a general employment contract. Under the specific contract the independent contractor will retain the copyright in the contracted work unless there has been an express agreement to the contrary.

Copyright is time-limited?

Copyright subsists in the work for the author's life, or in the case of joint authorship, the longest surviving author, plus fifty years. Joint authorship exists where the "contribution of one author is not distinct from the contribution of the other author or authors."[12]

The time periods for copyrighted works were devised long before the invention of digital information technologies. Their purpose was to provide a balance between paying the author for her creation while ensuring that society would also have access to the work. The peculiar characteristics of digital information technologies, and their high turnover, poses the question: should the protection period be lessened? A computer program is often obsolete in five years, let alone the author's life plus fifty years. Furthermore, given the market characteristics of computer programs, copyright holders stand to make super-normal returns. In 1984, facing a revision that eventually expressly placed computer programs under the jurisdiction of the Copyright Act in Canada, a governmental study proposed five years' protection for computer programs.[13] It died on the shelf. Thus the term of protection for computer programs under the Copyright Act is similar to other literary works, and consistent with the approach taken by other jurisdictions.[14]

What about simply rendering existing works, such as photographs, paintings or sounds, into digital form? Will these works become obsolete quicker just because they are expressed in digital form?

At first glance, digitized versions of traditional works such as paintings do not seem problematic. What has really changed, other than the medium or form of carriage? The ability of users to manipulate works rendered in digital form is the difference. This has added an entirely new dimension to the copyright problem. Traditionally, we worried only about copying. Although alteration of works was always possible, it was never at the forefront of the copyright debate. Instances of altered works were few. Today the situation is quite different. Many authors and publishers generate works in digital form precisely so the user may manipulate them, sizing, cropping or otherwise modifying the work. However, copyright holders may not want to allow all forms of alteration. These problems will create a host of difficulties for users, creators, researchers and courts.

But copyright holders who deal in digital works can set up their own contracts to give whatever rights they wish. Why does the law have to change?

This view may be right in theory, but wrong in practice. Copyright holders can indeed create licence agreements setting out their wishes. This is certainly true where there is a limited market, i.e., few buyers, for a product. Where a product is mass produced, however, the situation changes. In a mass market situation, creating and enforcing licences of this nature is expensive and difficult, if not impossible. Many believe that some reform of copyright law for digital works will be required as the technology proliferates. One popular theory of law ("form follows function") suggests that legal rules as they apply to commercial transactions should reflect industry practice. The law should try to facilitate the most common types of transactions. This reduces the costs to the parties transacting. If actual legal rules represent the parties' wishes, they will not have to create comprehensive and expensive contracts to render them legally enforceable. Also, it is not yet clear whether "shrink wrap licences" — agreements of adhesion that appear with mass produced works, especially computer programs — are enforceable under Canadian law.

The recent emergence of digital works may oblige us to rethink our views on information and associated proprietary rights created. Copyright law is a creature of statute. It is doubtful whether in Canada there is a natural law or fundamental right to copyright. Instead, the statute reflects the economic and utilitarian purposes discussed earlier. We are free to re-evaluate our copyright law and to change it so that it best reflects current needs and desires. Digital works and their interactivity are a relatively new phenomena. Do century-old copyright laws still reflect our society's views? Can they adapt to the realities of digital technology and the I-way?

How does the © symbol work?

In Canada there is no registration or marking the work (using the ©) requirement for works to be copyrightable; copyright exists upon the work's creation. Canada is a long-standing signatory to the Berne Convention on copyright. This international agreement amongst roughly 100 countries prohibits any requirement that works be registered or that the symbol be used in expressions of the work for copyright protection. One may, however, use the © or some other marking such as "copyright 1995" as a warning to would-be infringers.

Registration is not required. But is it advisable?

Yes. Once a work is created, and thus protected, the copyright holder may launch an action against anyone who copies, modifies, or reproduces the work without the holder's authorization. Although not mandatory, it is prudent to register a work for several reasons. First, registration provides an evidentiary record of the work should a dispute as to its authorship ever arise. Second, under Canadian law holders may have a broader range of remedies, e.g., damages, should there be an infringement. Therefore, where the work has commercial value, a copyright registration should be obtained. The cost of registration with the Department of Industry Canada is minimal, currently $35/work. The value of registration in an infringement action can be immense.

What constitutes copyright violation?

This occurs where the entire work, or a substantial part thereof, is reproduced without the holder's authorization. "Substantial" does not mean a strict percentage; it refers to the quality of the part taken. Therefore, a relatively small amount of the work's essence suffices. This is pertinent to browsing discussed earlier.

The Copyright Act's monopoly rights do not apply where a person independently creates a similar work. Accordingly, the jurisprudence on infringement requires a plaintiff to demonstrate both substantial similarity between her work and the defendant's, and a causal connection between the two.[15]

Where there is no evidence of actual copying, e.g., a witness who saw the copying occur, the courts employ a two-part test. First, they inquire: was there access to the work? If yes, they inquire: did a substantial portion of the work "reappear"? This latter test is performed by looking to see if the two works are substantially similar in the context of the genre of works in which they fit.

What happens if copyright is infringed?

The copyright holder may seek injunctory relief and/or damages. An injunction prevents further infringement. Damages, usually an accounting of profits, compensate the holder for lost revenues. One cannot commence a civil action "after the expiration of three years immediately following the infringement."[16] Where the Crown brings charges against infringers, the court may order a monetary penalty (civil remedy) or even jail (criminal remedy) in certain cases.

What is an injunction?

This is a discretionary remedy used in civil actions. The court prohibits the enjoined party from engaging in conduct such as continuing to copy. Injunctions may be obtained on an interim basis before trial. They may also form part of the court's final order at trial.

To obtain an injunction, an applicant must demonstrate that there is a serious issue to be tried, that irreparable harm may be caused, and, unless the case involves "blatant copying," that the balance of convenience favours the applicant. Damages, including exemplary or punitive damages in exceptional cases, are available where the copyright infringement causes economic loss to the plaintiff. An injunction is the only available remedy where the defendant was unaware or had no reasonable grounds for suspecting the existence of copyright in the work, unless the copyright was registered at the time of the infringement.[17] This is why it is wise to register one's work if one expects to use it for commercial purposes. This is also why the Copyright Act has struck a balance with this provision. If a copyright holder wishes to have the remedy of damages for infringement she must give "public" notice of the commercial value attached to the copyright through public registration.

Why is the criminal law used to punish copyright infringement?

In 1988, Parliament dramatically increased penalties for copyright infringement. The predecessor, the 1924 Act, provided a maximum fine of $10 per infringing copy, with a maximum fine of $200 and a possible sentence of hard labour. Because these penalties were too lenient to deter or punish in more severe cases of copying, Crown prosecution of copyright infringement was sometimes brought under the fraud provisions of the Criminal Code.[18] The Copyright Act did not give prosecutors the tools necessary effectively to combat organized commercial piracy. The recent toughening of copyright penalties was a response to increasing commercial piracy globally and strong lobbying by the software production and recording industries.[19] The criminal remedy applies only where the infringement is for commercial purposes;[20] it does not apply, e.g., to incidences of home copying for personal use.

Because of the weak penalties in the Copyright Act prior to the 1988 changes, in the past the Crown could choose to use Criminal Code fraud provisions to prosecute copyright infringers. As of 1988, using these has become unnecessary. The maximum penalties now depend on whether the Crown chooses to proceed summarily or by indictment (misdemeanor and felony using U.S. terms). On a summary conviction, a person may be sentenced to a fine not exceeding $25,000 or to a maximum of six months' imprisonment or both.[21] Where the Crown proceeds by way of indictment, the maximum penalty is a fine not exceeding $1 million or imprisonment not exceeding five years or both.[22]

Parliament's 1988 intent was to stigmatize copyright violation as criminal and tantamount to fraud. It expected that increased penalties would produce more frequent prosecutions under the Copyright Act. This demonstrates the increasing economic significance of ownership rights on the I-way. The Criminal Code itself contains no specific provision relating to copyright infringement.

What are the defences?

Several, from specific to general, exist.[23] For example, a specific exception for copyright infringement of computer programs is the backup exception, allowing a purchaser of a computer program to make a single copy for security or backup purposes. Another is the translation modification exception, allowing the purchaser to make a single copy that may be modified or adapted in order to make it function with a given computer.

The more general defence is the "fair dealing" exception. The U.S. Copyright Act contains a similar, but not identical, "fair use" section. It is often confused with its Canadian counterpart. Fair dealing is a general defence to copyright infringement that allows "any fair dealing with any work for the purposes of private study or research." The Canadian Copyright Act is silent as to the scope of the fair dealing exception, affording the courts greater flexibility as to its application. To date, however, our courts have given little elaboration.[24] The U.S. section, which receives more detailed mention in their copyright legislation, has been applied by American courts with much greater frequency, including areas that involve new technologies.[25] The U.S. section 107 provides guidelines for the courts. It states that:

In determining whether the use made of a work in any particular case is a fair use the factors to be considered shall include —

(1) the purpose and character of the use, including whether such use is of a commercial nature or is for non-profit educational purposes;

(2) the nature of the copyrighted work;

(3) the amount and substantiality of the portion used in relation to the copyrighted work as a whole; and

(4) the effect of the use upon the potential market for or value of the copyrighted work.

The fact that a work is unpublished shall not itself bar a finding of fair use if such finding is made upon consideration of all the above factors.

A final, lesser-known but nonetheless important, general defence to copyright infringement which may attain greater prominence in the digital age, especially as a defence to assertions of Crown copyright, is the public interest defence. This is not grounded in statutory law in Canada. It exists through limited mention in the case law. A public interest defence allows the infringer to claim that the purpose of the infringement was for the benefit of the public interest and should be allowed on the basis that its purpose supersedes the purposes of copyright law generally. The public interest exception has a more secure juridical history in the U.K. This may assist Canadian courts in applying it in the future.[26]

PATENTS

What about patent laws?

The terms copyright and patent are often misused by laypersons who wish to express the general idea of IP rights. The two regimes, however, are quite different in what and how they protect. Patents are monopoly rights granted by the federal government to inventors. These rights are limited in duration. They are fuelled by two basic policy objectives: to encourage further research and development by providing economic monopoly protection, and to create a system of knowledge sharing whereby the public may have access to patented technologies through a system of public disclosure of patent documents. As with copyright, obtaining a patent does not entitle one to specific sums of money *per se* or to any other reward. Rather, it gives one the right to exclude others from making or using the invention for the duration of the patent.

Patents sound very similar to copyright. What's the difference?

Patents apply to functional articles or processes that create a tangible product. They are not granted for the ideas at the core of these articles or processes. They are granted for the physical manifestation of the ideas. Examples of non-patentable items in Canada include mathematical theorems, computer programs (although this is slowly changing), scientific principles and medical treatments. Examples of patentable inventions are a staple remover, a revolutionary new garden tool, and a new drug cure for some illness. Patents, therefore, generally do not apply to the information that travels on the I-way, unless a patented computer program is being transmitted. Rather they apply to the technological innovation that makes the information highway function. For example, computers, routing devices that direct the data traffic, and even the adaptors that allow cables to connect, are all patentable.

At the present stage of I-way development, patents are extremely important to Canadian firms. They are, in several sectors, world leaders in developing information technology. This importance is increased by the I-way's global scope.

Consider a device that routes data packets on the information highway, e.g., that is adopted as the standard for information highway data transmission. If that router is patented, and the patent is drafted in such a way as to foreclose competitive devices from being used, the patent holder will reap monopoly profits. It will be the sole supplier of this necessary technology. Canadian companies such as Northern Telecom, Bell Canada and Newbridge Networks hold many patents for I-way technology. While Canada, due to its size, cannot always compete with larger countries such as the U.S. in all aspects of the I-way, it has many examples of comparative advantage in telecommunications technologies.

How does one obtain a patent?

The invention must possess three elements: novelty, utility and some measure of inventive step (also known as "non-obviousness"). Novelty requires that the applicant be the original inventor and that the invention be the first of its kind anywhere in the world. There must have been no public disclosure of the invention prior to the filing of the application, subject to a one-year exception in Canada. Utility requires that the invention or process has some useful function — it must work. Finally, the invention must be a result of ingenuity that would not have been obvious to a person of average skill in the industry. The degree of inventive step does not require that the invention be a revolutionary development; it may consist of an improvement on already existing technology. The rule of thumb for this final test is that the invention must elicit some reaction of marvel or amazement ("Why didn't I think of that?") by others in the industry. If the patent is an addition to an existing technology then any production of the invention will have to obtain the requisite authorization from patent holders of the existing technology usually in the form of licensing agreements.

Once the application is drafted, it must be submitted to the Commissioner of Patents with a written petition requesting that a patent be granted, accompanied by the prescribed fee. The filing date of a patent is extremely important in Canada. We have a "first to file" system. This means that the first person to file a successful patent application will be granted a patent even if she was not the first inventor. With respect to the making public of information, in Canada there is a one-year grace period granted prior to the filing of the patent application, during which the invention may have been disclosed without any prejudice to the subsequent application. This is to encourage research and the advancement of learning by putting important ideas into the public domain promptly. Eighteen months after filing the application, the application is made available to the public. Recall the knowledge-sharing policy objective discussed earlier. If the patent is infringed after the filing date but before being granted the patent, the eventual patent holder will be entitled to retroactive compensation.

Once examination has been requested, the waiting period is often several years before a decision as to patentability is received. Hence we see the term "patent pending."[27] A patent examiner, often a specialist in the invention's field, will then begin the process of examining the application and invention to determine whether it complies with the rules for granting patents and whether a patent already exists for parts claimed in the application ("a prior art"). Throughout the examination procedure, any member of the public may oppose the application by filing a protest or by filing a prior art.

How long does this patent monopoly last?

The term of protection in Canada is a maximum of twenty years from the date of filing. Obtaining a Canadian patent, however, does not grant patent protection abroad. To obtain foreign patent protection, one may either apply in each foreign jurisdiction, or file an application under the Patent Cooperation Treaty (PCT) in Canada. The PCT is a treaty respected by most industrialized nations. It provides for a standardized patent filing system. Once the PCT application is approved, the applicant must still file and pay the prescribed fees in each country. However, the application is likely to be accepted. Filing a PCT compliant application also qualifies as an application under the Canadian Patent Act. If a patent application is filed abroad, many countries respect the convention priority rule.[28] Once a patent application is filed in one's home country, that filing date will be used in each of the other countries that respect this rule, providing an application is filed in the other country within one year of the home country filing. The U.S. has its own rules regarding convention priority. If one obtains a patent in one's home country and fails to take advantage of the convention priority rules (i.e., file within time), one may be barred from obtaining certain foreign patents because the home country patent will be considered a disclosure to the public. Accordingly, the invention will fail the novelty requirement.

What are the remedies for patent infringement?

Under the Patent Act, the remedies available include damages and injunctory relief.[29] As a result of recent amendments, there is a six-year limit for claiming any remedy: in order to claim any remedy for infringement, one must bring a claim to court within six years of the act of infringement.[30] There are also criminal penalties for falsely holding oneself out as being a patent holder. Patent infringement, as with copyright infringement, is largely a civil matter; the criminal law does not play a great role in patent matters.

Other forms of IP, such as trademarks, exist as well. Given their marginal relevance to the I-way to date, we have not discussed these.

13

PRIVACY

"Privacy is the right to be alone —
the most comprehensive of rights,
and the right most valued by civilized man."
— Louis D. Brandeis

Public opinion surveys note that Canadians are increasingly worried about privacy on the I-way. This chapter focuses on that concern.

Why are Canadians worried about privacy?

As information is stored more and more in electronic, i.e., digital form, it can be shuttled around with relative ease. Information about individuals that may be considered private, such as health information or credit card spending habits, often has commercial value. The incentive to sell such information is high. Without adequate controls, the information will indeed be spread through its sale. Although the obvious target of proposed controls will be the large databases services dealing in this sort of information, control advocates propose that regulations must target small information transfers as well. With an interconnected network of networks, the information does not have to be present in one physical location. Inquisitive people seeking out the private information today have a wealth of computer search programs that can root out detail around the world and assemble it in a few minutes.

At the other end of the spectrum are free-speech advocates who feel that information, like ideas, should flow freely without government intervention. To impose privacy laws is to embark on a slippery slope where drawing firm lines is difficult. Who will decide what is private? The individual? The government? The administration of privacy rights is another tough issue altogether. What sanctions should be imposed? Civil? Criminal? The issue of privacy is complex and must be carefully considered.

What is privacy?

People often consider privacy to be a fundamental, guaranteed right. They equate it with freedom of expression or the right to equality. One can roughly define the limits of these latter two rights. Answers about the meaning of a right to privacy, however, are considerably more vague. Philosophers and lawmakers have debated the meaning of privacy for centuries with little success. A workable definition of privacy is:

the limits one has set on acquaintance with his personal affairs . . . [It is] the condition of not having undocumented personal knowledge about one possessed by others. A person's privacy is diminished exactly to the degree that others possess this kind of knowledge about him . . . personal information consists of facts which most persons in a given society choose not to reveal about themselves (except to close friends, family, . . .) or of facts about which a particular individual is acutely sensitive and which he therefore does not choose to reveal about himself, even though most people don't care if the same facts are widely known about themselves . . . What belongs in the public domain cannot without glaring paradox be called private; consequently it should not be incorporated within our concept of privacy . . . It is also important not to confuse documented facts as I define them here with facts about individuals which are kept on file for special purposes but which are not available for public consumption, for example, health records.[1]

The IHAC has defined privacy in two ways: "the right to be left alone, free from intrusion or interruption, and the right to exercise control over one's personal information."[2] All of these definitions share the view that personal information is somehow special to the individual. Its spread must be controlled for privacy to exist.

What specific privacy concerns does the I-way raise?

Privacy concerns are many and not new. As with other issues, such as intellectual property rights, the I-way has accelerated the debate and need for change. Privacy concerns include: access to existing records containing personal data; gathering and disclosure of transaction generated information; controlling monitoring and surveillance; the unauthorized use of personal information for non-approved purposes; and the security of information.

The issue of access to existing records containing personal data concerns both making the knowledge of a record's existence available to the subject as well as providing the ability to correct any mistakes. The most commonly raised example is the credit rating system. An erroneous credit rating can wreak havoc with an individual's financial welfare. The ability to correct mistakes is vital with this type of information and is currently supported by legislation.[3]

The ability to gather and disclose transaction generated information has been created largely as a result of the high incidence of transaction computerization. For example, checkout clerks at grocery stores often use bar-code scanners to read in the purchase price. These scanners read the data into a computer system that is linked to the store's accounting and inventory control systems. The store may add a marketing software module, which could track a person's purchasing habits, especially where credit card purchases are made. The store might track information about that person's purchasing for selective marketing to her, or the information could be sold to a third party for even more selective marketing.

Consider the recent appearance of "software moles." These are computer programs, contained within other computer programs, which users purchase and install on their computer systems. If the computer system is tied into a global network, such as the Internet, the software mole will relay information to the company selling the software. This information can be information about the user's use of the program, a report about other software on the user's disk, or even confidential files and information that the user may store. These moles can operate without the user's knowledge. The legality of using software moles, which seem to violate basic privacy principles, is not clear. At present, computer developers generally do not use these programs because of ethical and legal concerns, and because of the fear of a consumer backlash should they be discovered. There has been a great deal of press devoted to the recent release of Windows 95 by Microsoft and its inclusion of an online (voluntary) registration system. Some have accused Microsoft of starting what may become a disturbing trend.

Linked to these concerns is what rules govern the unauthorized use of personal information for non-approved purposes, such as the store purchase example where the information has been sold.

Another privacy concern arises with personnel monitoring and surveillance. Issues such as employee monitoring to achieve increased productivity currently remain largely unregulated.

Finally, the methods and controls associated with securing private information so that it does not fall into the wrong hands must also be considered in any discussion of privacy. We reviewed this issue earlier in Chapter 10 on security.

What laws protect privacy?

The laws that govern privacy and address the concerns as set out are largely underdeveloped. There is no comprehensive national law for privacy. Rather, privacy law is generally an afterthought, added to legislation which often has a completely independent issue as its primary thrust. Thus any discussion of privacy is piecemeal. We have attempted to draw together unrelated laws and distill a coherent and consistent approach to privacy. But it is highly artificial, and must be recognized as such.

Privacy law can be conceptually divided into two distinct components: privacy as between the state and the individual (public right), and privacy as between individuals (private right). The former has, to date, received a great deal of attention by lawmakers and the courts; the latter, little.

Explain the public right.

This governs all information held by government institutions, such as drivers' licences and tax returns. It also protects the individual's right to life, liberty and security of the person, and to be free from unreasonable search and seizures in dealing with the government. In Canada, the key pieces of legislation are the Privacy Act,[4] its provincial counterparts, and the Canadian Charter of Rights and Freedoms.[5]

1. The Privacy Act

The Privacy Act came into force in 1982, effectively replacing similar provisions contained in the Canadian Human Rights Act, 1977. The preamble and section 2 of the Act set out its purpose:

> An Act to extend the present laws of Canada that protect the privacy of individuals and that provide individuals with a right of access to personal information about themselves.
>
> S.2   The purpose of this act is to extend the present laws of Canada that protect the privacy of individuals with respect to

personal information about themselves held by a government institution that provide individuals with a right of access to that information.

S.8 of the Act states,

Personal information under the control of a government institution shall not, without the consent of the individual to whom it relates, be disclosed by the institution except in accordance with this section.

The government may only use the information for enumerated purposes that are consistent with good government. Government-held information is not available for public use.

Enforcement of the Act is overseen by the Privacy Commissioner, a post created under the earlier Canadian Human Rights Act, 1977. While the Privacy Act does support a right to privacy, it only applies as between an individual and government institutions. It does not extend to private parties.[6] Over the past few years, in addition to serving a watchdog role over government, in his annual report, the Privacy Commissioner has reported on the state of privacy law generally, including privacy between private parties. In addition to the Federal Privacy Commissioner, provinces may also have their own privacy commissioners who also serve as government watchdogs. Our constitution does not expressly deal with the power over privacy rights. Consequently, both the provinces and the federal government have exercised authority over privacy matters in different contexts. As with the federal Privacy Act, several provinces have enacted specific legislation to "protect the privacy of individuals with respect to personal information about themselves held by [government] institutions and to provide individuals with a right of access to that information."[7] Privacy legislation designed to protect individual information held by government also applies at the municipal level.[8] The U.S., like

Canada, protects individual information against government misuse through legislation, specifically the Privacy Act (1974).[9] Also like its Canadian counterpart, the American Act created a Privacy Protection Study Commission whose mandate has been to monitor issues of privacy between the state and individuals.[10]

2. The Canadian Charter of Rights and Freedoms

Another source of privacy law between individuals and the government can be found in the Canadian Charter of Rights and Freedoms. Three Charter rights have an impact on privacy.

Section 26 of the Charter states that the Charter "shall not be construed as denying the existence of any other rights or freedoms that exist in Canada." Some experts believe that this may allow the Courts to acknowledge a pre-existing privacy right, although, "a carefully drafted constitutional amendment would be far more effective in guaranteeing the protection of Canadians' privacy."[11] Section 7 states: "Everyone has the right to life, liberty and security of the person and the right not to be deprived thereof except in accordance with the principles of fundamental justice." The argument is that privacy is necessary to liberty and security of the person. Section 8 is more explicit. It states: "Everyone has the right to be secure against unreasonable search or seizure." Section 8 is frequently used to ensure that law enforcement officers take the proper steps prior to searching a person and his belongings. Without the requisite authority, such as during an arrest or with a search warrant, the police must respect an individual's right to privacy.

What about a right to privacy as between individuals — the private right?

There is no strong common law (judge-made law) of privacy *per se* in Canada. Private persons, although unable legally to tap into the databases of either level of government, which contain a wealth of information, remain relatively unhindered by privacy concerns. There are, however, a few exceptions.

There are some special privacy situations which are governed by provincial law, such as privately owned credit reporting agencies. In Ontario, for example, the Consumer Reporting Act restricts those agencies that gather and distribute consumer credit information. The Act specifically limits the type of information which can be gathered, as well as to whom such information may be given. Any person about whom information is being collected may request disclosure of this information. The Act also restricts anyone, who is not specifically listed under the Act, from "knowing[ly] obtain[ing] information from the files of a consumer reporting agency respecting a consumer . . ." While this Act is specifically aimed at controlling the privacy interests of individuals in a private party context, it is one of the few pieces of legislation that currently deals with private party privacy issues. As the I-way develops, and electronic databases become more prevalent, it seems likely that similar specific legislation will be enacted.

Another example of privacy legislation that concerns the I-way is the Federal Telecommunications Act. In its 1993 re-enactment it established a legislative right to privacy in communications, setting out that:

Canadian telecommunications policy has as [one of] its objectives . . .

(i) to contribute to the protection of the privacy of persons.[12]

Finally, Part VI of the Criminal Code makes it an indictable offence for any third party to intercept a private communication.[13] The maximum penalty under the Code is imprisonment not exceeding five years.[14] The term "private communication" is defined broadly as meaning "any oral communication, or any telecommunication . . . and includes any radio-based telephone communication that is treated electronically or otherwise for the purpose of preventing intelligible reception by any person other than the person intended by the originator to receive it."[15] In addition to preventing surreptitious wire-tapping by government agencies, these laws apply as between individuals as well.

Is there no general federal or provincial legislation that supports a broad right of privacy as between individuals?

Only Quebec has enacted several general acts. The Quebec *Charte des droits et libertés*, enacted in 1975, secures a right to privacy for residents of the province. This right has manifested itself in two further legislative enactments. Quebec's new *Code Civil*, which came into force in 1994, provides residents of Quebec with a right of action in cases where their informational, territorial or personal privacy is violated. In 1993, Quebec passed the *Loi sur la protection des renseignements personnels dans le secteur privé*. This operates as an access to information act concerning information held about individuals by private sector business operating within the province. Under this legislation, a resident has the right to request that the business provide her with access to information it holds about her.

What about foreign jurisdictions?

The most notable for the purposes of the I-way is the U.K.'s Data Protection Act, passed in July 1984. Under that Act, anyone holding or controlling "personally related data" which is "automatically processed" is required to register and provide a description of the data held as well as its intended use with the Data Registrar.[16] The maximum penalty for non-registration is a fine not exceeding £5,000 plus court costs at the Magistrates Court level, and an unlimited fine in the Higher Courts.

The Act also specifies "good data practice" principles. Upon a finding of non-compliance with data protection principles in the Act, the Registrar, in charge of administering the Act, may serve a notice of enforcement to the database holder.[17] Failure to comply with the notice results in a criminal offence under the Act. The Registrar has the power to deregister a database and prevent the database holder from holding personally related information. As with most administrative agencies, there lies an appeal to a tribunal, aptly titled the Data Protection Tribunal. Failing a successful appeal, a candidate may appeal to the courts.

Individuals can access these records via computer at the offices of the Registrar. The records held by the Registrar do not contain the actual information held in the registered database. They simply disclose what type of information the registered party holds.

With the steady increase in electronic databases, as a result of advances in information technology, the Registrar's office has been besieged with registration requests. This type of privacy protection requires direct regulatory intervention. The Quebec laws, on the other hand, create a legal right which can be enforced by the aggrieved citizen in the courts. It seems unlikely, given the current climate of government downsizing, that a regulatory system similar to that in the U.K. will be adopted in Canada. It is costly, highly bureaucratic and interventionist. It requires government to assume yet another function.

In addition to the U.K., most other countries of the European Union presently have data protection laws.[18] These laws, while serving to protect privacy interests, also interfere with the free flow of information across national boundaries, known as transborder data flow. This interference conflicts with the spirit of a common market. As a result, the European Commission has proposed a directive aimed at harmonizing these disparate regimes' protection. A comprehensive directive would force member-states to amend their laws so that they do not conflict with the directive's provisions. This illustrates a tension, not between privacy and free speech, but between privacy and trade.

What about the common law?

For the common law of privacy, the U.S. experience is far greater than our own. Historically, privacy as between individuals gained its first true champions in the United States in Samuel Warren and Louis Brandeis. In a famous 1890 *Harvard Law Review* article entitled "The Right to Privacy," Brandeis and Warren canvassed the case law and distilled a distinct principle which they called the right to privacy: "the right of a private individual to be let alone and protected from unauthorized publicity in his essentially private affairs."[19] This principle laid the foundation from which American laws of privacy evolved, although neither Canada nor the U.S. have comprehensive legal protections of privacy as between individuals. Nevertheless, the U.S. has developed its common law to a greater degree.

Examples?

The public disclosure of private facts, the employer–employee relationship, and the debtor–creditor relationship.[20] Of these private party privacy rules, the most relevant to users of the I-way is undoubtedly that governing the public disclosure of private information. In 1960, Professor William Prosser published a landmark article in the *University of California Law Review*. It examined the U.S. common law. Rather than one actionable tort, or civil right of action, for invasion of privacy, it found four: an intrusion into the plaintiff's private affairs, the public disclosure of private facts about the plaintiff, the appropriation of the plaintiff's personality, and publicity which places the plaintiff in a false light in the public eye.[21]

How do these common law rights protect individuals?

Protection against intrusion into one's private affairs protects individuals against unreasonable physical intrusions as well as eavesdropping.[22] One may not physically intrude upon another's private space (i.e., home, hotel room, etc.), tap telephones, read private mail, or engage in certain other surveillance techniques which intrude upon an individual's private affairs. To succeed in court, one must demonstrate that an intrusion into a private matter has occurred. If the matter is one which can reasonably be considered public, this claim will fail.[23]

On the I-way, information providers need not generally worry about this aspect of invasion of privacy as their business does not typically involve the surveillance of specific individuals; it is instead concerned with mass data collection.

The right of privacy concerning the public disclosure of private facts allows the plaintiff to recover damages where the defendant has revealed embarrassing facts which the plaintiff intended to keep private. The legal tests are difficult to meet. For example, one must demonstrate an unreasonable intrusion into one's affairs, as well as a subsequent publication of any private material gained.[24] One must demonstrate, for example, an exploitation or unwarranted appropriation of the private information resulting in an unauthorized endorsement of products or services.[25] Another possible cause of action lies in the claim that an information provider, or other person, has disseminated "information embarrassing to the person which, although wholly true, would be offensive to a person of ordinary sensibilities."[26] According to Professor Osborne,

> The disclosure must be such as to be highly offensive to the reasonable person, and it must be a disclosure of private facts; not matters which are already part of the public record. No liability is imposed if the disclosure is already part of the public record. No liability is imposed if the disclosure is of facts in which the public has a legitimate interest or where the plaintiff has consented to the disclosure.[27]

The requirement that the disclosure be public is important in discussing many I-way issues. The public/private legal distinction is a tricky one. Various laws each ascribe different tests as to what is considered public. In respect of privacy matters, U.S. courts have held that "public" requires some element of publicity. According to Professor Prosser, "it is an invasion of the right [of privacy] to publish in a newspaper that the plaintiff does not pay his debts, or to post a notice to that effect in a window on the public street or cry it aloud in the highway . . . it has been agreed that it is no invasion to communicate that fact to the plaintiff's employer, or to any other individual, or even to a small group, unless there is some breach of contract, trust or confidential relation which will afford an independent basis for relief."[28] In considering whether there has been an actionable public disclosure of private facts, one must also consider the status of the person about whom the facts are revealed, and whether they are properly considered to be public personalities or merely private persons. A public personality, such as a celebrity or public official, has a much narrower scope of that which is considered private than would the average person. Consequently, public personalities have less privacy.

The tort concerning the unauthorized appropriation of the plaintiff's personality is aimed at preventing the use of individuals' personalities for commercial gain without their consent. Actionable situations might involve advertising one's product using a celebrity impersonator in the advertisement, or stating that an individual endorses one's product without that person's authorization to do so.[29]

The fourth and final head of Prosser's tort of privacy occurs where a defendant intentionally claims facts about the plaintiff which are both untrue and offensive to the sensibilities of the reasonable person. For a database provider on the I-way, this privacy test may raise cause for concern since the database provider's business is to provide information about various subjects and individuals. If a database provider should falsely attribute a statement, opinion, or any other matter to an individual in his/her database which is untrue and has the effect of placing that individual in a false light in the public eye, then the mistake may give rise to legal proceedings.

It should be stressed that Prosser's torts of privacy exist in an American context and do not necessarily exist in a Canadian one. However, Canadian courts often find their American counterparts to be helpful in dealing with new high-technology issues.

Do we not have similar laws in Canada?

Other common law heads of liability may, potentially, be used in Canada to argue the same points. For example, for the tort of intrusion, Prosser's first category, the laws of trespass and nuisance, with some further development, may be used as a substitute.[30]

Prosser's second category, the public disclosure of private facts, which is of some concern to information providers who operate in the United States, does not exist in any form in Canadian law.[31] According to Professor Osborne:

> The only possible protection is provided by the rule in *Wilkinson v. Downton* which provides a remedy for the infliction of nervous shock. The ability of this tort to protect privacy has been restricted by requiring the plaintiff to establish that he has suffered nervous shock of such seriousness as to manifest itself in physical consequences. There is no liability for transient anxiety, embarrassment or humiliation. The Canadian courts have shown no inclination to dispense with this limitation.[32]

Prosser's appropriation of personality category receives protection in Canada under several legal principles. First, the common law holds that one's goodwill is worthy of protection and cannot be misappropriated. Other applicable rules include defamation as well as the unauthorized exposure of the plaintiff to legal or financial risk.[33] As stated above, the appropriation of personality category does not raise much concern in the case of information providers on the I-way.

Prosser's fourth and final category, placing the plaintiff in a false light in the public eye, does not receive any protection in Canada under privacy laws. Rather it falls within the domain of the tort of defamation, and more specifically libel. Defamation covers two elements: slander and libel. Libel occurs where a publisher prints a false statement about an individual and the statement causes harm to the individual. Slander is similar but concerns the spoken word. In the

U.S., a suit for defamation requires that the plaintiff show malice on the part of the defendant. In Canada there is no malice requirement. Rather, demonstrating malice will be used by the court to assess damages. Defamation laws are therefore broader in Canada than in the United States, covering more causes of action than their American counterparts. As a result, Canadian defamation laws provide a fairly good substitute for the American tort of placing the plaintiff in a false light in the public eye. This is, of course, no comfort to information providers, who are constantly at risk of disseminating erroneous information about individuals to the public.

Although the legal tests enumerated above are complex and numerous, they should not be of great worry to information providers who simply gather up all but the most private of information about individuals. Instituting procedures whereby editorial or other questionable data is verified will provide a strong measure of prevention from such legal entanglements occurring. Canadian laws are clearly in need of further development in comparison with their American counterparts. Consequently, information providers face a situation where they may be able to get away with more questionable conduct in Canada than in the U.S. In both countries, however, claiming that the individual has consented to the information's use will serve as a solid defence in each of the instances mentioned above.[34] Americans are also substantially more litigious than Canadians.

Legal rules, other than privacy, may also cause information providers concern. These include, in addition to defamation, disclosure of confidential information, and most recently product liability law.[35]

Can you summarize how privacy relates to the information highway?

IHAC considered this broad question. It raised ten specific questions:[36]

    (1)   Is legislation required to establish an individual's right to privacy or to vast ownership of personal information with the individual? Or should we rely on voluntary

compliance to protection guidelines, leaving the individual to settle ownership contractually with data gatherers?

(2) Should any limit be placed on an individual's ability to trade or sell personal information or on the ability of organizations to trade or reuse this information?

(3) Who owns the electronic transaction records of consumer purchases? Should government intervene to regulate the subsequent or third-party use of transactional data?

(4) Under what circumstances should law enforcement or other public officials be able to access unrelated information on an individual?

(5) Should governments intervene to regulate the use of electronic surveillance? What limits, if any, should be placed on the ability to electronically monitor behaviour using information technologies?

(6) Is a uniform national level of privacy protection needed to ensure consistent rights and treatment across Canada, and give Canada a competitive trade advantage?

(7) Are different levels of privacy protection needed for different tasks or different types of information? Can the same rules cover all personal information and all carriers and information service providers?

(8) What should be done to improve the consumer's awareness of the threats to privacy and ability to protect his or her privacy?

(9) What standards, networks configurations or technologies should be explored in the design of the information highway to better allow individuals to protect their privacy? Who should bear the cost for improved privacy protection?

(10) Should the privacy implications of all new technologies be explored before their commercial introduction? If so, how should this be done?

IHAC responded to these questions with a broad set of recommendations aimed at developing a national strategy or framework that can guide lawmakers in devising privacy legislation. Briefly, IHAC recommended that Canada adopt guidelines to ensure that privacy laws preserve the dignity of Canadians. These laws must balance this dignity with the public benefits of ensuring the free flow of information which might assist research both in the natural and social sciences. The method by which this balancing may be achieved must take into account the public it serves. Users of private information should develop methods by which the public is educated and informed about the manner in which data is "collected, managed, accessed, retained, disposed, linked and analyzed."[37] IHAC recommended developing a workable national privacy strategy primarily through consultation with the private sector, including non-governmental organizations, as being the preferred manner in which to proceed.

What are some possible concrete solutions to the problems of privacy?

IHAC proposed four: legislation, education, voluntary codes of conduct and technological solutions.[38] Adoption of any of these solutions must be tempered or guided by considerations of openness, disclosure (access), secondary usage, correction, reliability and security. These latter principles were developed by the U.S. Department of Health, Education and Welfare in a 1973 report which dealt with the automation of personal data, entitled the Fair Information Practices Guidelines.

The principles are easily defined. Openness requires that the very existence of an information database be disclosed. There can be no secret record keeping. Disclosure requires that individuals about whom information is being gathered and stored be given access to the information. Secondary usage deals with the resale and transfer of information once it has been compiled. Individuals should have rights to prevent any transfer from occurring. Correction refers to the individual's ability to correct any wrong information that has been stored that concerns her. Finally, reliability and security require that bodies who gather personal information be forced to maintain that information securely. Clearly, the level of security required will vary with the type of information gathered or stored. These principles provide sound guidance in dealing with privacy issues.

Of the possible solutions to the privacy problem, clearly the most controversial is legislation. Creating a broad privacy right through legislative enactment poses a tricky balancing act. Preventing the disclosure of information must be balanced against free-speech rights, and should also be concerned with economic impact. The issue of privacy is in its infancy and its limits have yet to be determined.

The use of voluntary codes of conduct allows society to test out principles of protection without being forced to adhere to them. A system of voluntary codes of conduct, such as the 1981 OECD Guidelines, updated frequently to take into account new concerns, is to be preferred, and is more realistic than imposing legislation at this early stage.

Technological solutions are often touted as the best way to keep technological progress in check. This involves private sector development of privacy tools, such as encryption methods. These could be used to ensure privacy whether or not there is government backing. Unfortunately, without some government regulation, technology can also be used to defeat these devices. A good example of technology outsmarting technology concerns the appearance of television decoders. These can decode encrypted cable signals, such as those used on pay-per-view channels. These decoders are available on the black market for a relatively low price. If not for laws preventing this action, these decoders would be prevalent, and cable companies would be forced to spend more money for better encryption. Consumers ultimately pay for this.

Finally, improving education about privacy rights may be the easiest and most effective way to combat poor information privacy practices. The ability of consumers to exercise their power will be enhanced by the evolving I-way. Individuals already use the Internet to spread their message. Although we have had only a brief opportunity to gauge user behaviour on the Internet, it seems clear that consumers are becoming more aware of and proactive about their rights. Enhancing privacy education is already becoming a reality. Government need do little to supplement this growing movement.

IV

THE ISSUES

14

THE ECONOMIC IMPACT

"Employment, which Galen calls 'nature's physician,'
is so essential to human happiness that indolence
is justly considered as the mother of misery."
— Richard E. Burton

The information highway is a rapidly evolving phenomenon. The full dimensions of its economic impact are uncertain.[1] There is a dearth of empirical analysis and little time to adjust. This chapter considers the economic impact of the I-way from three interconnected standpoints: (1) economic growth, (2) the marketplace and (3) the workplace. We wish to illustrate how the information highway is transforming our economy and to try to assess whether this transformation bodes well or ill for Canada.

ECONOMIC GROWTH

How is the information revolution shaping the economy?

Digitization and the convergence of technologies are structurally transforming our economy, with three results: privatization, deregulation and globalization. As illustrated by the changing roles of Canadian telecommunications carriers, the privatization and deregulation of information technology industries are central to this transformative process.[2] Traditional telecommunications monopolies and quasi-monopolies are crumbling while entrepreneurialism and competition are flourishing. This is largely a product of technological progress. Moreover, time and distance are shrinking dramatically. As national borders fade, competition occurs increasingly in an international forum. To compete, companies must keep pace with technological change and must be innovative.

Explain the importance of innovation.

Economists typically use economic models to describe the cause-and-effect relationship between different aspects of the economy. The information era has transformed the economic model for prosperity. Consider the neo-classical economic model's formula for growth:

capital + labour = economic growth

Traditional economic theory presupposes that capital accumulation combined with labour are the driving forces behind economic growth. Accordingly, the extent of wealth creation corresponds primarily to the modernity of the machines and production equipment and to the level of workers' physical and mental efforts. Productivity explains how effectively capital and labour are combined to generate output. In a knowledge-based economy, however, there is an additional prerequisite to economic growth: innovation. The modern equation is:

capital + labour + innovation = economic growth

Without innovation in products, services and processes, businesses cannot compete and will not prosper. Economists Mark Potter and Marc Lee explain that "[n]ew developments in growth theory are centred around explaining growth at a microeconomic or firm level by focusing on technology and the underlying innovation process. . . . The centrality of innovation points to the fundamental role of information, learning and R&D in economic growth, as well as better organizational and institutional structures to accommodate and encourage innovation."[3]

What are concrete examples of the impact of the information highway on the Canadian economy?

Let's consider two. A first is the steady shift from a cash to a credit economy with the development of electronic payment systems. The credit card initiated this process. The consumer may purchase goods and services on "credit" and pay back the outstanding balance at a later date. Secure electronic transmission of the purchase value and credit card number to the bank permits verification of the account and credit limit. A more recent innovation is the debit card, e.g., Interac payment. Withdrawal is made immediately on purchase by electronically identifying and debiting the cardholder's bank account, i.e., instantly removing the funds from the account. Electronic bill payment through telephone banking, automatic tellers, automatic salary deposits and "smart" cash cards periodically credited electronically from one's account with fixed amounts of "cash" by one machine for crediting the vendor's machine on a purchase, all plunge us deeper into a cashless economy. These examples illustrate but one dimension of innovation that is reshaping the economic relationships.

The emerging cashless economy is one aspect of how the information highway is altering the links between buyers and sellers. Rapidly emerging virtual malls, banks and corporations advertise, purchase and transact electronically on the Internet. New virtual relationships have emerged due to the integrative force of electronic commerce. They are collaborative webs of vendors and consumers linked via computer and telecommunications facilities. Wal-Mart Stores, based in a small Arkansas town, is a leading example.

Closer to home (though Wal-Mart has arrived close to home with its purchase of the Woolco Canada Inc. chain of discount stores), Calgary Stockyards Inc. sells cattle by electronic auction. Formerly, cattle merchants from all across the country had to be physically present at a Calgary auction to see and bid on cattle transported there. Long-distance travel both for cattle and human beings can be inefficient. Consider a cattle seller from Prince Albert, Saskatchewan, and a buyer from nearby Saskatoon doing business in Calgary. The cattle would be shipped to the Calgary stockyard and then back to Saskatchewan. And so would the buyer. The electronic auction allows the buyer to assess and purchase the cattle online, using high-tech imagery, without travelling the long distances. Cattle can stay on the farm or at a nearby video centre. Buyers can stay at their computer-equipped home offices. This saves both time and money. In Quebec, the cable company Videotron Ltd. is working in concert with the provincial government, Hydro-Quebec, National Bank, Canada Post and many vendors to launch UBI (universal, bidirectional, interactive), a home communications network providing interactive shopping, banking and other services. Videotron is scheduled to introduce UBI into 30,000 homes in the Lac-St-Jean region in 1996.

How deep and broad is this virtual economy?

It is very comprehensive. Consider New Brunswick, where the rapid application of advanced telecommunications has dramatically changed a regional, largely rural and resource-based economy. Premier Frank McKenna envisions information technology transforming New Brunswick. One of his cabinet ministers, George Corriveau, became the world's first "Information Highway Minister." With government encouragement, NBTel established fibre-optic transmission throughout the province. The Education Ministry overhauled its primary and secondary school curriculum to ensure computer literacy. The Health Minister has initiated a $500,000 per year telemedicine project in Moncton and the three surrounding counties to "field" patients' health inquiries via telephone and computer. The Finance Ministry offers attractive incentives for high-tech companies to invest in the province. To demonstrate that the effort begins at the top, New Brunswick's toll free number for economic development information is 1-800-MCKENNA.

Are these initiatives paying off in New Brunswick?

Initial indications suggest they are. Numerous Canadian and global companies, e.g., Sears Canada, Royal Bank, Canada Trust and U.P.S., have located call centres in Moncton, St. John and Fredericton (all with substantial bilingual capacity). The test, however, will be whether Premier McKenna can exploit the information economy to end a century of "have-not" status in the Canadian confederation and turn New Brunswick into a "have" province within a decade. His recent re-election for a third conservative mandate confirms his popular appeal.

You've spoken of a province. What makes a city attractive for high-tech companies?

The August 1995 *Globe and Mail* supplement *Report on Business* magazine discussed just this. It published the fourth annual survey of Canada's best cities for business, entitled "Smart Cities."[4] Researchers sought out cities with brainpower. The Report explained that:

[f]irms want research oriented analytical problem solvers who are a source of innovation, new product ideas and confidence in coping with change — in short, knowledge workers. Likewise, many CEOs who want their companies to grow, begin to feel anxious if there isn't a research-based university within 15 kilometres or an established base of innovative companies. And they throw up their hands if the telecommunications system prevents them from executing high-speed data transfers.

The determinants of a smart city differed from previous years. A first and essential component was the presence of a research university with close ties to the business community. A second ingredient was a high ratio of university-educated people and a community emphasis on continuing education. The presence of a hub of high-tech companies and a municipal-private sector coordinating body for the city's telecommunications infrastructure were positive indicators. Researchers examined as well computer facilities in high schools and sought out diverse cultural entertainment and easy proximity to cottages and ski hills. The more traditional business interests, e.g., cost, transportation and the degree to which a city was business-friendly, were also considered.

The results?

According to the Report, the best five cities for business were:

(1) Toronto, which, despite its high-cost environment, retains some of the country's top finance, communications and medical minds;

(2) Ottawa-Carleton, the Canadian "silicon valley" home to many successful software and telecommunications companies;

(3) Saskatoon, whose status as an agricultural biotech centre put it in the top five;

(4) Halifax, where knowledge workers outnumber other workers 3 to 1; and

(5) Edmonton, which enjoys ongoing cooperation between the University of Alberta and the business community.

Calgary, Kitchener-Waterloo, Montreal, Victoria and Fredericton received honorary mentions as strong contenders. There were no surprises to Nuala Beck, author of *Excelerate: Growing in the New Economy*, quoted in the same article:

Smart cities are cities where an uplink to a satellite matters 10 times more than having a divided highway running through town. They realize that the new economy companies have no burning desire to be located in a strip mall and that it helps to have excellent educational facilities close at hand. But instead of sending students away the moment the ink is dry on their degrees, these university towns need to give young graduates a reason to stay.[5]

How can one evaluate the economic impact of the information highway?

Productivity is a well-recognized yardstick.

What is productivity?

It is a relationship between inputs and outputs mitigated by technological innovation, education and training of employees. Accordingly, as new technologies enter the workplace, increased productivity can be measured. Take the following simple example. An auto manufacturer introduces new computer-controlled robots that weld pieces for car bodies. To ascertain the resulting productivity differential, one calculates and compares the number of cars produced daily prior to and after the addition of the machines, the production cost per car and the product's quality. These measurements are affected, of course, by a host of other determinants such as worker productivity, machine breakdowns and cost of capital. These other factors can be strikingly important. For example, an automobile assembly plant in one Ontario town has one-sixth the worker absenteeism rate of another plant 150 kilometres down the road. Imagine the impact on productivity.

What is the effect of globalization on the Canadian economy?

Canada is among the world's largest traders on the basis of total per capita imports and exports. The gradual falling of trade barriers diminishes impediments to international trade. Telecommunications and computers are eliminating the barriers of time and distance. Together, technology and freer trade have produced a more sophisticated and integrated global market.[6] Therefore, Canada must compete globally if it is to compete at all. The challenge of equipping Canadians with the intellectual and technological tools to compete in an increasingly global market will directly determine the Canadian standard of living. The presence of an advanced information and communications infrastructure is a key driver. These elements come together in a virtuous circle where improved productivity increases competitiveness which enhances growth, wealth creation, higher value-added employment and increased standard of living.

THE MARKETPLACE

Consider the two principal players in the marketplace: individuals and firms. The I-way has affected both.

How so?

The effective use of telecommunications has become a key ingredient to business success over the past couple of decades. History shows that innovations, both great and small, can yield a wealth of unseen opportunities — the serendipity factor — for business and consumers. Consider an earlier technological breakthrough of this century, the automobile, and its impact over the past 100 years.

The German inventors Daimler and Benz introduced the "horseless carriage" in 1886. Automobile use gradually spread among the European elite. In the early 1900s, a forecast set an upper limit of one million for the number of automobiles that could be used in Europe. This calculation was based upon the number of mechanics who could be trained as chauffeurs. No lady or gentleman could be expected to drive her or his own car.

Henry Ford's Model T, however, fundamentally and irreversibly changed the notion of an automobile from a horseless carriage chauffeured by a skilled mechanic to a mass-produced and widely available commodity. As a result, more than 100 million vehicles are driven in North America today — one for every three people. We now take for granted the automobile as a way of life for any middle-class family. Contemporary North American society is heavily dependent upon automotive transportation. This is reflected in the importance of highways, suburbs, cottages, rural communities and our society's need for rapid transportation.

Daimler-Benz introduced the automobile. Ford made it affordable and more user friendly. The advent of the automobile was both a boon for capitalism and a breakthrough for consumers. The I-way is undergoing a similar transformation and aiming for similar objectives: easy operability and accessibility. Computers, cable, television, VCRs and cellular telephones originated as luxury items. As they became more affordable and user friendly, however, they became a way of life. The Internet was originally accessible only to an elite group of military and academic researchers. But the pool of network users continues to expand rapidly and irreversibly. The Freenet movement, with thirty-five Canadian cities now online, symbolizes its grassroots reach. Much like the fax machine, the Internet will become a necessary and invaluable component of any Canadian business, particularly once concerns such as security are resolved. However, the Internet has the added benefit of cost-efficiency. Whereas phone and fax communications can be quite expensive, particularly for businesses, Internet access can require only a flat monthly fee irrespective of the amount of use. Digital communications through "packet switching" tends to be less costly because the data travels along the fastest and generally least expensive route.

What type of business can best take advantage of the information highway?

There are special opportunities for small business. As large corporations have contracted in size, partly due to technology adoption and the elimination of layers of hierarchy, small business has been the engine of job growth in Canada. Between 1979 and 1989, businesses with less than 100 employees provided over 2.3 million net jobs to Canadians. This represented over 87 percent of overall employment growth for that period.[7] By virtue of their small size and typically flat management structure, they are more adaptable and have greater potential for innovation.[8] These characteristics make them well suited to take advantage of the I-way to seize new business opportunities.

How does such a business transformation occur?

Technology allows for more sophisticated and more efficient business transactions. The use of computerized bar-codes on retail products, e.g., vastly improved operating efficiency and cost-effectiveness in many retail industries. When the consumer purchases a product, the requisite information, e.g., price, model and amount, is entered automatically into inventory and payment control. Virtual auctions eliminate inefficiencies due to time and distance constraints. Three years ago, the international consulting firm Arthur Andersen launched the Knowledge Exchange system. It links 2,000 databases storing the collective experience and knowledge of specialized consulting groups working on various projects. This virtual library is accessible to Andersen's 30,000 employees worldwide to provide quick solutions to recurrent problems and to reduce "reinventions of the wheel."

Despite the I-way's asserted benefits for small and mid-sized businesses, they face challenges. In Canada, many small businesses have been slow to innovate. They often lack the time or human and financial resources to employ technology to its full potential. Largely as a result of business's failure to keep pace with technological change and to exploit effectively the available technology until the last several years, increased accessibility did not translate into faster economy-wide productivity growth.[9] A 1987 Economic Council of Canada report observed that "Canada's persistent lag in the introduction and use of computer-based technologies is an urgent national problem of major proportions. The diffusion of process technologies is too slow."[10] But there have been helpful signs since the 1991–92 recession. A 1993 Statistics Canada survey indicated that one-fifth of the manufacturing plants surveyed intended to add computer networks.[11]

Small and medium-sized companies require network technology to compete with big business. According to one telecommunications specialist, however, small and mid-sized businesses have fallen prey to Canada's lack of low-cost high-speed telecommunications connections.[12] Because Canada has more distance to cover and a smaller population to service and has been slower to deregulate, high-speed telecommunications is more expensive in Canada than in the U.S. We have a daunting challenge: to enhance accessibility and bring down costs to levels equal to or less than our major competition's. Yet, Canada has one of the most sophisticated telecommunications infrastructures and one of the highest penetration rates in the world. Almost 99 percent of Canadian households have telephones resulting from the commitment to universal service. The U.S. figure is 94 percent. In addition, current Canadian government policy aims to increase the levels of competition to drive prices down, especially for high-speed telecommunications.[13]

How will electronic commerce change the marketplace?

It should stimulate businesses of all sizes and types in Canada. It will improve efficiency in service delivery and expand access to markets. It will tend to eliminate intermediaries between producers and consumers, thereby reducing transaction costs. In this decade, to succeed, businesses must provide additional value to the consumer in better selection, more efficient service and higher quality while being cost-competitive.[14] Electronic commerce eliminates geographic constraints and widens the market to less-populated areas. Electronic malls, or "E-malls," will transform the nature of consumerism, much like the Eaton's catalogue did in the early 1900s. They will offer more consumer choice and provide greater accessibility. Electronic commerce on the Internet, through World Wide Web home pages, is becoming an excellent marketing tool.[15]

The reduction of transaction costs between buyer and seller and wider consumer choice will generate demand leading to economic growth.[16] If Canada is to remain a world trade leader, it is vital that all our corporate sectors embrace electronic commerce to improve their operations, discover new and faster ways to deliver their products and services to consumers.

Nonetheless, there are numerous hurdles to jump before electronic commerce is fully integrated into the marketplace. First, commerce over the Internet is largely unregulated. Consequently, there are few recourses for victims of false advertising. Second, poor security is a major concern. Invariably, consumers will be reluctant to divulge their credit card numbers and other confidential information without a guarantee of privacy and protection. Third, there is a learning curve both for business and consumers. It shapes how quickly businesses will make the necessary investment in technology and user-friendliness and the consumer in *savoir-faire*. But when the connection is made, there is usually a snowball effect. The pace can be painstakingly slow and then aggravatingly fast. Making the correct judgment of when, where and how is a formidable task.

THE WORKPLACE

Will the information highway create or destroy jobs?

Both. To date, there is considerable disagreement regarding the impact of information technology on employment. Part of this disagreement stems from the fact that comprehensive empirical studies are in short supply.[17] Moreover, it is unrealistic to believe we could predict at this stage its full effect on the work force.

Optimists assert that the advent of the I-way will surely stimulate job creation, as it will lead, not only to productivity improvements, but also to the emergence of entirely new and innovative products and services. A more foreboding and cautionary outlook is that technology supplants human labour. Two competing influences — automation and a growing labour market — are threatening low-skilled jobs and creating an uncertain employment future.[18] One consultant observed:

> While history has proven that technological change has led to long-term job creation through gains in productivity and innovation, we cannot make the assumption that the diffusion of information technology (through the creation of a national Information Highway or otherwise) will serve as a panacea for our current economic difficulties. This is because:

- information technology is far more pervasive than any other technological change experienced thus far;
- it is being introduced much faster than were earlier technologies, leaving society less time to adjust to the inevitable job losses which will occur and less time to train people for the new jobs that might be created; and,
- because it is transparent to distance and time, the technology makes jobs more portable, enhancing the ability to export jobs to low-wage jurisdictions.[19]

Won't automation largely eliminate the need for human labour?

At least since the advent of the first Industrial Revolution in the eighteenth century, people have warned that automation would cause massive job loss. The 1811–16 Luddite movement arose in response to the Industrial Revolution's disruptive effects. It was rooted in fear. The English Luddites believed that the introduction of machinery into the workplace reduced wages and increased unemployment and fundamentally changed their way of life. They smashed the mechanized weaving looms to stop automation and save their jobs. Luddites exist in every country's history pages.

Yes, automation eliminates jobs. Increased reliance on machines reduces need for human effort to perform certain tasks. The phrase "chips for neurons" has replaced the slogan "steam power for human labour." Computerization shrinks or even extinguishes some sectors of the work force. Consider telephone operators. Since the advent of the telephone, human operators have been essential for the routing of calls. Today, that process is almost entirely computerized. Recall, e.g., the recent announcement by Bell Canada, the "phone" company, of 10,000 of its 45,000 jobs to be cut over the next three years in the "fast growing" telecommunications industry.

But, simultaneously, machines have increased dramatically productivity and efficiency.[20] The concern with technological change is not so much the net loss of jobs as it is the fundamental alteration of the job market and the prospects of short-term job displacement. Job displacement underlies the importance of economic restructuring to allow adjustment to technology and market changes.[21] As Goss Gilroy Inc. observed:

> While there has certainly been a period of shedding during the introduction of new technologies, history demonstrates that the diffusion of these technologies into the economy has, in fact, increased productivity and created new employment in whole new industries, which more than offset the initial, transient job displacements.[22]

Technology, therefore, is a double-edged sword which both creates and destroys jobs. When new technology penetrates the workplace, there is inevitably an initial job displacement effect. This results from the obsolescence of certain jobs. Job creation occurs only when the new technology is exploited to its full potential so as to improve productivity, quality and efficiency. Most of the economic literature studying the employment impact of technology focuses on two key factors: (1) the rate of diffusion in each sector and (2) the effective or appropriate application of technology which is defined by corresponding human and organizational adjustments. Studies tend to conclude that it is by maintaining the status quo and by *not* applying new technology that firms become less competitive and shed jobs.

Explain job displacement.

With labour restructuring, job locations and employing sectors may change. The I-way will change demographics. Workers will be required to pack up and move to different centres and even countries. Effective adjustment to change requires a certain degree of labour mobility. Consider this in an historical context. The North American open frontier spread populations to isolated homesteads and small villages over previously vast and unsettled areas. Then, the first two Industrial Revolutions produced urbanization. Families migrated to the city for more lucrative employment in new mass-production industries. As the I-way conquers distance, it may again reverse this historical pattern of centripetal migration. With the assistance of computers, many workers need not commute to or live in urban centres, and certainly not in high-rise towers clustered in the downtown core. This opens new avenues for the growth and prosperity of Canada's traditionally disadvantaged regions. Job displacement is more than a geographical phenomenon, however. It is essentially a movement of jobs from low- to high-skilled sectors.

Explain this workforce restructuring.

The high-skilled and knowledge-intensive sectors of the job market provide the best employment prospects. Many of the jobs created by technological change will be in different sectors and in new or different industries. Initial workforce restructuring will induce *short-term* job loss in many low-skilled vocations or functions. Conversely, however, technological change should bring about *long-term* job creation, at least for those societies which can adapt and embrace it, and if it takes root.

Who is being displaced by new technologies and who is replacing them?

Traditional industry-based labourers, such as low- or moderately skilled assembly line or clerical workers, are being replaced. For example, automobile manufacturers rely increasingly on computers to design and build cars. A new car's electronics currently exceed the value of its steel. Simultaneously, the information technology and telecommunications industries are booming. In 1993, these sectors employed 484,000 Canadians and generated revenues of $50 billion. In fact, for two decades, knowledge-intensive job sectors have contributed disproportionately to employment growth in our country.[23] A Department of Finance study indicated that they produced 53 percent of Canada's employment growth between 1984 and 1991.[24]

Won't the speed with which technology is changing aggravate structural unemployment?

The current technological transformation of the workplace is occurring at a much more rapid pace than in previous periods of major change. Consequently, there is a very real concern that the necessary retraining and skills development cannot be accomplished quickly enough to fill the new jobs. Moreover, many in the present low-skilled workforce lack the educational base to adjust. As the *Report on Business* magazine review of Canada's best business cities noted, corporations seek out hubs with "knowledge workers." This creates a tragic temporal gap between initial job destruction due to obsolescence and long-term job creation with properly trained employees.[25]

According to a 1993 Department of Human Resources study, in the next decade, approximately half of the new jobs will require sixteen or more years of education.[26] In 1991, the figure was at roughly 30 percent. Currently, one quarter of the Canadian population is enrolled in full-time learning and training programs, 83 percent at the elementary and secondary levels, 8 percent in community colleges and vocational schools and 9 percent in universities.[27]

Because many new jobs will be in different sectors of the economy or in different geographic regions, workers who intend to remain in the workforce for that length of time may require retraining and may be forced to uproot themselves. As an ironic example, a recent front-page newspaper headline declared: "3,500 at job centres face axe: Ottawa plans self-serve computer terminals for employment seekers, pensioners."[28] The article detailed a reduction from 450 Canada Employment Centres to 300 Human Resource Centres as the largest part of a 5,000-person job cut in the federal Human Resources Department, in order to save $2.8 billion over three years. The moves are designed both to save money and to improve service. Employment program information will be delivered via electronic kiosks and telephones. It will provide "one-stop shopping" for currently separate groups, i.e., students, pensioners, job seekers.

How will the information economy transform the structure of the workplace?

Two key effects are telework, or telecommuting, and the democratization of the workplace.

Explain telework.

Applying information technology permits more flexible work patterns. The newly coined terms "telework" and "telecommuting" reflect the changing nature of employment today. People can now work out of their homes or on the road. This can be very positive. First, it may enhance family life by increasing the time available for children and spouses. Second, it will create new employment opportunities for people unable to commute to employment hubs, e.g., parents with young children, the disabled and people living in rural or remote areas, thus diversifying the workforce and stimulating regional development.

However, telework can also be detrimental. First, it can cause isolation in the home. Interaction with fellow workers can be a healthy ingredient of working life. Eliminating this aspect of one's work environment could damage an employee's state of mind. Second, telework may hinder a worker's ability to assert his or her employment rights through a collective voice. It furnishes the potential for abuse through longer hours and reduced wages. And, at the same time, it reduces the opportunities for workers to communicate and organize for the purposes of labour relations. Third, jobs can be exported to other communities, cities, provinces and countries where wages are lower.[29]

But can technology not be used to empower workers?

Yes. New technologies can help equalize the power structure of employment relationships. Because technology can facilitate access to information, it can transcend the traditional vertical hierarchy of knowledge and power within the workplace. Consequently, it has the ability to eliminate invisible barriers between more senior and lower level employees. As well, it improves proximity to the client.

While global management control of the enterprise is maintained, knowledge is no longer seen as the exclusive preserve of the few; the structure and culture of the company is changed with revived entrepreneurial spirit when lower managers feel empowered, by access to information, to resolve issues of their own; power moves down the hierarchy. A change management process is introduced. Managing it successfully is a new challenge.[30]

What public policy measures are appropriate given the magnitude of the change?

IHAC wrestled with exactly this question — how to address the job creation/job loss dichotomy. The result: a majority and a minority position. The majority, made up of all the members except the representative of organized labour, made several major recommendations to reduce the employment gap by (1) establishing a competitive business climate that allows firms to maximize job creation and (2) updating labour legislation to minimize the I-way's negative impacts on employment standards. To this end, the majority report endorsed various mechanisms such as implementing retraining programs, facilitating worker mobility and coordinating job searching nationally. The minority report, by Jean-Claude Parrot, Executive Vice-President, Canadian Labour Congress, provided a detailed agenda for much more proactive government initiatives. He concluded that market-driven solutions to unemployment did not work, much more substantial labour standards protection was required, international-level social charters should be developed, and legislated mandatory training and employment impact assessments for corporate plans were required to integrate technological change.

It is appropriate to end this chapter on this note of fundamental disagreement. Solutions will not emerge either with blinding clarity or universal appeal.

15

THE SOCIAL IMPACT

> "Things do not change,
> we do."
> — Henry David Thoreau

How can you describe the social impact of the information revolution?

There are at least three plausible answers:

* You can't.
* It's too early to tell.[1]
* We see through a glass darkly. All we can do now is to sketch out some of the shadows of answers.

Let's try the third answer. We begin this chapter with a simple diagnosis of our social situation, some sweeping and largely illustrative observations that flow from that diagnosis, some broad prescriptions of what to do. Then, as the shadows begin to lighten and the picture emerges into clearer patterns, we identify a few initiatives which can improve our chances of winning. But this chapter ends abruptly with these few. It is for all of us to complete our own picture.

So what is the diagnosis?

We begin with the observation that opened this book — we have embarked on a voyage buffeted by profound change, and like Columbus sailing west 500 years ago, there are few navigational guides.

But history has seen change before — even profound and concentrated change. What is so different about this one?

A convergence of factors. Principally, its pace, breadth and depth, the shrinkage of time, impersonality and uncertainty as to outcomes. Let's examine these generalizations.

First, pace?

Gutenberg's printing press has profoundly affected our society. But its pace was gradual. Even his original invention of moveable type in 1440 precariously staggered out of his bankruptcy. It took some years to achieve commercial respectability. It took decades and centuries to permeate through society and transform it. Perhaps its greatest single institutional influence, at least in the European context, was on the Church — opening the scriptures to non-clergy, and some decades later producing the reformation of the Church, the most influential socio-political institution of its time. It is no accident that the Church strenuously tried to suppress and control this invention, to maintain the Church's monopoly on knowledge and learning and the language — Latin — used to communicate this knowledge. Its power was threatened.[2] The pace of the information revolution may be best quantified by Moore's Law, named after the chief of Intel, the computer-chip maker: the capacity of a microchip to store information doubles every eighteen months.

Next, time?

Perhaps the best illustration of the information revolution's conquest of time in the recent past was a spoken phrase and a television image: "That's one small step for man; one giant leap for mankind," uttered by Neil Armstrong as he stepped onto the moon in 1969. How remarkable that the voice and the image of that step were broadcast almost instantaneously over hundreds of thousands of miles. Time is overcome in other ways. Consider the capacity of the information revolution to reduce and eliminate institutions built up over decades with enormous effort, in minutes and seconds. Consider the fall of the Berlin Wall in 1989; and the disintegration of the Soviet Union and the collapse of Communism in the weeks immediately after. Consider also the capacity of information to transform financial values in hours. A good example is the 50 percent devaluation of the Mexican peso in a few hours over Christmas 1994, indicating that capital can flee massively with a phone call or electronic transfer.

Next, its impersonality?

A recent *New Yorker* cartoon featured two dogs sitting in front of a computer screen marked "Internet." While one dog's paw was about to press a key, the other said, "Go ahead, they won't know you're a dog." While information flow of human communication is rapidly increasing, it is also becoming increasingly impersonal. We don't really know who sits at the sending and receiving ends. We are identified not by our hair colour or family name but by a digital address.

One illustration of this impersonality is machines replacing human beings. As Joseph Wood Krutch observed: "As machines get to be more and more like men, men will come to be more like machines." Even more ominous is the power of technology to transform, even to the point of substituting itself for knowledge. Marshall McLuhan's phrase "the medium is the message" captures this transforming quality. A further perceived drawback is the all-encompassing capacity of the machine to absorb and lock users into a world of their own with little face-to-face contact with other human beings in the real world. Information technology is proliferating both laterally and vertically. Most homes have televisions, more and more people are buying computers, modems and related services. Consider the explosion of the television, telephone, VCRs, cellular telephones, computers and modems.

Next, its depth and breadth?

The information revolution transforms both deeply and widely all institutions — economic, social, cultural and political. Who would have guessed as recently as seven years ago that the Berlin Wall would fall, then the Soviet Union and then Communism. It is interesting that President Mikhail Gorbachev began with political reform — *perestroika* and *glasnost*, restructuring and openness — before economic reform in the Soviet Union. The momentum grew beyond his control. In China the reverse occurred. Reform, at least after the Cultural Revolution ended in the late 1970s, was directed primarily at the economy. It introduced the curious and confused but apparently effective "socialist market" economy. But when economic openness spilled over into the political arena, particularly Tienanmen Square in June 1989, the most repressive measures were taken to suppress communication and arrest the growing free market in information.

Perhaps the single factor that contributed most to the unpopularity and eventual U.S. defeat in Vietnam was the fact that the war and its most senseless acts were seen directly in living rooms every evening in American homes. A more recent and perhaps notorious example is the broadcast of the O. J. Simpson trial directly into North American homes. Marshall McLuhan's phrase "the global village" aptly captures this.

Finally, uncertainty of outcome?

Enormous change is occurring in such a short period of time that it is very difficult, if not impossible, to see ten, twenty or fifty years down the road. Will our society by able to adapt quickly enough? Perhaps the best answer to this question is to leave it unanswered.

With that diagnosis, what do we do to avoid losing the ability to direct our own society, to turn the social impact of the information revolution into positive consequences?
The federal government answered this by proposing a national strategy for the information highway and identifying three objectives for its advisory council:

(1) Create jobs through innovation and investment;
(2) Reinforce Canadian cultural identity and sovereignty;
(3) Ensure accessibility on the information highway.

In its report, IHAC made over 300 recommendations largely directed at government in response. But governments today have less capacity to act and must concentrate their greatest efforts on helping individuals to be more self-reliant.

The balance of this chapter takes this approach. It sketches out the social impact of the information highway at four levels: accessibility, education, health and government. It asks some basic questions: Will the information revolution exacerbate the division of a society into "haves" and "have-nots"? Will it lift the living standards and civic opportunities of all, and at the same time reduce disparities? Will it use the limited powers of government to increase self-reliance in the information age?

An underlying theme is choice. Another is equality of opportunity. A third is adaptability, capacity to cope and self-reliance. All are honoured Canadian values. We, as a society, each of us as individuals, have the opportunity to use the I-way for the betterment of ourselves and our neighbours — or neglect it at our peril. The role of the state is also key and shifting. The comparative wealth-generating capacity of the Canadian economy has diminished by roughly 25 percent over the past two decades. Yet, we have a system of social programs and expectations geared to those better times. The state today can provide less by way of direct intervention. The challenge is to do more in ensuring that all citizens are aware of the dramatic transition through which we are passing, in creating conditions for equality of opportunity to act on that awareness to the individual's and the nation's advantage, and helping us all to be more self-reliant in the face of great change. Accessibility to the I-way is a first step.

What does accessibility mean?

How can the information highway be made as accessible as possible with the highest possible quality and extent of services at the lowest possible cost?[3] In doing so, how do we deal with disparity of opportunity between city and rural areas, within a country, economic strata and within the world at large as it increasingly becomes a global village? In posing the question this way, there is already an individual focus but a collective responsibility. Sorting out individual rights and responsibilities and those of the collectivity or community is the fundamental value choice on which all of the other decisions are based.

How can we achieve universal access to the I-way?

IHAC considered this at great length. It proposed a national access strategy with the following principles:

- universal, affordable and equitable access;
- consumer choice and diversity of information;
- competency and citizens' participation; and
- open and interactive networks.[4]

It summarized its expectations by saying, "Basic access to the Information Highway should be as universal and relevant to Canadians as telephone and television services are today."

What about the pervasive role of government services?

Governments everywhere are under increasing pressure to do more with less, to increase the effectiveness, penetration and quality of their services while reducing costs. The problem is exacerbated in Canada today with high government debt levels. Solutions that tinker at the edges are often counterproductive, leaving the worst of both worlds. Re-engineering of the entire service, using technology where appropriate and with careful attention to the skill base of both deliverer and recipient of the services, is essential. Information technology offers considerable promise if aggressively and intelligently used.[5] IHAC gave considerable attention to government services and made the following broad recommendations:

- The federal government should accelerate the "single window" concept with electronic access for a majority of Canadians, and pricing and access of electronic services should be regularly reviewed;
- Electronic directories should exist for all services and information, and electronic interaction with all departments;
- Strategic I-way partnerships with community and client groups should be pursued;
- Periodic revision of policies and alternative electronic points for services to the disabled should be undertaken.

What are the implications of the I-way for education and training?

Canada currently spends $35 billion annually on public education. When education and training by employers and private sector organizations are factored in, that figure is probably doubled, or approximately 10 percent of GDP. Even before considering the I-way, we understand that all is not well in this fundamental sector. Consider the following observations that suggest our foundation is critically weak:

- Near-bottom performance in internationally comparative achievement tests in mathematics, science and literacy, in spite of public expenditure per capita on primary and secondary education second only to Denmark amongst OECD countries;

- Industry training budgets considerably smaller than our major competitors';
- High school drop-out rates of 20–30 percent across the country;
- Adult illiteracy rate exceeding 25 percent by some tests such as the capacity to fill out a driver's permit application; 38 percent of Canadian adults are not sufficiently literate for today's workplace;
- Inadequate apprenticeship systems to prepare skilled tradespeople for jobs where significant shortages exist;
- A primary and secondary school year of 170–175 days, a five-day school week, and a school day of less than five hours of learning. The Japanese have a 240–260 day school year, six-day school week, and seven to eight hours of learning per day, supplemented with extra tutorials and intensive school entrance exam preparation;
- National unemployment rates of 10 percent, in some regions exceeding 20 percent, with a social security system that does not encourage unemployed people to find permanent work or develop the skills to find work; and
- A social security system under review but without clear new patterns, and comprehensive solutions impeded by federal-provincial jurisdictional concerns.

There are specific imbalances in the information highway context:

- A gender imbalance, with substantially higher percentages of boys taking mathematics and science, playing with and using computers;
- A male/female ratio of Canadian Internet use estimated at 4:1;
- An anglophone/francophone ratio of Canadian Internet use estimated at 3:1;
- Significantly higher ratios of computers to students in English

versus French primary and secondary schools;
- Younger people are much more adept at using new technology, e.g., as studies of banks' ATMs repeatedly show; and
- Disabled persons have obvious difficulty in using tools and techniques not designed with their special needs in mind, such as fees based on online time of access rather than actual contact time with a database.

This is not a propitious trampoline for the knowledge-based society of the twenty-first century. But the message is clear. We must give serious attention to improving our basic education and training systems, intensifying rigour, if the mass of our population — particularly the next generation — is to use new tools of information technology effectively. There is no magic in this. It begins in each home and in each neighbourhood school. Simply put, we must raise our expectations.

Special efforts are needed to identify and respond to special needs. To some extent, the marketplace, with a customer-centred bias as opposed to a technology-driven design, can do this if imagination and efforts are shown to appeal to the diverse needs of different customers. But, there must also be a clear appreciation that the marketplace will not meet all requirements, and broader government initiative at all levels will be essential.

Who should do what?

IHAC responded to this question in the form of an issue: "What consumer awareness and learning opportunities should be provided to enable Canadians to be effective users of the Information Highway?"[6] It set out recommendations directed to the federal government but with a careful recognition that education is a provincial responsibility. The highlights include:

- Lifelong learning should be a key design element in building the information highway;

- Learning and training are integral parts of the knowledge economy. Canada should provide an environment for lifelong learning with the widest possible access to learning opportunities;

- A comprehensive national strategy should be developed with all levels of government and industry participants to ensure affordable learning and training access to the information highway and to recognize the role of technologies in learning and training, to foster new media-based learning, to stimulate the creation of Canadian content on the I-way, and to support more R&D for new media-based learning and training products;

- As a condition of graduation, new entrants to the teaching profession should be well versed and capable in information technology learning products, and programs should be developed for existing professionals to meet this requirement within five years.

Are there any particular initiatives which illustrate some of these principles in action?

There are many. We select four that deserve close scrutiny as models of innovation. The first is "SchoolNet." Several years ago, the Ministry of Industry launched the SchoolNet initiative with a budget of $50 million. Through SchoolNet, the federal government plans to link Canada's 16,500 elementary and secondary schools, 3,400 libraries and 200 colleges and universities to the Internet by 1998. To date, over 5,000 schools are online.[7] This is a formidable achievement. The U.S. hopes to accomplish the same by the year 2000. Some estimate their cost at $50 billion U.S., 1,000 times higher than Canada's. The Japanese propose to link all their schools and homes with fibre-optic capacity by 2015.

A grave Canadian concern, however, is that accessibility to School-Net may become prohibitively expensive in rural and remote areas due to the high cost of servicing these distant areas. While urban schools have access to the Internet via local telephone networks, remote schools must pay long-distance fees for online access via telephone lines. Consequently, if SchoolNet is to be universally accessible, government will have to arrange for some type of subsidization or rate reductions for rural Canada.

But education falls under provincial jurisdiction. How can a federal initiative succeed?
By innovative, wise, low-profile, functional collaboration. In fact, this is a model for government that concentrates on needs and pragmatic solutions and ignores partisan advantage. A few federal department officials, working closely with provincial ministries of education, local school boards and library authorities and many private sector partners have simply gone ahead with the job, contributing services and facilities and minimizing expenditures. Linking schools with the I-way's world of knowledge, however, is only part of the battle. Now, we must transform our teachers from content providers to coaches or enablers who will instil in each student the excitement of discovery and self-advancement for him- or herself.

And the second initiative?
This is CANARIE Inc., the Canadian Network for the Advancement of Research, Industry and Education (see Chapter 2), launched in March 1993 with $26 million of Industry Canada money matched by $125 million from the private sector. It is an industry-led consortium of businesses, research and educational institutions and government organizations. Its objectives are to develop broadband high-speed networks, to stimulate research and development on them, to forge strategic alliances between private- and public-sector entities and to commercialize cutting-edge technologies, products, applications and services in information technology. The underlying aim is to help develop the Canadian communications infrastructure in a knowledge-based society, thereby enhancing Canadian competitiveness and job and wealth creation.

The first phase engaged over 200 Canadian companies, education and research institutions. CANARIE regional networks also provide the Canadian Internet connections. By comparison, the U.S. government is spending $2 billion over two years for wide-capacity test networks under its High Performance Computing and Communications Program. An $80 million federal expenditure in CANARIE's Phase II, from 1995 to 1999, will generate $400 million in matching funds from the provinces and private sector. Incremental jobs from 1993 over ten years are estimated at 24,000 persons fully employed. Again, federal-provincial-territorial collaboration and cooperation with the private sector, as well as a sense of entrepreneurialism and innovation, are responsible.

The third initiative?

"Distance education" telecommunications networks now service remote communities. They operate in every province and territory. This is a distinctive Canadian tradition. The Tele-Education New Brunswick initiative, e.g., links thirty sites across the province. In its first two years, Newfoundland's StemNet has made the Internet accessible to more than 80 percent of its schools. This is an especially positive movement in a sparsely populated province where small communities are widely dispersed across its territory.

The International Institute for Sustainable Development, based in Winnipeg, has entered a unique relationship with the 500 university members of the International Association of Universities and the Earth Council, a non-governmental successor organization to the 1992 U.N. Earth Summit at Rio de Janeiro, to put teaching, research and informational materials about sustainable development "on line" through the Internet. This will connect universities around the world, allowing them to trade their experience in understanding and promoting sustainable development, and through them penetrate colleges, training institutes and schools in every corner of the globe. But the exchange is a two-way street. Poorest and richest each can contribute knowledge and enhance the other.

And the final initiative?

FreeNet is a movement to create community-based computer networking projects. They provide low- or no-cost modem-based access to E-mail, business and community information and services in a city using "no-cost" local telephone service. They are an economical way to promote broad-based community and individual participation in the information era. The FreeNet movement began over a decade ago in Ohio. Today, thirty-five Canadian cities, beginning with Ottawa, have FreeNet associations. Canada has the fastest growing FreeNet movement in the world. A national FreeNet association coordinates and encourages new ones. The relatively moderate costs of starting and maintaining these community networks are covered by public and private grants and donations. They simply permit people of modest means to operate on an electronic highway designed for their own community and its needs.

Let's turn to the health sector. What are the information highway implications?

Canada currently spends $70 billion — 10 percent of GDP — on health care. This contrasts with almost 14 percent of GDP in the U.S. and 5–7 percent in countries like Japan (which has the highest longevity in the world), the U.K. and France. Universal accessibility is a cherished feature of Canadian health care. But, financial pressures have begun to compromise accessibility and quality. Major shifts are taking place. They include a move from health care and cure to health promotion and disease prevention, from urban-centre concentration to regionalization and integration across sectors, from acute to long-term care, from institutional to home and self-managed care, from reliance on specialists to consumers taking greater responsibility for their health care and assuming greater involvement in decisions about it.

IHAC proposed a national health information infrastructure to lead this shift that would:

(1) Allow online diagnostic consultation in a timely fashion, improve the quality of care and reduce costs;

(2) Provide care closer to homes, preventing costs incurred by unnecessary transportation;

(3) Provide essential health services to currently underserved populations;

(4) Provide online information to empower consumers to make informed decisions about personal health and health intervention; and

(5) Promote the development of a national, standardized, longitudinal health information database accessible to researchers and policy makers.

The Council also proposed an investment fund to support trials and demonstrations for networking technologies and, as with recommendations for the educational sector, reduced telecommunications tariffs for the health sector to make these initiatives affordable.

How has the information revolution influenced medical research and treatment?

Above all, it has vastly improved efficiency. Telemedicine is the foremost illustration. Technology helps to diagnose and treat patients and to provide long-distance medical consultations, particularly beneficial to rural Canada. For example, a Toronto-based corporation, CardioLink Inc., enables heart-disease sufferers to receive virtually instantaneous diagnoses of chest pains from anywhere in the world. Subscribers attach electrodes from a pocket-sized electrocardiogram unit to their body. ECG signals are then transmitted to a CardioLink medical centre through the phone lines. If the doctor determines that the subscriber is having heart trouble, his or her entire medical history can be transmitted electronically, via facsimile or via the

Internet, to the nearest hospital emergency room.

The Ontario Air Ambulance Services use Canada's Mobile Satellite services to transmit vital medical information about patients being transported from remote areas to a city hospital. In New Brunswick, a Moncton-based project, Tele-Care, performs triage via telephone and computer. Bilingual and experienced emergency nurses receive telephone calls. Using diagnostic software, they help callers determine whether their medical condition constitutes an emergency. With an initial setup cost of $150,000 and annual operating costs of $500,000, the aim is to reduce expensive emergency room visits and to provide more reassuring medical care. Similar systems exist in Montreal and Toronto, but New Brunswick's initiative makes the most extensive use of computers.[8]

In the U.S., NASA and the National Cancer Institute have collaborated to employ aerospace and military image-processing techniques for use in mammography. As a result of this three-year research collaboration, technology that enables the Hubble space telescope to peer deep into galaxies thousands of light-years from Earth should soon enhance the ability of radiologists to screen for breast cancer. High-contrast digital detectors identify breast cancer at early stages, when it is still too small to be detected with conventional radiology equipment. This illustrates the rapid transition in fundamental research to applied development in a variety of fields. As with the Internet, research originally intended for national defence was subsequently exploited to benefit society more tangibly, another illustration of swords into ploughshares.

SmartHealth is an entrepreneurial venture that brings together government services and health care using the I-way. This Winnipeg-based subsidiary of the Royal Bank won in a tendering process to develop and manage a health information network for Manitoba. The network will be built by modules. One is an electronic health profile for each patient. It enables a doctor electronically to call up that patient's record and then quickly access data relevant to treatment from all sources to eliminate unnecessary tests. It can provide crucial information when a patient is unconscious. Special care must be taken re confidentiality. A second module will generate statistical information from existing patient records to enable medical researchers to study specific illnesses and treatments and determine which treatments are more effective. These results will be distributed to physicians to make better treatment decisions. A third module will identify rising trends in specific preventable illnesses and target educational information to reduce these incidents.

Canadian governments can serve as model laboratories. Manitoba On-Line, e.g., provides a single-point access to government information and services including land registry, the Legislative Assembly proceedings and the Western Purchasing Information Network with calls for tenders on supplies and services required by the Western provincial governments.

The way ahead?

We give the final word to IHAC and its "key messages":

Canadians need to recognize that we are at a turning point in history. We are challenged to make a confident, positive choice toward a more civil society by seizing the new tools of the information revolution and employing them to the advantage of every Canadian.

To the federal government:

- Create an environment in which the private sector can innovate, create wealth and jobs to the benefit of all Canadians.
- Address market imperfections. Ensure a prominent place for Canadian content and culture. Ensure that Canadians have equitable access to the I-way both as users and as providers of content.
- Set an example as a model user of information and information

technologies. Use the power of government procurement to help Canadian firms to compete globally.

To the private sector:

- Get on with it! In the new world of the I-way, firms that invest in technology and people will prosper. Those that do not will fail.

To each of us as individual Canadians:

- Get involved as users of information technology. Take charge of our own education. Regard the I-way not as a threat but as an opportunity to enhance our lives and independence.
- Think about what kind of society we want to live in. Do what we can to see that vision reflected on the I-way. Work for the values we care about.

EṈDṈOTES

PART I – THE HIGHWAY

Chapter 1 – What Is the Information Highway?

[1] *The Globe and Mail*, 24 May, 1995, Telecommunications supplement, at 4.

[2] Industry Canada, *The Canadian Information Highway: Building Canada's Information and Communications Infrastructure* (Ottawa: Supply and Services Canada, April 1994), at 1.

[3] Elizabeth Angus and Duncan McKie, *Canada's Information Highway: Services, Accessibility and Affordability*, a policy study prepared for New Media Branch and Information Technologies Industry Branch, Industry Canada, May 1994, at 14 [hereinafter Angus-McKie Report].

[4] Roger Darlington, *The Information Highway: An International Trade Union View*, paper prepared for Postal, Telegraph and Telephone International, 1995, at 4 [unpublished].

[5] Information Highway Advisory Council, *Canada's Information Highway: Building Canada's Information and Communications Infrastructure*, Progress Report (Ottawa: Supply and Services Canada, November 1994), at 3 [hereinafter Advisory Council Progress Report].

[6] Ibid.

[7] Telecommunications Act, S.C. 1993, c.38.

[8] Broadcasting Act, R.S.C. 1991, c.11 B-9.01.

[9] Canadian Radio-television and Telecommunications Commission, *Competition and Culture on Canada's Information Highway: Managing the Realities of Transition*, report (Ottawa: Supply and Services Canada, 1995) (Chair: Keith Spicer) [hereinafter CRTC Report].

[10] Angus-McKie Report, *supra*, at 13.

[11] Goss Gilroy Inc., *Impacts of the Information Highway on Employment and the Workplace* (Ottawa: Goss Gilroy Inc., 1995), at 10 [hereinafter Goss Gilroy].

[12] Ibid.

¹³Ibid.

¹⁴Pierre Berton, *The Last Spike: The Great Railway 1881–1885* (Toronto: McClelland & Stewart, 1971).

¹⁵Information Highway Advisory Council, Final Report: *Connection, Community, Content, Challenge* (Ottawa: Supply and Services Canada, September 1995) (Chair: David Johnston), at 2 [hereinafter IHAC Final Report].

¹⁶Ibid. "Except as one of the largest users and consequently, a persuasive role model, governments in Canada should stand aside to allow the private sector to drive the development of the highway and to do what it does best — invest, innovate and create jobs."

¹⁷IHAC Final Report, *supra*.

¹⁸Patrick G. McKeown, *Living with Computers* (Orlando, Florida: Harcourt Brace Jovanovich, Inc., 1986) at 6; refering to John Naisbitt, *Megatrends* (New York: Warner Books, 1984), at 1–33.

¹⁹Gaston Lionel Franco & Henry J. Novy, eds., *World Communications: Ways and Means to Global Integration* (Italy: Gaston Lionel Franco Publications, 1994), at 278.

²⁰IHAC Progress Report, *supra*, at 3.

²¹Angus-McKie Report, *supra*, at 13.

Chapter 2 – The Internet

¹Michel Marriott, "Super Cyber Surfers," *Newsweek*, 20 March, 1995, at 43.

²*The Globe and Mail*, 24 May, 1995, Telecommunications supplement, at 4.

³*The* (Montreal) *Gazette*, 15 March, 1995, C4 reprint of *New York Times* article.

⁴Philip Baczewski et al., *The Internet Unleashed* (Indianapolis: SAMS Publishing, 1994), at 4–5.

⁵*The Globe and Mail*, 12 May, 1995, C3, C7.

⁶Ed Krol, *The Whole Internet User's Guide and Catalog*, 2nd ed. (Sebastopol, California: O'Reilly & Associates Inc., 1994), at 17.

⁷Mark Potter and Marc Lee, *Economic Impacts of the Information Highway: An Overview*, paper presented to the Information Technology and Telecommunications Sector, Industry Canada, July 1995.

⁸Angus-McKie Report, *supra*, at 88.

⁹These regional networks are: Newfoundland and Labrador Network (NLnet), Nova Scotia Technology Network (NSTN), Prince Edward Island Network (PEINet), NB★net, Réseau interordinateurs scientifique Québécois (RISQ), ONet, MBnet, SASK#net, Alberta Research Network (ARnet), BCnet.

¹⁰Angus-McKie Report, *supra*, at 90.

¹¹Stevanne Ruth Lehrman, *Local Area Networking with Microcomputers* (Prentice Hall Press: New York, 1986), at 10.

¹²Lehrman, *supra*, at 12.

¹³Krol, *supra*, at 24.

¹⁴Ibid.

¹⁵Lynda Covello, *Reaping the Whirlwind: IP on the Infobahn*, memorandum to the Information Highway Advisory Council [unpublished].

¹⁶Baczewski et al., *supra*, at 30.

¹⁷Krol, *supra*, at 16.

¹⁸Covello, *supra*, at 2.

¹⁹James Stevenson, "Jewels sparkle on network," *The Edmonton Journal*, 16 March, 1995, at 16.

PART II – THE METHODS
Chapter 3 – The Quality of Understanding

¹Section 2, R.S.C. 1985, c. C-42, as amended.

²*The Random House Dictionary of the English Language* (Toronto: Random House Inc., 1987), at 1064.

³At its most mechanical level, justice may be thought of as being composed of a set of strict, unalterable rules. The utilitarian notion of justice formulated by Bentham, and later refined by Mill, holds that the "standard of what is right in conduct, is not the agent's own happiness, but that of all concerned." J. S. Mill, "Utilitarianism," *Encyclopaedia Britannica* (Chicago, 1952), at 453. This ethic of justice, given a question as to which course of action is just, implies a mechanical aggregation of "happiness" and comparison on the basis of the higher total. Although it may be argued that happiness is a purely human determination, happiness may be substituted for other more objective criteria such as money or power, depending on one's approach to utilitarianism.

Chapter 4 – Science Basics

¹John S. Mayo, "Evolution of the Intelligent Network," in Tom Forester, ed., *The Information Technology Revolution* (Cambridge, Massachusetts: The MIT Press, 1985), at 111.

²Nancy Stern & Robert Stern, *Computers in Society* (Englewood Cliffs, New Jersey: Prentice-Hall Inc., 1983), at 13.

³Nancy Stern & Robert Stern, *supra*, at 13.

Chapter 5 – The Inner Workings of a Computer

¹We use the term to refer to both computers as well as those other devices that
• operate using microprocessor technology.

²*Delrina Corp. v. Triolet Systems Inc.* (1993), 47 C.P.R. 1, at 51, gives a simple, but

useful, definition of "memory":

[Memory is defined as a]n area of the computer's circuitry that holds applications and any data generated with those applications. Information held in Random Access Memory (RAM) is erased whenever the computer is turned off. Information held in Read Only Memory (ROM) is retained even when the computer is off. Memory usually refers to the high speed semiconductor storage within a computer that is used to temporarily store data while it is being processed or examined. The term "memory" is also generically extended to refer to data that is stored externally on disks and tapes.

[3]Associated Press, *The Globe and Mail*, "Compact Disc Format Extends to Videos," August 26, 1993, at B8.

[4]The word "Disc" is used where the term forms part of the proper name of the media, whereas "disk" is used when describing the media in a generic sense.

Chapter 6 – Transmission Methods

[1]Lehrman, *supra*, at 68.

[2]Lehrman, *supra*, at 71.

[3]Gilbert Held, *Understanding Data Communications,* 3rd ed. (Indiana: SAMS, 1992), at 76.

[4]Gilbert Held, *supra*, at 92.

[5]Andrew S. Tanenbaum, *Computer Networks* (New Jersey: Prentice-Hall).

[6]*End-User Computing, supra*, at p. 571.

[7]Ibid.

[8]In actual fact, more than one telephone company's circuits may be involved.

[9]Ed Krol, *The Whole Internet Catalog & User's Guide* (U.S.A.: O'Reilly & Associates, Inc., 1993), at 20.

[10]"Newbridge Plays a Key Role in European Videoconferencing," *Newbridge MainStreet International News*, Newbridge Networks, January 1993, at 12.

[11]*Newbridge Mainstreet International News, supra*, at 3.

[12]Although there are limits to the clarity and size of the images due to bandwidth constraints.

Chapter 7 – Standards

[1]*The Random House Dictionary of the English Language, supra*.

[2]IHAC Final Report, *supra*, at 107.

[3]When it is introduced, Canadian digital radio will be transmitted in the L-Band, between 1452 and 1492 Megahertz.

[4]IHAC Final Report, *supra*, at 107.

[5]Policy Review Panel, "Direct-to-Home Satellite Broadcasting," report to the

Minister of Canadian Heritage, April 1995, at 28.

[6]Harvey Enchin, "Cable TV rivals hit roadblock," *The Globe and Mail,* 14 August, 1995, at B3.

[7]Anthony M. Rutkowski, "Today's Cooperative Competitive Standards Environment For Open Information and Telecommunications Networks and the Internet Standards-Making Model," paper presented to the Standards Development and Information Infrastructure Workshop, June 1994 [unpublished].

[8]Bill Gates, "Who needs government-imposed speed limits on the information highway?", *The* (Montreal) *Gazette,* 28 June, 1995, at F4.

[9]Mark Tran, "Computer giants join to fight Microsoft in business market," *The* (Montreal) *Gazette,* 18 August, 1995, at D7.

[10]The Task Force on the Introduction of Digital Radio, "Digital Radio's place in the Information Highway," paper presented to the Minister of Canadian Heritage, February 1995, at 9–10.

[11]Gaston Lionel Franco & Henry J. Novy, eds., *supra,* at 38.

[12]Apple's iconic interface, coupled with the use of a mouse and pointer on the screen, was first developed by the Xerox Palo Alto Research Center and the Stanford Research Institute in the 1960s and 1970s. Lotus, originally written in 1982, was based on the Visicalc spreadsheet originally developed by Daniel Bricklin, a Harvard Business School student, for the Apple II computer in the late 1970s.

PART III – THE PLAYERS AND THE CONTROLS
Chapter 8 – The Carriers

[1]John S. Mayo, *supra,* at 114–115.

[2]Ian and Liz Angus, "Canada Calling II: Sustainable Competition," *The Globe and Mail,* Supplement, 24 May, 1995, at 2.

[3]CRTC Decision 94-19, 16 September, 1994; CRTC Report, *supra.*

[4]Unitel, which has less than 5 percent of the $5 billion long-distance phone market compared with Bell's 85 percent, lost $240 million in 1994 and a further $100 million in the first quarter of 1995. Canadian Pacific offered its 48 percent stake in Unitel for $210 million. It was refused, prompting CP's CEO, Bill Stinson, to remark: "What you have today is an industry in total disarray . . . We are not going to invest any more money in this business." Rogers Communications chief CEO, Ted Rogers, has declared publicly that he is prepared to abandon his 29.5 percent stake in a $500 million investment in Unitel. And AT&T, which owns the remaining 22.5 percent, has sent in a new CEO with a reputation for aggressive turnarounds. September 1995's *Globe and Mail Report on Business,* at 108, reported that, recently, two of the smaller players in the long-distance market, TelRoute Communications Inc. and STN Inc., have gone bankrupt. One analyst

of First Marathon Securities Ltd. observed: ". . . what the [Paul] Martin budget told us is that the government is finally willing to play by the rules of the free market. And, in the free market, failing companies are allowed to fail."

[5]Telecommunications Act, S.C. 1993, c.38.

[6]Radiocommunication Act, R.S.C. 1985, c.R–2.

[7]Broadcasting Act, R.S.C. 1991, c.11 B-9.01.

[8]The Act is divided into four parts. Part I of the Act (ss. 2–4) provides the introductory backdrop to broadcasting in Canada. It defines the relevant terms in the Act, sets out the "cornerstone of the Act," frames a statement of Canadian broadcasting policy and the objectives of the Act, and outlines its scope. Part II of the Broadcasting Act (ss. 5–34) delineates the powers and purpose of the CRTC with respect to broadcasting.

[9]*The Globe and Mail*, 25 August, 1995, at B3.

[10]IHAC Final Report, *supra*, Recommendation 2.5.

[11]IHAC Final Report, *supra*, Chapter 8, Recommendation 1.7.

[12]CRTC Decision 94-19, 16 September, 1994.

[13]Cableco versus Telco revenues are $2 billion versus $14 billion.

[14]IHAC Final Report, *supra*.

[15]The panel was chaired by Gordon Ritchie, the former senior civil sevant who was number two in command of the U.S. and North American free trade negotiations. He was joined by Robert Rabinovitch, former deputy minister of Communications, and Roger Tassé, former deputy minister of Justice, both now in the private sector.

[16]IHAC Final Report, *supra*.

[17]Ibid.

[18]Ibid.

[19]*United States v. AT&T*, 552 F. Supp. 131 (D.D.C. 1982) *aff'd subnom., Maryland v. United States*, 460 U.S. 1001 (1983).

Chapter 9 – Content and Culture

[1]Cable companies are often hybrid utilities — comprising both telecom and broadcasting operations.

[2]Working Group on Culture and Content, draft report to the Information Highway Advisory Council, 25 May, 1995, at 6 [unpublished]. The public/private distinction is crucial to many areas of administrative law and to the fundamental issue of whether the state should intervene to "protect the public." For example, in securities regulation, to protect the consumer in the purchase of securities, elaborate licensing requirements are imposed once a sale or distribution of securities to the public occurs. See David Johnston, *Canadian Securities Regulation* (Toronto:

Butterworths, 1977) at 148–155.

[3]Working Group on Canadian Programming and Private Television, *The Future of Canadian Programming and the Role of Private Television: Keeping Canada on the Information Highway*, report to the Minister of Canadian Heritage, March 1995, at 3 [hereinafter Working Group on Canadian Programming and Private Television Report].

[4]"Telecommunications, Radiocommunication, Broadcasting and Copyright Acts: Linkages," notes on the text, March 4, 1994, at 2 [unpublished].

[5]Telecommunications Act, S.C. 1993, c.38.

[6]Broadcasting Act, R.S.C. 1991, c.11 B-9.01. Note that the CRTC administers both Acts.

[7]A third statute, the Radiocommunication Act, R.S.C. 1985, c.R-2., plays a complementary but subsidiary role. It has a technological orientation. Section 5 stipulates: ". . . the Minister may have regard to s.7 of the Telecommunications Act . . . and to the orderly development and efficient operation of radiocommunication in Canada."

[8]"Telecommunications, Radiocommunication, Broadcasting and Copyright Acts: Linkages," *supra*, at 2.

[9]The Honourable Michel Dupuy, P.C., M.P., Minister of Canadian Heritage, address to the Advisory Council on the Information Highway, Ottawa, 30 September, 1994 [unpublished].

[10]John Gray, *Billy Bishop Goes to War* (Vancouver: Talonbooks, 1981).

[11]Canadian Content and Culture Working Group, draft report, *supra*, at 3.

[12]IHAC Final Report, *supra*, Issue 13.

[13]The Broadcasting Act regulates the broadcasting operations of "distribution undertakings" such as cable companies.

[14]CRTC Report, *supra*, at 33.

[15]CRTC Report, *supra*, at 28.

[16]CRTC Report, *supra*, at 29.

[17]Working Group on Content and Culture, draft report, *supra*, at 9.

[18]André Bureau, "Reinforcing our sovereignty and identity on the Canadian information highway" (oral remarks to the CRTC, Ottawa, 30 March, 1995), at 3.

[19]CRTC Report, *supra*, at 27.

[20]CRTC Report, *supra*, at 27–28.

[21]André Bureau, *supra*, at 5–6.

[22]Anna Porter, "*Canadian Culture and Content on the Information Highway: Toward a New Cultural Framework*" (address to the Information Highway Advisory Council, Ottawa, 20 February, 1994) [unpublished].

[23]Jim Boothroyd, "Canadian publishers feel federal cuts," *The* (Montreal) *Gazette*, 9

June, 1995, at D5.

[24]IHAC Final Report, *supra*, ch. 8, rec. 7.4.

[25]IHAC Final Report, *supra*.

[26]Working Group on Content and Culture, draft report, *supra*, at 5.

[27]André Bureau, *supra*, at 5.

[28]Working Group on Content and Culture, draft report, *supra*, at 4.

[29]Ibid. At present, Canadian content has a minimal presence online.

[30]Working Group on Content and Culture, draft report, *supra*, at 8.

[31]Ibid.

[32]Working Group on Content and Culture, draft report, *supra*, at 5.

[33]IHAC Final Report, *supra*, ch. 8, rec. 2.18.

[34]CRTC Report, *supra*, at 33–34.

[35]Ibid.

[36]CRTC Report, *supra*, at 34.

[37]Working Group on Content and Culture, draft report, *supra*, at 4.

Chapter 10 – Security on the Information Highway

[1]Coalition for Public Information, *Future Knowledge: The Report*, response to the CRTC and IHAC reports, June 1995, at 13.

[2]Sections 184 and 193 of the Criminal Code criminalize the unauthorized interception (s.184) and disclosure (s.193) of private communications.

[3]Invasion of privacy and copyright infringement on the information highway are treated in separate chapters. Chapter 12 discusses intellectual property rights. Chapter 13 considers questions of privacy.

[4]Clifford Stoll, *Silicon Snake Oil* (New York: Doubleday, 1995); excerpts reprinted in *Report on Business* magazine, June 1995, at 73.

[5]Joe Chidley, "Cracking the Net," *Maclean's*, May 22, 1995, at 54–55.

[6]Gayle MacDonald, "Toll fraud $300 million a year, may hit 25% of firms," *The Financial Post*, 1 April, 1995, at 37.

[7]IHAC Final Report, at 145.

[8]Twisted-pair wiring, widely used in the telephone system and in some local area networks, are poorly insulated. Hence, the data they transmit is broadcast as if the cable was an antenna and thus easily intercepted. Broadband coaxial cable, used by cable companies, and fiber-optic cable do not broadcast signals. Hence, one must physically tap into these cables to intercept communications. Consequently, there is a greater risk of detection. Baseband cable is not as well insulated and thus easier to tap.

[9]Gilbert Held, *supra*, at 82.

[10]IHAC recommended various legislative measures to counter this type of behaviour.

IHAC Final Report, *supra*, Recommendations 10.5–10.7.

[11]Criminal Code, R.S.C. 1985, c. C-46.

[12]Copyright Act, R.S.C. 1985, c. C-42. This latter avenue is explored in Chapter 11.

[13]Parliament has the power to create and classify offences in the Criminal Code. Prosecution is left up to the provincial Attorneys General. With hybrid offences, the Crown prosecutor has an unfettered discretion to proceed either by way of indictment or on summary conviction. The choice of proceedings has a number of effects including the trial and appeal procedures, the level of trial court and the maximum penalties available at law.

[14]By virtue of s.334 of the Criminal Code, where the value of what is stolen exceeds $1,000, theft is an indictable offence. Where the value does not exceed $1,000, theft may be prosecuted summarily or by way of indictment, at the discretion of the prosecutor. As an indictable offence, theft under $1,000 carries a maximum sentence of two years' imprisonment.

[15]*R. v. McLaughlin* (1980), 53 C.C.C. (2d) 417, [1980] 2 S.C.R. 331, 18 C.R. (3d) 339.

[16]Consider, e.g., the time required to plot and execute a bank robbery.

[17]Jim Carroll, *Canadian Internet Handbook* (Scarborough, Ont.: Prentice-Hall Canada, 1995).

[18]Jim Carroll, "I know the Internet, and it's not a cauldron of evils," *The Globe and Mail*, 22 March, 1995, at A19.

Chapter 11 – Controlling Content

[1]Peter Lewis, "Despite a New Plan for Cooling It Off, Cybersex Stays Hot," *The New York Times,* 26 March, 1995.

[2]Simon Wiesenthal Center, "The Need for Regulation of the Information Highway (Bigotry on the Internet)" position paper presented to the Solicitor General's Department and the ministries of Justice, Heritage and Industry Canada, June 12–13, 1995 [hereinafter Simon Wiesenthal Center].

[3]Simon Wiesenthal Center, *supra*, at 4.

[4]Warren Caragata, "Crime in Cybercity," *Maclean's*, 22 May, 1995, at 50.

[5]*R. v. Pecciarich* (1995), 22 O.R. (3d) 748 (Ont. Ct. (Prov. Div.)).

[6]Four others were charged in addition to Pecciarich. Two BBS operators pleaded guilty to the offence of obscenity. They were both given conditional discharges and required to make contributions to the community (to a rape crisis centre for one and donation of computer equipment for the other). A fourth was convicted of distributing obscene pictures and was fined $500.

[7]Keith Schneider, "Hate Groups Use Tools of the Electronic Trade," *New York Times*, 15 March, 1995, at A12.

⁸Bertrand Marotte, "Nassau-based Internet casino about to open," *The* (Montreal) *Gazette,* 17 March, 1995, C10.

⁹For analogous cross-jurisdictional offences in securities regulation, see *Quebec Securities Commission v. Gregoire* and *R. v. Mackenzie Securities* (cites in Johnston's Securities Regulation)

¹⁰Section 7 of the Canadian Charter of Rights and Freedoms guarantees the right to a fair trial. Section 11(d) safeguards the presumption of innocence.

¹¹IHAC Final Report, June 27, 1995, *supra*, at 48.

¹²The Criminal Code, R.S.C. 1985 c. C-48.

¹³The Canadian Charter of Rights and Freedoms, Part I of the Constitution Act, 1982, Schedule B of the Canada Act 1982 (U.K.), 1982, c.11.

¹⁴The Broadcasting Act, R.S.C. 1991, c.38 B-9.01.

¹⁵The Telecommunications Act, S.C. 1993, c.38.

¹⁶The Canadian Human Rights Act, R.S.C. 1985, c.33 H-6.

¹⁷The Customs Act, R.S. 1985, c.1.

¹⁸IHAC Final Report, *supra*, at 48.

¹⁹Section 31(1).

²⁰Section 2.

²¹Diane Rinehart, "Anti-racists urge Ottawa to regulate Internet," *The* (Montreal) *Gazette,* 15 June, 1995.

²²Diane Rinehart, *supra.*

²³IHAC Final Report, *supra*, ch.8, rec. 7.18, 2.19.

²⁴*Webster's Ninth New Collegiate Dictionary* (Markham: Thomas Allen & Sons Ltd., 1989) at 942.

²⁵IHAC Final Report, *supra*, at 48.

²⁶Section 163 of the Criminal Code.

²⁷*R. v. Pecciarich, supra*, at 765.

²⁸Subsection 163(8).

²⁹*R. v. Butler* (1992), 70 C.C.C. (3d) 129, 11 C.R. (4th) 137, [1992] 1 S.C.R. 452.

³⁰*Butler, supra*, at 144ff.

³¹*Butler, supra.*

³²Section 319 of the Criminal Code.

³³Section 318 of the Criminal Code.

³⁴Criminal Code section 318(4). Note that gender-based hate discrimination was excluded.

³⁵Section 319(7) of the Criminal Code.

³⁶Simon Wiesenthal Center, *supra*, at 4.

³⁷Section 241 of the Criminal Code.

³⁸Section 22(3) of the Criminal Code.

³⁹Canadian Charter of Rights and Freedoms, Part I of the Constitution Act, 1982, Schedule B of the Canada Act 1982 (U.K.), 1982, c.11.

⁴⁰*Striking a Balance, supra,* at 107.

⁴¹See, e.g., *Re Ontario Film and Video Appreciation Society and Ontario Board of Censors* (1983), 34 C.R. (3d) 73, 147 D.L.R. (3d) 58, 41 O.R. (2d) 583 (Div. Ct.), aff'd 38 C.R. (3d) 271.

⁴²*Striking a Balance, supra,* at 107.

⁴³*R. v. Oakes* (1986), 24 C.C.C. (3d) 321, [1986] 1 S.C.R. 103, 50 C.R. (3d) 1; fleshes out the section 1 requirements, known as the "Oakes test."

⁴⁴*R. v. Butler, supra.; R. v. Keegstra* (1990), 61 C.C.C. (3d) 1, [1991] 2 W.W.R. 1, 1 C.R. (4th) 129 (S.C.C.).

⁴⁵European Convention for the Protection of Human Rights and Fundamental Freedoms, opened for signature 4 November, 1950.

⁴⁶U.S. Const. amend. I.

⁴⁷Don Sellar, "A media virus from Internet," *Toronto Star,* 13 May, 1995.

⁴⁸To illustrate the potential danger of untested information, consider the following case. A Carleton University journalism student posted a false message that the rock band Pearl Jam was about to announce a Canadian tour, providing dates and locations. The *Toronto Star* picked up and published the news. It subsequently learned that the story was untrue and retracted it.

⁴⁹Jeremy S. Williams, *The Law of Libel and Slander in Canada* (Toronto: Butterworths, 1987), at 49.

⁵⁰Warren Caragata, *supra,* at 50.

⁵¹Comments by Paul Saffo.

⁵²Warren Caragata, *supra,* at 50.

⁵³Michael Martineau, Vice-President of NSTN Inc., a company that provides Internet connections, quoted in Warren Caragata, *supra,* at 50.

⁵⁴Warren Caragata, *supra.*

⁵⁵A California-based software company is designing a new program, called Surf Watch, which would alert users to material they may not want to view.

⁵⁶IHAC Final Report, *supra,* at 49.

⁵⁷Laura Bobak, "Cullen backs FreeNet," *The Ottawa Sun,* 14 March, 1995.

⁵⁸This is a problem for many areas of the law. For example, securities regulations establish onerous licensing conditions for the sale of securities to the "public" but exempt "private" transactions.

⁵⁹Warren Caragata, *supra.*

Chapter 12 – Intellectual Property

¹*R. v. Stewart,* [1988] 1 S.C.R. 963.

[2]R.S.C. 1985, c. C-42, as amended.

[3]S. 2 of the Copyright Act, added by S.C. 1993, c. 44, s. 53(3), expressly protects compilations of data, although it is arguable that, prior to 1993, such works were already protected as collective works, or as compilations under the classification of literary works.

[4]Copyright Act, ss. 14.1, 28.1 and 28.2.

[5]IHAC's Final Report recommended that:

Crown copyright should be maintained;

The Crown in Right of Canada should, as a rule, place federal government information and data in the public domain;

Where Crown copyright is asserted for generating revenue, licensing should be based on the principles of non-exclusivity and the recovery of no more than the marginal costs incurred in the reproduction of the information or data (except information or works produced by Crown agencies or corporations such as the CBC or National Film Board).

Information Highway Advisory Council, final report of the Copyright Subcommittee (Ottawa: Industry Canada, 1995), at 23–24.

[6]United States Copyright Act, s. 105.

[7]In *Canadian Admiral Corp. Ltd. v. Rediffusion Inc,* [1954] Ex.C.R. 382, the Court ruled that "for copyright to subsist in a 'work' it must be expressed to some extent at least in some material form, capable of identification and having a more or less permanent endurance." (At 394).

[8]17 U.S.C. § 102.

[9]Copyright Act, s. 2.

[10]Copyright Act, s. 5.

[11]Clifford Chance, *The European Software Directive* (London: Clifford Chance, 1991), at 19.

[12]Copyright Act, s. 2.

[13]Consumer and Corporate Affairs, *From Gutenberg to Telidon: A White Paper on Copyright* (Ottawa: Department of Communications, 1984), at Section XII.

[14]Sub-Committee on the Revision of Copyright, *A Charter of Rights for Creators* (Ottawa: House of Commons, Government of Canada, 1985), at Recommendation 60.

[15]*Gondos v. Hardy* (1982), 64 C.P.R. (2d) 145 (Ontario. H.C.); *Francis Day & Hunter Ltd. v. Bron,* [1963] Ch. 587 (C.A.).

[16]Copyright Act, s. 41.

[17]Copyright Act, s. 39.

[18]Criminal Code, s. 380.

[19]Copyright Act, s. 42.

[20]Subsection 42(1) makes it a hybrid offence for any person to knowingly:

(a) make infringing copies of a work for sale or hire;

(b) sell or let for hire, by way of trade, expose or offer for sale or hire infringing copies;

(c) distribute infringing copies for the purpose of trade or to such an extent as to affect prejudicially the owner of the copyright;

(d) exhibit infringing copies in public by way of trade; or

(e) import infringing copies for sale or hire into Canada.

[21]Copyright Act, s. 42.

[22]Ibid.

[23]Copyright Act, s. 27(2).

[24]The Canadian Information Highway Advisory Council has recommended "specific criteria and guidelines be provided" in the Copyright Act for fair dealing "including explicit clarification that [it] applies to the making of an electronic copy of a work and to the storage and transmission of that copy by electronic means." IHAC Final Report, Chapter 8, s. 6.5, at 22.

[25]Examples of U.S. fair use cases include: *Sega Enterprises Ltd. v. Accolade Inc.*, 977 F.2d 1510 (9th Cir. 1992); *Feist Publications, Inc. v. Rural Telephone Service Company*, 499 U.S. 340, 113 L. Ed. (2d) 358 (1991); and *Harper & Row Publishers, Inc. v. Nation Enterprises*, 471 U.S. 539 at 562–63, 85 L. Ed. (2d) 588 (1985).

[26]The public-interest defence has not yet been raised successfully in Canada with respect to copyright. It has gained judicial recognition in *R. v. James Lorimer & Co.*, [1984] 1 F.C. 1065, 77 C.P.R. (2d) 262 (C.A.). It has been considered at greater length by the U.K. courts: *Hubbard v. Vosper*, [1972] 1 All E.R. 1023 (C.A.); *Beloff v. Pressdram*, [1973] 1 All E.R. 241 (Ch. D.); and *Lion Laboratories Ltd. v. Evans*, [1985] Q.B. 526 (C.A.).

[27]Marking a patent with terms such as "patent pending" and "patented" is not required by law in Canada.

[28]These rights exist under the Paris Convention for the Protection of Industrial Property, U.N.T.S. No. 11851, vol. 828, at 305–388.

[29]Patent Act, sections 55 and 57.

[30]Patent Act, section 55.01.

Chapter 13 – Privacy

[1]Hyman Gross, "Privacy and Autonomy," from *Nomos XIII, Privacy*, ed. by John Chapman and J. Roland Pennock (New York: Lieber-Atherton, 1971), 169–182, as found in Joel Feinberg & Hyman Gross, *Philosophy of Law*, 3rd ed., (Belmont, Ca.: Wadsworth Publishing Co., 1975), at 291–298.

[2]IHAC, *Privacy and the Canadian Information Highway* (Ottawa: Industry Canada,

1994), at 5.

[3]For example, Ontario's Consumer Reporting Act, R.S.O. 1990, c.C.33.

[4]1980–81–82–83, c.111, Sch. II "1."

[5]Part I of Constitution Act, 1982.

[6]S. 60(1)(c) does, however, give the Privacy Commissioner the power to extend his/her investigations to "persons or bodies, other than government institutions, that come within the legislative authority of Parliament."

[7]Freedom of Information & Protection of Privacy Act (Ontario), R.S.O. 1990, c. F.31, s.2.

[8]For example, Municipal Freedom of Information and Protection of Privacy Act, R.S.O, c. M.56.

[9]54 U.S.C. 522a.

[10]Warren Freedman, *The Right of Privacy in the Computer Age* (New York: Quorum Books, 1977).

[11]David H. Flaherty, *Protecting Privacy in Two-way Electronic Services* (New York: Knowledge Industry Publications, 1984).

[12]Telecommunications Act, S.C. 1993, s. 7.

[13]Criminal Code, s. 184. Additionally, s. 184.5 applies specifically to radio-based telephone communications.

[14]Criminal Code, ss. 184(1) and 184.5(1).

[15]Criminal Code, s. 183.

[16]A small fee is charged for this registration.

[17]Ibid.

[18]Examples include: the Netherlands' Data Protection Act, 1988; Belgium's Law on the Protection of Private Life Regarding the Processing of Personal Data, 1992; Luxembourg's The Use of Name Linked Data in Computer Processing Act, 1979; Sweden's Data Act; and Spain's Law on the Regulation of the Automated Processing of Personal Data.

[19]William Prosser et al., *Torts: Cases and Materials,* 7th ed. (New York: The Foundation Press, Inc., 1982), at 1083.

[20]*The Right of Privacy in the Computer Age, supra,* Chapter 1.

[21]Prosser, "Privacy" (1960), Cal. L.R., 383, at 389. Prosser's four-part privacy tort test was later adopted by the American Law Institute's Restatement of the Law of Torts, and has been widely accepted by numerous courts.

[22]"Privacy," *supra,* at 390.

[23]Philip H. Osborne, "The Privacy Acts of British Columbia, Manitoba and Saskatchewan," as contained in Dale Gibson, *Aspects of Privacy Law* (Toronto: Butterworths, 1980), at 75.

[24]*Tureen v. Equifax, Inc.* (1978), 571 F2d 411 (8th Cir. C.A.).

[25]*Shibley v. Time, Inc.* (1975), 341 NE2d 339.

[26]John T. Soma and Jay Batson, "The Legal Environment of Commercial Database Administration," Spring 1987, Jurimetrics Journal 297, at 311, as taken from *Cox Broadcasting Corp. v. Cohn* (1979), 420 U.S. 469.

[27]"The Privacy Acts of British Columbia, Manitoba and Saskatchewan," *supra*, at 76.

[28]"Privacy," *supra*, at 393–394.

[29]"The Privacy Acts of British Columbia, Manitoba and Saskatchewan," *supra*, at 77.

[30]Ibid, at 78–79.

[31]Ibid, at 79.

[32]Ibid.

[33]Ibid, at 80, as found in Pannam, "Unauthorized Use of Names or Photographs in Advertisements" (1966), 40 Aust. L.J. 4.

[34]"The Legal Environment of Commercial Database Administration," *supra*, at 311.

[35]"The Legal Environment of Commercial Database Administration," *supra*, at 310–311.

[36]IHAC, *Privacy and the Canadian Information Highway, supra*; IHAC Final Report, ch. 8, sec. 10.20–10.23.

[37]IHAC Final Report, ch. 8, sec. 10.22.

[38]IHAC, *Privacy and the Canadian Information Highway, supra*, at 15–18.

PART IV – THE ISSUES
Chapter 14 – The Economic Impact

[1]Potter and Lee, *supra*, at 1.

[2]For a more in-depth discussion of privatization and deregulation, see Chapter 8 on carriers.

[3]Potter and Lee, *supra*, at 8–9.

[4]"Smart Cities," *Report on Business* magazine, *The Globe and Mail* supplement, August 1995, at 45.

[5]Ibid, at 70.

[6]Potter and Lee, *supra*, at 2.

[7]For an in-depth analysis of small firms' impact on employment, see G. Picot, J. Baldwin & R. Dupuy, "Have small firms created a disproportionate share of jobs in Canada: a reassessment of the facts," paper presented for Statistics Canada, November 1994.

[8]This is particularly attractive for Canada, where small and medium-sized firms play such a prominent role in the national economy.

[9]David Crane, *The Next Canadian Century* (Toronto: Stoddart Publishing, 1992), at 28.

[10]Economic Council of Canada, *Making technology work: innovation and jobs in Canada: a statement* (Ottawa: Supply and Services Canada, 1987).

[11]The challenge, of course, will be to ensure that these intentions become more widespread and come to fruition. But, there is often a significant lag between the introduction of new information technology and increased productivity. For example, the level of training and adaptability of the people using the technology will affect the level of productivity.

[12]Roberta Fox, telecommunications specialist with Hewlett-Packard (Canada) Ltd., quoted in Gordon Arnaut, "Small business stands to benefit from reforms, report suggests," Report on Telecommunications, *The Globe and Mail*, 20 September, 1994, at C9.

[13]Perhaps the best evidence of this policy is the mandate for the Canadian Government's Information Highway Advisory Council. See, for example, two of its three objectives: create jobs through investment and innovation, and accessibility. As well, three of its original four operating principles are competition, public-private sector collaboration, interconnection and interoperability.

[14]Potter and Lee, *supra*, at 2.

[15]Potter and Lee, *supra*, at 4. Online magazines have sprouted on the Net. In addition to publicizing their product, they contain advertisements for other companies.

[16]Potter and Lee, *supra*, at 2.

[17]OECD, "Technology, Innovation and Employment," October 1994, draft report, Paris.

[18]Goss Gilroy, *supra*, at 1.

[19]Goss Gilroy, *supra*, at 5. The dilemma is well set out in the following comment at 15:

Shifts in the economy resulting from adjustments to the nature and composition of the work force, usually accompany high rates of structural change. (15, Conference Board of Canada, "Jobs in the Knowledge-based Economy: Information Technology and the Impact on Employment," November 1994) These shifts, in turn, result in a rise in demand for labour and wages which offset the job loss. Structural unemployment is an unfortunate and arguably inevitable side effect of labour displacement resulting from technological change.

[20]Goss Gilroy, *supra*, at 14.

[21]Ibid.

[22]Ibid.

[23]Potter and Lee, *supra*, at 20.

[24]Ibid.

[25]Goss Gilroy, *supra*, at 18; summary of the 1994 Conference Board of Canada report and the 1994 Job Creation and Skills Working Group Report:

While both theory and evidence indicate that, in the long run, information technology should create more jobs than it destroys, there is a very real concern about protracted time lag between the cycles of job destruction and job creation. It is recognized that these consequences of a prolonged lag between these cycles must be addressed, along with the fact that the new jobs created may be inappropriate for the displaced workers.

[26]Department of Human Resources, *Canadian Occupational Projection Systems*, 1993, cited in IHAC Final Report, *supra*.

[27]IHAC Final Report, *supra*.

[28]*The Globe and Mail*, 3 August, 1995, at A1.

[29]Goss Gilroy, *supra*, at 4.

[30]Gaston Lionel Franco & Henry J. Novy, eds., *supra*, at 276.

Chapter 15 – The Social Impact

[1]This is a facile answer. One remembers that telling cross-cultural remark attributed to China's senior leader under Chairman Mao Ze Dong, Chou En Lai: when asked what he thought were the lasting consequences of the French Revolution, he replied, "It is too early to tell."

[2]Some opponents of controls on the information highway — See Chapter 11 — suggest that the Church's current substitute, national governments, are embarked on similar retrograde campaigns on the information highway. Consider Umberto Eco's compelling novel *The Name of the Rose*, chronicling the desperate efforts of the Church to maintain a tight monopoly on knowledge before the printing press.

[3]IHAC Final Report. The three IHAC objectives were job creation, reinforcement of Canadian identity and sovereignty, and accessibility.

[4]IHAC Final Report, *supra*, ch. 8, rec. 13.1–2.

[5]See list of IHAC recommendations.

[6]IHAC Final Report, ch.8, at 75, rec. 14.4–6.

[7]Doug Hull, Industry Canada, March 1995, ITAC Conference.

[8]Jane Coutts, "New Brunswick tried out telephone triage," *The Globe and Mail*, 28 July, 1995, at A3.

GLOSSARY

ATM – 1) Asynchronous Transfer Mode: a high-speed networking technology for broadband communications.

2) Automated Teller Machine: an unattended terminal-type device that provides simple banking services, such as cash withdrawals, transfer of funds between accounts and account balance inquiries.

Bandwidth – The range of frequencies required for the transmission of a signal, usually given in hertz. More bandwidth is required for carrying more complex signals. For example, more bandwidth is required to carry full-motion video than simple voice messages.

BBS – (See Electronic Bulletin Board.)

Binary – Where only two values or states are possible for a particular condition, such as "ON" or "OFF," or "1" or "0."

Bit – A contraction of the term "binary digit." A unit of information represented by a 0 or 1. The speed of information transmission is measured in bits per second (bps).

Bottleneck – Refers to local communications company network service, function or facility currently subject to some degree of monopoly control, that competitors cannot economically duplicate, but require access to in order to compete.

Broadband Services – A range of communications services that require and use larger bandwidth than traditional voice messaging. A broadband communication system can simultaneously accommodate television, voice, data and many other services.

Broadcasting – Any transmission of programs, whether or not encrypted, by radiowaves or other means of telecommunication for reception by the public by means of a broadcasting receiving apparatus, but does not include any such transmission of programs that is made solely for performance or display in a public place.

Bundling – The practice of combining separate hardware, software and services into a package offered at a single price.

CANARIE – The Canadian Network for the Advancement of Research, Industry and Education: a public- and private-sector initiative for a national high-speed digital network that allows research scientists to communicate in multimedia formats on R&D projects.

CAN-LINKED Consortium – Representatives from the Canada Institute for Scientific and Technical Information (CISTI), the National Library of Canada and ten Canadian universities involved in a pilot project for electronic access to information and documentation in domestic research libraries.

CD-ROM – Compact Disc with Read-Only Memory. Compatible with computers, Compact Discs are inexpensive high-capacity storage devices for data, text and video.

Certification Authority – A trusted authority that assigns a unique name to each user and issues a certificate containing the name and the user's public key for purposes of security of messaging.

Coaxial Cable – High-capacity cable used in television distribution, communications and video, commonly called co-ax, to carry great quantities of information.

Convergence – The "coming together" of formerly distinct technologies, industries or activities; most common usage refers to the convergence of computing, communications and broadcasting technologies.

Cross-Certification – Occurs when a corporation which is legally certified to provide products and services in one industry (or marketplace) is also certified (as a legitimate or legal entity) to provide products or services in another industry.

Cross-Ownership – Refers to the practice of one corporation exercising partial or complete control of the operation of another industry, through purchase or ownership of the stock in the latter corporation.

Cross-Subsidization – Refers to the practice of applying revenues from an operation or line of business to another operation, to lower the price of the latter operation. For example, local telephone rates have remained low because they were subsidized by long-distance revenues.

Cryptographic Algorithm – Also called a cipher, this is a mathematical function used for encoding and decoding a message.

CSA – The Canadian Standards Association: one of five standards-writing organizations in Canada that are accredited by the Standards Council of Canada.

Cyberspace – The three-dimensional expanse of computer networks in which all audio and video electronic signals travel and users can, with the proper addresses and codes, explore and download information.

Digital – Information expressed in binary patterns of 1s and 0s.

Digital Radio – Microwave transmission of digital data via radio transmitters or radio broadcasting using a digital signal.

Digital Scanner – A device that allows users to monitor radiocommunication frequencies automatically.

Digital Signature – Data, appended to a part of a message, that enables a recipient to verify the integrity and origin of a message.

Digitization – The conversion of analog or continuous signal into a series of 1s and 0s, i.e., into a digital format.

Direct-to-Home – A TV signal broadcast by satellite and received directly in a subscriber's home via a small dish antenna.

Distance Education (Tele-Education) – Education using different media (correspondence, radio, television and others) but requiring little or no physical attendance at the institution offering the courses and accredited certification.

EDI – Electronic Data Interchange: electronic preparation, communication and processing of business transactions in a predefined structured format, using computers and telecommunications.

Electronic Bulletin Board – An electronic messaging system and an information storage area shared by several users, each having access to all messages left or posted in that area.

Electronic Commerce – Consumer and business transactions conducted over a network, using computers and telecommunications.

Encryption – The coding of data for privacy protection or security considerations when transmitted over telecommunications links so that only the person to whom it is sent can read it.

Fibre-Optic Communications – A modern transmission technology using lasers to produce a beam of light which can be modulated to carry large amounts of information through fine glass or acrylic fibres.

Freenet – A non-profit community organization that provides free access to electronic mail and information services and to computer networks such as the Internet.

Full-Motion Video – Video that is perceived to provide smooth and continuous motion.

GII – Global Information Infrastructure: a global information highway initiative put forward by the United States to G7 countries.

HDTV – High-Definition Television: television with greater resolution than the current 525-line television standard.

Hertz – A unit of frequency, one cycle per second.

Hypermedia – Use of data, text, graphics, video and voice as elements in a hypertext system. All the forms of information are linked together so that a user can easily move from one to another.

Hypertext – Text that contains embedded links to other documents or information.

Intellectual Property (IP) – A collective term used to refer to new ideas, inventions, designs, writings, films, etc., and is protected by copyright, patents, trademarks, etc.

Internet – A vast international network of networks that enables computers of all kinds to share services and communicate directly.

ISDN – Integrated Services Digital Network: A set of digital telecommunication network standards.

ISO – The International Organization for Standardization: a specialized international agency for standardization. It has a membership of standards bodies in eighty-nine countries.

ITU – The International Telecommunication Union: United Nations organization overseeing multi-nation telecommunications and radiocommunication standards and interconnectibility.

Key Escrow Policy – A United States policy concerning the technology that has been developed to address the concern that widespread use of encryption would make lawfully authorized electronic surveillance more difficult. It involves granting designated third parties special keys needed for law enforcement agencies to gain access, under court warrant, to encrypted communications or transactions.

Local Area Network (LAN) – A private data network in which serial transmission is used without store and forward techniques for direct data communication among stations located within the user's premises.

Local Loop – Designates the part of a communications circuit between the subscriber's equipment and the line termination equipment in the exchange facility.

Modem – A contraction of the words *mo*dulator and *dem*odulator. Accessory that allows computers and terminal equipment to communicate through telephone lines or cable. The modem converts analog data to the digital language of computers.

Narrowband – A relatively restricted frequency band normally used for a single purpose or made available to a single user.

Number Portability – The ability to maintain the same user number when transferring among various networks and service providers.

OECD – The Organization for Economic Cooperation and Development: a United Nations organization of which Canada is a member. The OECD is responsible for issues in international development including information and communications technologies and related standards.

PCS – Personal Communications Services: a family of radiocommunications services provided through personal user radio terminals operating in a mobile or portable mode.

PKI – Public Key Infrastructure: a network of connected third-party certification authorities that allows the movement of data and information between organizations that have their own security architecture or system.

Protocols – Sets of technology language rules that determine how various components of communications systems interact.

Rate Rebalancing – A process aimed at increasing prices for local telephone service that are subsidized by long-distance revenues and reducing subsidies paid by long-distance service providers. (See also Cross-Subsidization.)

Spectrum – The range of electromagnetic frequencies capable of traversing space without the benefit of physical interconnection.

Structural Separation – Refers to the setting up of a separate but affiliated company to provide a specific line of business. Structural separation is one approach to dealing with cross-subsidization or undue preference.

TSACC – The Telecommunications Standards Advisory Council of Canada: a government/industry-led body establishing commonality of standards.

Unbundled – Services, programs, software and training sold separately from the hardware.

Universal Access – The ability to get online to a network from anywhere.

Universal Service – A policy that local rates should be kept low enough to ensure that the maximum number of persons are able to afford basic telephone service.

Video Compression – A term that describes the process of contracting data so that more can be stored and transmitted.

Video-Dial-Tone (VDT) – Refers to the two-way, or "switched," broadband carriage of information. VDT technology will provide the platform for video-on-demand services. A switched communications system is one that allows the two-way, point-to-point exchange of information.

Video-On-Demand Service – A service that allows the user to dial in to a video-dial-tone system, choose a video and play it.

Virtual Reality – An interactive, simultaneous electronic representation of a real or imaginary world where, through sight, sound, and even touch, the user is given the impression of becoming part of what is represented.

Wide Area Network (WAN) – A communications network made up of a number of Local Area Networks (LANs) and/or Metropolitan Area Networks (MANs), allowing access to data physically located at great distances.

INDEX